Dedicated to Dawn,

My creative and romantic soulmate and personal salty siren.

Welcome to the depths, Matey!

*Many of these pirate women are known to us from history;
be sure to google a few of these names to learn more of their fascinating stories!
The rest of these salty sirens live unknown, beneath the tide of time...
enjoy bringing them to the surface, sparkling with light and color!*

Copyright © 2020 Matt Davidson
Published by Prevail Press

All rights reserved.
No part of this book may be reproduced in any form or by any electronic or mechanical means including information storage and retrieval systems, without permission in writing from the author.
The only exception is by a reviewer, who may quote short excerpts in a review.

ISBN: 978-1-948824-13-2

Salty Sirens of the Seven Seas

Immerse yourself in the world of the Pirates and Mermaids, of history and mystery, beauty and danger, swords and seduction! Here unknown treasures lie waiting… to be colored with your imagination!

Welcome to Atlantis

Anne Bonney Victorious

Catch of the Day...maybe

The Rescue and Awakening

A moment to treasure

A Mermaid's Kiss

Her own terms

Deep Gazing

French Corsaire

Aquilla and her steed, Morceffyl

The Raven Feathers her Nest

Delicacies of the Deep

Song of the Sea

Luminous Depths

Captain Isabella avenges her father

Settling a Disagreement

Anguilles and her Serpents

Jacquotte Delahaye
Back from the Dead

Part of the Family

A Waste of Good Rum

Riches Reclaimed

Jewels of the Sea

Be Ye Ready for Volume II, Matey?

The Artist and his wench, er, wife!

I've personally known many famous and fashionable "Pyrates" and Mermaids, having designed many for Disney over the past 30 years, but my love for them goes back to my childhood. What began as a romantic and then historical fascination became romantic again when I met my creative soul mate. Here we are at a Key West pirate celebration whilst we be courting. — *Matthew Davidson*

Many thanks to Lisa Mitrokhin, who colored the image on our back cover; you can find her tutorial at her Youtube channel by searching for "How to Color Jellyfish - Mermay Madness"

Share your masterpieces! Join us on social media:
Instagram: dawndavidsonart
Facebook: The Davidson Duo Official Coloring Group
See more coloring books and pages at our etsy shop:
www.etsy.com/shop/dawndavidsonart

Swatch and Scribble
Test your colors here!

Made in the USA
Columbia, SC
09 September 2020

The Official Handbook for Health Club Sales

Strengthen Membership Sales In 30 Days

Manny Butera

Dr. David Lill

Jennifer Lill

 Sundog, Ltd. • Nashville, TN 37206

The Official Handbook for Health Club Sales: Strengthen Membership Sales in 30 Days.

Manny Butera
Dr. David Lill
Jennifer Lill

 Published by Sundog, Ltd., Nashville, TN 37206

The Official Handbook for Health Club Sales copyright ©2005 by Manny Butera, Dr. David Lill, and Jennifer Lill. All rights reserved. No part of this book may be used, reproduced, or transmitted in any manner whatsoever without prior permission in writing except in the case of brief quotations embodied in critical articles and reviews. Queries regarding rights and permissions should be addressed to Sundog, Ltd., 1505 Stratton Avenue, Nashville, TN 37206

This book may be purchased for educational, business, or sales promotional use. For information or to order, please contact Sundog, Ltd., or Express Media Corporation, Inc., 1419 Donelson Pike, Nashville, TN 37217. Phone: 800-336-2631; email: fulfillment@expressmedia.com

FIRST EDITION

The Library of Congress Cataloging-in-Publication data

Butera, Manny
Lill, David
Lill, Jennifer

The Official Handbook for Health Club Sales: Strengthen Membership Sales in 30 Days. / Manny Butera / Dr. David Lill / Jennifer Lill. – 1st ed.

ISBN 1-932203-96-6 (paper)

1. Business 2. Sales training 3. Career development 4. Self help

I.Title.

Library of Congress Control Number: 2004110397

Dedication

This book is dedicated to my dad, Tony Butera. The unconditional love and devotion he gave to his family taught me how to be a leader, a father and a husband.

– Manny Butera

To the perfect father and grandfather, Deryl Bass. The dignified and Godly way he lived means more to us than he could ever realize. It is an honor to have known him.

– David and Jennifer Lill

Special Thanks to:

Chris Cunningham - Cover Design
The Warehouse Multimedia Studios
Phone: 615-851-9179
www.thewrhse.com

Jolene Reynolds - Layout Design
Express Media, Inc.
Phone: 615-360-6400
www.expressmedia.com

BRIEF CONTENTS

Table of Contents   iv

Preface   ix

About the Authors   xiv

PART I   Relationship Building and the Sales Cycle Framework

1   Your Career in Professional Fitness Sales   4

2   Relationship Selling   16

PART II   Cultivating an Ethics Climate and Developing Communication Skills

3   Ethical Issues in Selling   34

4   Purchase Behavior and Communication   48

5   Finding Your Selling Style   64

PART III   Gaining Knowledge, Preparing, and Planning for the Presentation

6   Preparation for Success in Fitness Sales   86

7   Becoming a Master Prospector   106

8   Preapproach and Telephone Techniques   126

PART IV   The Face-to-Face Relationship Model of Selling

9   Approaching the Prospect   144

10   Identifying Needs Through Questioning and Listening   162

11   Making the Presentation   182

12   Handling Objections   202

13   Closing the Sale   228

PART V   Management Aspects: Personal and Organizational

14   Service After the Sale   252

15   Time Management   268

THE OFFICIAL HANDBOOK FOR HEALTH CLUB SALES

TABLE OF CONTENTS

Preface . . . . **ix**
About the Authors . . . . **xiv**

PART I Relationship Building and the Sales Cycle Framework

1 Your Career in Professional Fitness Sales

Everybody Sells **4**
The Value of Salespeople **5**
Positive Attitudes Toward Professional Selling **6**
Definition of Personal Selling **7**
Rewards of a Sales Career **8**
Characteristics of Highly Successful Salespeople **10**

2 Relationship Selling

Chapter 2 Sponsored by Cybex

Value Creation Through Relationship Selling **16**
Relationship Selling Versus Traditional Selling **19**
Sales Cycle Framework for Relationship Selling **21**
Continuous Quality Improvement **25**
Team Selling **28**

PART II Cultivating an Ethics Climate and Developing Communication Skills

3 Ethical Issues in Selling

Chapter 3 Sponsored by Fitness Underwriters

The Ethical Dilemma **34**
Influences on a Fitness Consultant's Ethics **36**
Developing a Personal Code of Ethics **38**
Ethics and Job Tenure **40**
Sexual Harassment **42**
Ethics as Good Business **43**

4 Purchase Behavior and Communication

Chapter 4 Sponsored by Intrannuity

Caution: Small Words at Work **48**
Why Prospects Join **49**
Influences on the Decision Making Process **51**
The Communication Agenda **53**
Using Your Voice as a Selling Tool **57**
Selling Without Words **58**

5 Finding Your Selling Style

Chapter 5 Sponsored by Innovative Fitness Systems

A Difference in Social Style **64**

Table of Contents **v**

TABLE OF CONTENTS

The Social Styles Model 66
Identifying the Four Behavioral Styles 71
Versatility as a Communication Tool 76
Gender Style Differences 79

PART III Gaining Knowledge, Preparing, and Planning for the Presentation

6 Preparation For Success in Fitness Sales
Chapter 6 Sponsored by Free Motion
Preparing To Sell 86
Fitness Knowledge 87
Product Knowledge 93
Product Positioning 94
Motivation and Goal Setting 96
Success and the Total Person 101

7 Becoming a Master Prospector
Chapter 7 Sponsored by Colliers International
The Concept of Prospecting 106
Qualifying the Prospect 107
Methods of Prospecting 109
Internal Prospecting 111
External Prospecting 115
Managing Prospect Information 121

8 Preapproach and Telephone Techniques
Chapter 8 Sponsored by Life Fitness
Preparation and Preapproach 126
Telephone Techniques 129
The Six-Step Telephone Track 133
Sample Telephone Script 138

PART IV The Face-to-Face Relationship Model of Selling

9 Approaching the Prospect
Chapter 9 Sponsored by Star Trac
Purpose of the Approach 144
First Impressions. 146
Surface Language 148
The Proper Greeting. 150
Types of Approaches. 155

10 Identifying Needs Through Questioning and Listening
Chapter 10 Sponsored by Lorex
The Purpose of Asking Questions. 162
Strategic Recommendations. 169
Common Questioning Techniques 170
Classification of Questioning Techniques 174
Listening 177

THE OFFICIAL HANDBOOK FOR HEALTH CLUB SALES

TABLE OF CONTENTS

11 Making the Presentation
Chapter 11 Sponsored by Strive
Developing a Persuasive Presentation 182
Presentation Styles 185
Product-Analysis Worksheet 188
Five Steps to a Successful Presentation 192
Adjust the Presentation to Unique Circumstances 197
Price Presentation 198

12 Handling Objections
Chapter 12 Sponsored by Total Fitness Systems
The Truth about Objections...................................202
Types of Objections 203
Getting to the Heart of Sales Resistance 206
When to Answer Objections 208
A Six-Step Plan For Dealing with Buyers' Concerns................211
Five Specific Techniques for Negotiating Objections...............215
A Mindset for Negotiating Price Resistance 219
Three Methods for Overcoming the Question of Price 221

13 Closing the Sale
A Closing Frame of Mind 228
Functions of the Close 230
A Closing Consciousness 231
When to Close 235
Recognizing Buying Signals 236
Types of Closes 239

PART V Management Aspects: Personal and Organizational

14 Service After the Sale
Building Partnerships with Total Customer Service 252
Customer Service Techniques that Support the Relationship 255
Retain or Win Back Unhappy Customers 257
Follow-Up Activities for Membership Retention 262

15 Time Management
Developing a Time Management Attitude 268
Procedure for Getting Organized 271
An Organizing System 275
Maintaining a Positive Attitude Toward Time 280

THE OFFICIAL HANDBOOK FOR HEALTH CLUB SALES

Preface

INTRODUCTION

The Official Handbook for Health Club Sales is your guide for success in the competitive environment of the health and fitness industry. Becoming a great fitness consultant involves no less a commitment to your profession than does becoming a great physician, lawyer, or teacher. Follow our 30-day plan for reading this book, and then review key chapters periodically to refresh in your mind the principles of relationship selling. Before you know it, applying the principles in your club will be natural and become a part of who you are as a fitness sales professional.

Success begins by taking a single step. It begins by learning the correct principles and gaining the proper knowledge to lead you down the right path toward success. We believe that your path begins here by reading *The Official Handbook for Health Club Sales*.

Congratulations on purchasing the *new authority on gym membership sales!* This handbook is designed to strengthen your knowledge and selling ability. Experts in the health and fitness industry know that it is not always the amount of time you spend exercising; rather it is the *type of exercise* you do that makes the difference. That is why you can make a dramatic change in your *membership sales in just 30 days.*

Treat this handbook like a workout routine. Give your mind a *workout* by reading a chapter, and then spend the next day absorbing what you read, giving your "mental muscles" time to refresh and absorb the information. Using this method, after 15 chapters and 30 days, you will see real, tangible results. Like resistance loading in weight training, *building up* your arsenal of effective techniques will bring maximum results in the most efficient and explosive way.

We developed this handbook so every professional fitness consultant will have access to a training tool that offers the most comprehensive study of the relationship style of selling. Our goal was to find a way to break the process into its most basic components, in an attempt to simplify the complex interaction that takes place in an actual selling situation in your club.

The result is an eight-step sales cycle model that we explore in depth in over one-half of the handbook. This relationship-building style spells success for a fitness consultant operating in the highly competitive health club industry and dealing with today's health conscious buyers who demand correct answers to complex problems.

Because attitude is so important for achieving success in selling, we included verbal and nonverbal communication and social style technology as foundation stones in the relationship model of selling, as well as providing an ethical framework upon which a profitable and lasting career in fitness sales can be built.

Throughout this handbook, you will see the "world" of selling through current sales literature, personal experience, and stories of successful, active sales fitness consultants who put the theory contained in this handbook into everyday practice in their clubs. As one leading sales pro relayed to us, *"Practice without theory is blind and theory without practice is sterile."*

This handbook is divided into five sections. We urge you to read one chapter at a time to fully digest the material. Interact with it. Personalize it. Take plenty of notes in the margin, and at the end of each section, think about the practical applications to your sales career.

Read the following section descriptions so that you understand the sequence and how you can get the most out of the organization of the chapters. Remember, this is your handbook, your own personal "workout" for sharpened mental muscles, focus, and success in relationship selling.

PART I — Relationship Building and the Sales Cycle Framework

Chapter 1 discusses the consultative nature and problem-solving approach to selling and details the characteristics that successful fitness consultants possess. Relationship selling is interactive, involves two-way communication, encourages prospect participation, employs empathy, and promotes a win-win environment. Today's style of selling favors building close and trusting long-term relationships. Positioning yourself as a consultant creates a partnership with your members.

You gain a better understanding of the complete selling situation and the problems it generates by breaking the sale into its basic tasks. There are several steps to achieving a successful sale. An eight-step sales cycle is introduced in chapter 2 and explained in detail in chapters 7 to 14. It makes sense that if you understand what the steps are in the Sales Cycle Framework for Relationship Selling, and what is required to make each step a successful endeavor, you will become a professional in selling much quicker than those who are simply stumbling through the process trying to figure it out. The chapters included in this section are:

1. Your Career in Professional Fitness Sales
2. Relationship Selling

PART II — Cultivating an Ethical Climate and Developing Communication Skills

Few professions give you more opportunities for rejection on a daily basis than does the field of sales. Chapter 3 discusses the need for a strong ethical and moral character to sustain a sales career. Honest and caring service brings members back, assures more referrals, and ensures your success.

Success in professional selling also depends upon your ability to have a *productive exchange of information* with prospects and members. As detailed in chapter 4, the more you understand about potential members and their decision making process, the more readily you can discover what they need and want. Because success in relationship selling depends on accurately getting your message across to prospects, chapter 4 also describes how to break through communication barriers.

An especially useful tool for gaining insight into how the prospect is thinking is knowledge of the *social styles model*, presented in chapter 5. A social style is the way a person sends and receives information. It is a method for finding the best way to approach a prospect and to set up a working relationship with that person. The chapters included in this section are:

3. Ethical Issues in Fitness Sales
4. Purchase Behavior and Communication
5. Finding Your Selling Style

PART III — Gaining Knowledge, Preparing, and Planning for the Presentation

The information in chapter 6 prepares you for success in a sales career by focusing on gaining product knowledge, developing a plan for self-motivation, and goal setting.

Chapters 7 and 8 discuss the procedures for locating and qualifying prospects and identify the information needed to prepare for an effective club presentation. Chapter 7 is a very thorough look at the topic of prospecting. As the saying goes, "I'd rather be a master prospector than a wizard of speech and have no one to tell my story to."

Chapter 8 discusses the process of gathering preapproach information and presents a six-step telephone track for making appointments for that all important club presentation. The chapters in this section are:

6. Preparation for Success in Fitness Sales
7. Becoming a Master Prospector
8. Preapproach and Telephone Techniques

PART IV — The Face-to-Face Relationship Model of Selling

Chapters 9 to 13 are the very heart of professional selling. This is considered the "how to" portion of the handbook. We refer to this as the face-to-face portion of the sales cycle. It is the valuable time spent in the actual presentation – the time when a membership commitment is obtained and kept.

What happens in the opening moments is crucial to the overall success of the club presentation. Chapter 9 focuses on the approach. Chapter 10 is devoted to the art of asking questions and listening effectively. A questioning sequence and listening guidelines are presented to carry through the entire sales interview. Chapter 11 details the techniques to use in making the actual presentation. Units of conviction are the building blocks for creating and making a meaningful sales presentation. The five elements that comprise a complete unit of conviction are explained and illustrated.

Chapters 12 and 13 present the psychology behind handling objections and closing the sale. A plan to handle objections is introduced, while a separate section in chapter 12 explains several ways of dealing with the difficult price objection. Chapter 13 stresses that closing the sale is the natural conclusion to a successful sales interview. A special section presents specific ways that help a fitness consultant deal with the rejection so common in selling. The chapters in this section are:

   9. Approaching the Prospect
10. Identifying Needs Through Questioning and Listening
11. Making the Presentation
12. Handling Objections
13. Closing the Sale

PART V — Management Aspects: Personal and Organizational

The service you give members after they have joined can be as important, or even more important, than the sale itself. Keeping current members happy and regaining lost clients is the focus of chapter 14. Your club's members absolutely define quality in every transaction. Great salespeople don't *talk* customer service – they *live* perfect service.

Chapter 15 shows you how to get better control of your time and your activities. The chapter really is all about personal organization and self-management. You cannot manage time, but you can manage yourself and your personal activities. Administrative ability on the part of the salesperson is fundamental to success. The chapters in this section are:

14. Service After the Sale
15. Time Management

This saying rings so true in the health and fitness industry: *You only get out of something what you put into it.* We challenge you to achieve the maximum benefits of this powerful resource. Remember, there is no substitute for relationship selling. Commit to this – for yourself, your members, and your club. Good luck in your pursuit of sales success.

Here's the prescription for strengthening membership sales in 30 days!

ABOUT THE AUTHORS

Manny Butera is the CEO and founder of Total Fitness Systems LLC and managing Partner of Fitness Express LLC, a holding company that owns 6 health clubs in Tennessee. Mr. Butera has spent more than 15 years in the health and fitness club industry.

He has owned, opened, operated, and overseen the management of over 125 clubs in his career. Mr. Butera is an acknowledged industry expert in the field of club sales and marketing, and has conducted seminars on those subjects for over 10 years. Currently Mr. Butera is the director of the *World Gym Work Experience.*

Mr. Butera graduated with a BA in Business Administration from Faulkner University. He was awarded a full hockey scholarship and went on to play Professional Hockey in Canada and Italy. Mr. Butera is a proud father of four – Mackenzie, Cade, Addie Grace, and Maggie – along with his wife of nine years, Jennifer.

David J. Lill has a combined 30 years of sales, sales training, and teaching experience. He has taught selling classes at Baylor University, New Mexico State University and Belmont University. He earned his Ph.D. degree in Marketing from the University of Alabama. Dr. Lill is also a business consultant specializing in sales, advertising, and communications skills development.

Dr. Lill has won awards for excellence in teaching. He currently spends his time conducting seminars and training courses on sales and marketing related topics. His relationship selling model is being successfully used by companies throughout the country in a wide variety of industries including insurance, telecommunications, real estate, publishing, banking, hospitality, chemical, and automotive.

Dr. Lill is the author of the highly acclaimed college textbook, *Selling: The Profession,* now in its 4th edition, and is the co-author of *The Handbook for Relationship Selling: Acquire The Selling Focus.* Dr. Lill has published over 85 articles in various academic, trade and professional publications. These include: *Selling Power, Journal of Advertising, Journal of the Academy of Marketing Science, Sales & Marketing Management, Business Topics, Nashville Business Journal,* and the *Journal of Pharmaceutical Marketing & Management.*

Jennifer Lill received her first sales training while still in college as an independent contractor for the Southwestern Company. Ms. Lill also has training in human resources management from her work with Mercedes Benz U.S. International.

She attended the University of Alabama, graduating Summa Cum Laude with honors. While there, Ms. Lill was a research assistant and co-authored a finance textbook with an elite group of students and professors. She is currently a marketing developer for Synergistic Learning and serves on their Board of Advisors.

In addition, Ms. Lill is the co-author of *The Handbook for Relationship Selling: Acquire The Selling Focus*. She also has real estate industry experience and has plans to return to school for her Ph.D., while continuing to write and conduct sales training classes and seminars.

Part I

Relationship Building and the Sales Cycle Framework

Get Focused, and you can . . .

CHANGE is often desirable, frequently necessary, and always inevitable.

REMEMBER . . . only you can give yourself permission to approve of you. Free your mind from negative thinking.

ENVISION yourself as a success. What you think about, you become.

ATTITUDE does determine your altitude. It is what's inside that makes you rise.

THE right angle to solve a problem is the try-angle.

ELIMINATE failure as an option, and progress naturally occurs.

THE best is yet to come. Yesterday's impossibilities are today's possibilities.

HAVE your dreams. They are the stuff great people are made of. Reach for the stars, but keep your feet on the ground.

EXTRAORDINARY desire and persistence drive ordinary people to achieve great things. Achievers are not extraordinary people.

SEVEN days without laughter makes one weak.

A smile is the shortest distance between two people.

LISTEN twice as much as you talk. You have two ears and one tongue.

ENCOURAGING feedback is a process for learning about your impact on those around you.

SUCCESS is the progressive realization of worthwhile, predetermined, personal goals.

EXCUSES are for losers. Winners have ways. May we all find the way.

DETERMINE never to give up. It's when things seem worse that you must not quit.

GOALS are dreams with a due date.

EXPECT the best of yourself. Be somebody special. The best never consider success optional.

Chapter 1

Your Career in Professional Fitness Sales

FOCAL POINTS

- **The role of selling in our economy.**
- **The purpose of personal selling.**
- **Personal attributes of a fitness consultant.**
- **Opportunities gained by selling in the health and fitness industry.**

EVERYBODY SELLS

Many interactions between people involve selling. Of course, some are universally recognized as selling: Retail salespeople sell you clothes, furniture, or cameras; a salesperson sells you the car you drive; and your insurance agent sells you a policy. Nothing happens in business until somebody sells something. However, many other common transactions not usually recognized as selling involve the same skills, goals, and behavior patterns that professional salespeople use: Waiters attempt to sell you on trying a particular entrée, or adding a dessert to your order; politicians want to convince constituents to vote for them or convince other politicians to join them in promoting certain projects; and family members influence decisions such as where to live, who can use the family car tonight, and what to cook for dinner. In other words, you are already selling. You are selling yourself, your ideas, and your desire for cooperation and companionship to almost everyone you engage in anything more than the most casual conversation.

Chapter 1 — Your Career in Professional Fitness Sales

THE VALUE OF SALESPEOPLE

The growth of the health and fitness industry has been extraordinary. Americans realize and appreciate the benefits of a fit and healthy lifestyle. The growth continues at an accelerated rate, which has caused an increasing competitiveness among the world's major fitness providers. Competing with yesterday's sales strategies is dangerous as competitors battle each other. Clubs that build value for their members are the ones that continue to grow, regardless of the competition. The latest and best sales practices are essential in gaining new customers and in retaining those you currently serve. The fitness consultant must rise to the challenge because, as Will Rogers said, "Even if you're on the right track, you'll get run over if you just sit there."

It is crucial to understand the health and fitness world today and what challenges customers face so you can really become a *solutions provider*. You can demonstrate your value to customers by being actively involved in a fitness program as well. Exercise regularly and watch your diet. In other words, practice what you preach, especially if you are asking other people to pay for it.

Reliance on Salespeople

Your club relies on you to keep prospects and members informed of improved products and services the fitness industry and your club offer. To do that, your job is to identify customer needs, to determine ways those needs could be met by the services your facilities have to offer, and then to provide that information to the members. You are a facilitator of information that keeps you and your health club competitive. You have the opportunity to change the lives of so many people by helping them see the benefits of a fit and active lifestyle.

Importance of Sales Training

In today's extremely competitive selling environment the most successful health and fitness clubs provide continuing sales training on a regular basis. And many of these clubs spend considerable amounts of money for training. Their reason is simple: they see sales training as the basis for gaining an advantage over the competition.

Health clubs know that it is essential to spend money on training productive salespeople who will be long-term assets to the organization. In a survey of 250 sales organizations conducted by the Krannert School of Management at Purdue University, the cost of replacing a single sales rep (including recruitment, training, and lost-opportunity costs) ranges from $50,000 to $75,000. A well-trained fitness consultant is truly indispensible!

POSITIVE ATTITUDES TOWARD PROFESSIONAL SELLING

More accurate information and education today is helping to improve attitudes toward sales as a career. Individuals responding to recent surveys now support the view that selling requires more creativity, offers improved career opportunities, fosters increasing integrity, and provides better financial incentives than ever before.

An understanding of the personal attributes that a career in professional selling actually requires quickly dispels any outdated myths an individual may still possess. Four areas of your personality are involved:

Personal Integrity. Continued success in sales requires the highest possible ethical standards when dealing with prospects, members, and your own club. A fitness consultant who lies or deceives customers in order to complete a sale is soon out of a job because prospects do not join and get the word out that this person is not to be trusted. A professional salesperson has high values and always operates in the most ethical manner.

Personality Structure. Sales is a demanding career, which is why you must have a confident personality, a positive self-image, and a sense of self-worth. A fitness consultant who is unable to accept the reality that not every prospect becomes a member will be devastated by failures and feel an overwhelming sense of personal rejection. Successful consultants have instead a driving desire and sincere belief in helping others make positive decisions regarding their health and fitness goals.

Personal Relationships. Successful salespeople are recognized as productive, capable professionals. Selling need never be personally degrading. You are not required to pretend, to abdicate your own personality or needs, or to become doormats for customers. Success in the professional world of health and fitness does not call for assuming an inferior position. The most successful salespeople find that their members become friends with whom they form personal relationships.

Personal Abilities. Success in sales requires high levels of intellect and developed skills. You must be able to understand, sometimes quickly and almost intuitively, a customer's specific needs and problems. Then you must interpret those needs even if customers themselves do not have a clear picture of their own needs or

Chapter 1 — Your Career in Professional Fitness Sales 6

cannot verbalize them clearly. Develop a broad knowledge of health, fitness, and nutrition, and understand how to relate to people positively. The development of these skills requires not only intelligence but also continuous training.

DEFINITION OF PERSONAL SELLING

- Personal selling is the process of **seeking** out people who have a particular need, **assisting** them to recognize and define that need, **demonstrating** to them how your particular service fills that need, and **persuading** them to make a decision to use that service.

Because every sales situation is unique, your career in sales is an exciting and demanding career in which every day brings opportunities to develop new skills and sales strategies and ways to refine existing ones. The potential for personal and professional growth never ends. Because different prospects have varying needs, interests, ability to pay, and authority to make a decision, selling is different in every situation – it is constantly changing, bringing with it new possibilities.

Becoming a Master Salesperson

Too many people involved in selling have not attempted to learn the basic skills needed for success in the profession. They cop out by saying that they weren't born to be salespeople. They are called the "90-day wonders" because after ninety days they wonder why they ever got into the sales business. Professional salespeople read books, take courses, ask questions, study the techniques of successful salespeople, work for their customers, and continually strive to outperform themselves.

Selling requires a working knowledge of psychology, sociology, communication, and persuasion. It is not a natural process to "close" asking for a membership. It is a skill to be learned just like anything else. Salespeople can fail if they get to the point where they think they know it all. Success in selling is a contant learning process. You must be a student of your profession. Successful salespeople are made, not born, and they are made with concentrated attention, repeated practice, and goal-directed action.

We are all like computers in that we are only as good as we have programmed ourselves to be philosophically, emotionally, and intellectually. Becoming a real master salesperson takes a long time. The very best salespeople continue to adapt and refine their professional skills throughout their careers.

REWARDS OF A SALES CAREER

The once popular "Wide World of Sports" television program promised the viewer "the thrill of victory–the agony of defeat." This thrill of victory makes sales an exciting and satisfying career, but the thrill is not just that of earning the monetary rewards or beating out the competition. That is actually a minor part of the satisfaction of successful selling.

The true victory you will enjoy as a successful fitness consultant consists of moving up to satisfy higher personal needs. Maslow's hierarchy of needs presented in Figure 1.1 has special significance for you. In the beginning, salespeople concentrate on supplying their lower-order needs: earning a living, providing security for themselves and their families, and being accepted socially by their peers. As they satisfy these basic needs, salespeople can concentrate on the higher-level needs: self-acceptance (a positive self-image), making a contribution to community life, and self-actualization (becoming all one can be; knowledge and achievement for its own sake).

Sense of Independence and Variety

A sales career frees you from a mundane daily routine. You are likely to work a variety of hours and deal with prospects who have widely different personalities. What works with one prospect may antagonize another. Consequently, you must always be aware of every element of the environment and adjust quickly. Selling is never boring.

You can exercise a greater measure of control over your time and activities than many other professional people. Sales is not a nine-to-five job. The hours are usually flexible, long one day and short another. Because your job is not structured just for you, you must be a self-starter and stay motivated.

Security

Health clubs will always need fitness consultants. In fact, the demand appears to be steadily increasing rather than decreasing. Ambitious salespeople are eagerly sought, and most health clubs provide excellent rewards and benefits for their top sales performers. They know that quality salespeople who become dissatisfied can easily go to work for a competitor.

Because you are usually paid according to performance, you can directly affect your own income by deciding how much time and effort to invest in the job. Thus, your security comes from your own personal decisions about how hard and

Chapter 1 — Your Career in Professional Fitness Sales   **8**

how efficiently you want to work. *Work, in many ways, is like money; if you are willing to expend enough of it, you can have almost anything you want.*

Entrepreneurship

Sales is an ideal career for those planning to one day own and run their own business. No business can survive without a viable marketing organization. An owner or chief executive who has been involved in sales truly understands this part of the business and is in an excellent position to launch and manage a new enterprise successfully.

Figure 1.1

Hierarchy of Personal Needs

Self-Actualization
Fulfillment of Full Personal Potential

Personal Esteem Needs
Self-Acceptance

Social Needs
Affiliation — Group Membership — Acceptance by Others

Safety Needs
Physical Safety — Job Security — Satisfying Personal Relationships — Psychological Security

Physiological Needs
Adequate Food — Water — Shelter — Air to Breathe — Sexual Satisfaction

Compensation Potential

Because of their vital role in business, salespeople are among the best-paid employees of a company. More salespeople earn above $100,000 annually than people in any other profession. The top performers are walking away with the fattest wallets by far, averaging $139,826 in total compensation. Some salespeople make less, some make considerably more. Salespeople are the catalysts of the economy. They are responsible for keeping goods, services, and ideas flowing.

CHARACTERISTICS OF HIGHLY SUCCESSFUL SALESPEOPLE

No single list of traits exactly describes every successful salesperson. They are as diverse as members of any other profession. They include both extroverts and introverts—and all the degrees in between, shy and outspoken, talkative and quiet. However, certain core characteristics seem to be present to some degree in most successful salespeople, despite the numerous ways individuals express those characteristics and adapt them to their own styles. Focus on the following ten attributes that enhance the likelihood of success for you in the health and fitness industry:

Enthusiasm

Ralph Waldo Emerson said, "Nothing great was ever achieved without enthusiasm." One of the most important characteristics in new salespeople is enthusiasm, but a distinction must be made between people who are enthusiastic about their club and those who are merely eager to take someone's money. Your enthusiasm is based on a genuine belief in your health club and a conviction that it will serve the needs of the members. Such enthusiasm is communicated both verbally and nonverbally to the prospect in terms of your own personality. Enthusiasm may be expressed as calm, quiet confidence or excited activity. However it is demonstrated, real enthusiasm is highly attractive and reassuring to prospects.

Empathy

Empathy, the ability to understand another person's concerns, opinions, and needs, whether sharing them or not, provides salespeople with the *sales edge* of being able to think and understand "with" the prospect during a tour of the facilities. In order to accurately understand what a person is really saying, you must temporarily set aside your own preconceived notions. It is essential in the initial contact to uncover the basic needs or requirements they might have before dis-

Chapter 1 — Your Career in Professional Fitness Sales

cussing a workout routine. By careful listening, effective salespeople absorb prospects' reactions, generate an upbeat environment, and sell themselves to customers. The combination of sincerity and empathy enables them to tailor their presentation to mesh precisely with the prospect's stated lifestyle and fitness goals.

Goal Direction

Stay focused on your goals and daily activities. A half-dozen things make 80 percent of the difference between success and failure. Ask yourself what things contribute the most to your success. Goal-directed salespeople often respond positively to incentives such as money, prestige, recognition, and pride of accomplishment, which they see as tools they can use to reach their overall goals. When these incentives fit into their overall plan for achieving the goals that represent self-actualization for them, salespeople go all out to win them.

Ability to Ask Questions

Good fitness consultants ask questions; poor ones just keep talking. You need to remain in control of the tour, and the person who is asking questions is the one in control. When you learn to ask the right kinds of questions you gain new prospects, discover valuable qualifying information, uncover prospects' buying motives, and are able to anticipate most objections. Asking questions is your best tool for keeping the appointment on track and moving toward a successful close, while also giving the prospect the feeling of remaining in control of the situation.

Resourcefulness

Top salespeople are resourceful. On the spur of the moment, they can think of new ways to make an old point, new applications and creative uses for their health club, and unique reasons for a particular prospect to join. They can think on their feet under pressure. Resourcefulness operates like a reflex action, an automatic response.

"Nothing can stop the man with the right mental attitude from achieving his goal; nothing on earth can help the man with the wrong mental attitude."

-Thomas Jefferson

Resourcefulness comes from an agile and analytical mind and allows you to stay on the right side of *the fine line between being just right and very wrong.* In the sales situation, the right word or phrase clears away the fog and reveals the solutions. The wrong word or phrase is like putting a drop of ink into a glass of water; it obscures everything. Resourceful salespeople always seem to have at hand a barrelful of ideas and strategies.

Administrative Ability

Efficient self-management, especially the management of time, is essential to success in fitness sales. Your most productive time is spent face-to-face with prospects. But you are also required to attend meetings, prepare for gym tours, read, study, do paperwork, and conduct after-sale follow-up and member services. Efficient time management can make the difference between success and failure.

Initiative

All great salespeople have a powerful, unrelenting, internal drive to excel. This intrinsic motivation can be shaped and molded, but it cannot be taught. Successful salespeople are self-motivated. They are self-starters who exercise initiative. They do not wait to be told to prospect, to be assigned tours to give, or to be urged to end the presentation with a close. They see the work that needs to be done and take personal responsibility for doing it. Creative ideas that surface during a club tour must be implemented then and there—without time to ask their manager for advice. Salespeople who have self-confidence supported by solid product knowledge and belief in their own ability to succeed feel free to exercise initiative.

Perseverance

Setbacks often outnumber triumphs, and salespeople must have reserves of strength and resilience to fall back on when this happens. The number of sales closed compared to the number of presentations made usually ranges from 5 percent to 50 percent or more. Salespeople need perseverance in several areas:

- The ability to keep going to another prospect no matter how many decide not to join.

- The ability to make repeated presentations to the same prospect over a period of time.

- The ability to continue asking for an appointment to make a sales presentation until one is finally granted.

Self Discipline

Salespeople that are truly successful have developed a tremendous amount of self-discipline. Most of the time you will not have your club sales manager continually checking in to make sure you are always on time and working hard all day. Yet it is still crucial to plan your work and execute your plan with diligence

Chapter 1 — Your Career in Professional Fitness Sales   12

each and every day. By staying efficient and on track you are less likely to give up memberships to competitors.

Pleasant Personality

The way to make a friend is to be one. The fitness consultant with a pleasant, outgoing disposition is remembered and favored. A key to forming a pleasant personality is to like people and genuinely enjoy knowing as many different kinds of people as possible. People respond to those who like them.

Department store entrepreneur J.C. Penney said, "All great business is built on friendship." How do you build friendships in today's tough competitive sales climate? Find out what the potential member needs, then make every effort to deliver it. Ask yourself: "What would I do if I really wanted to be friends with this person?" The answer will tell you how to build a long-term relationship.

Your Career In Professional Fitness Sales

REFOCUS

- Selling is a basic component of all human interaction and involves discovering needs and providing products or services that satisfy those needs.

- Salespeople are among the highest-paid professionals and make the greatest impact on profitability and success for a health club.

- An understanding of the benefits of health and fitness is essential in helping others identify their health and exercise goals.

- All personality types can be successful as fitness consultants, but focus on these characteristics that enhance the likelihood of success: enthusiasm, empathy, goal direction, ability to ask questions, resourcefulness, administrative ability, initiative, perseverance, self discipline, and a pleasant personality.

- Selling is a demanding career that offers substantial rewards with outstanding opportunities for personal achievement.

Chapter 1 — Your Career in Professional Fitness Sales

Experience the Total Body Arc Trainer, the revolutionary cross-trainer that significantly increases the effectiveness of your upper and lower body workout. Nothing else allows you to personalize the intensity of your workout or reach your goals this fast. The Total Body Arc Trainer is the result of five decades perfecting the science of biomechanics and challenging the limits of human performance. Cybex engineers define the industry with groundbreaking technology; we differentiate ourselves from the competition through unyielding dedication and passion to create the most empowering fitness products in the world.

equipment | financing | service | customization

Chapter 2

Relationship Selling

VALUE CREATION THROUGH RELATIONSHIP SELLING

Over the past few decades there has been a revolution occurring in professional sales. This revolution is in the relationship selling process where the buyer requires advice and expertise. The same is true in the health and fitness industry. Consumers want to deal with trained and knowledgeable fitness consultants. This new selling is all about value creation: how the selling process itself can be used to create value for the customer.

It is important to recognize the "ABC's" of the fitness industry, the basics that will always be an effective approach to club sales. Arnold Schwarzenegger, in his book *Modern Bodybuilding,* states that the bench press is one of the fundamentals of basic exercise. He says, "The bench press is the king of upper body movement when it comes to size, period." The same applies to professional fitness consultants. Sure you can try the new techniques, listen to self-improvement tapes, read books written by Zig Ziglar, Brian Tracy, and all the experts. As a matter of fact, that is recommended. However, as soon as you forget about the basics of the sales cycle outlined in this hand-

FOCAL POINTS

- **The role of relationship selling and stereotypes of selling.**
- **Steps in relationship selling.**
- **Relationship selling versus the traditional sales model.**
- **Total quality management in your health club.**
- **Building relationships through team selling.**

> Your professionalism is defined not by the business you are in, but by the way you are in business.
>
> — Dr. Tony Alessandra

book your sales production will decrease without a shadow of a doubt.

Relationship selling–in which fitness consultants demonstrate not just a club's features, but how it can help its members reach fitness and lifestyle goals–isn't a new idea. Yet experts say that few health clubs have truly adopted this method of selling. Positioning yourself as a professional consultant creates a more equal relationship with prospects and members. Exhibit 2.1 illustrates the key elements that can build or break this trust-bond relationship between you and a potential member.

Build or Break a Relationship

Partnership is a positive word that makes customers and members feel that you are looking out for their best interests. The partnership formed between the buyer and seller is not a "legal" partnership. Rather it is a part of the continuous qual-

Exhibit 2.1

How to Build or Break a Relationship

Relationship Builders
- Treat members like lifelong partners.
- Become a solutions provider.
- Deliver more service than you promise.
- Seek out members to ask about their progress.
- Develop open and honest communication.
- Use the "we can" approach.
- Take responsibility for mistakes made.

Relationship Breakers
- Focus only on getting the membership.
- Simply wait for a problem to develop.
- Lie or make exaggerated claims.
- Wait for prospects to call you.
- Focus on your own personal monetary gain.
- Use the "us-versus-them" approach.
- Blame somebody else. Knock a competitor.

ity improvement process that successful health clubs are implementing. To be successful, take time to get to know the customer's situation, needs, decision-making process, and the competitive environment. In health and fitness sales, a partnership is a living demonstration of the attitudes sales reps have toward their members. Relationship selling allows you to grasp a person's fitness needs by putting yourself in their shoes. You are first a *diagnostician.*

Relationship fitness conslutants create an information transfer, a support for members' goals, and enthusiasm for their success. Chris Elkins, a fitness consultant in North Carolina, believes that we need to get away from a selling mentality and let the members tell us their needs. He states that we should strive to build a relationship, based on a trust in our expertise that can help members reach their goals. When this occurs, Elkins says, "We talk about our approach to solving our members' problems and sometimes don't even need to ask for the membership. The prospect often asks us."

To be a consultant rather than just a salesperson you have to be a creative resource, a value provider, and a friend to members. The relationship fitness consultant works hard helping others succeed–not just helping them join. Unless you are willing to commit to excellence, consultation will not occur. Here are some key characteristics of relationship selling:

- Discover and understand potential members' problems and needs.

- Partner with your members and become a valuable resource for information.

- Demonstrate to prospects how they can achieve their goals at your club.

- Have a true conviction that your club and its services are the best for your members.

- Believe in yourself because a positive attitude makes it all work.

In professional selling, as in medicine, prescription before diagnosis is malpractice.

Chapter 2 — Relationship Selling

RELATIONSHIP SELLING VERSUS TRADITIONAL SELLING

It just makes sense that if you understand what the steps are in the *Relationship Model of Selling,* and what it takes to make each step a successful endeavor, then you will become a professional in selling much more quickly than those individuals who are simply stumbling through the process trying to figure it out. The *sales cycle model* in the actual face-to-face meeting between you and the prospect includes these 4 steps:

1. Approach
2. Identifying Needs
3. Making the Presentation
4. Handling Objections and Gaining Commitment

Figure 2.1 contrasts the amount of time the relationship salesperson and the traditional salesperson spend in each step. You can see from the figure that the old pyramid model of selling has been turned upside down. The 40 percent of the equation for the traditional model that used to be closing is now *building trust* in the relationship model. Meanwhile *reassuring the customer and closing* has shrunk to just 10 percent in the new model.

The relationship fitness consultant spends the vast majority of time in the first two steps, whereas the traditional salesperson exerts most of the effort and the majority of time on presenting features and trying to close. The goal is to learn how to communicate and establish an alliance that is extensive in scope and relevant to the potential member's fitness goals.

Customers Buy Solutions

Low-end selling – essentially *order taking* – continues to shift away from traditional sales forces into the more efficient, cost-effective, and faster setting provided by the Internet. But this doesn't mean that the Internet will replace the professional fitness consultant. Selling is simply becoming more strategic. Prospects can read a brochure or visit a club's website and join, but they don't. They are looking for a place to come several times a week, a place that has to feel comfortable in terms of both environment and people. Their impression of the club will be formed by you, and that is why an *order taker* doesn't successfully sell memberships, a professional and knowledgeable fitness consultant does.

Figure 2.1

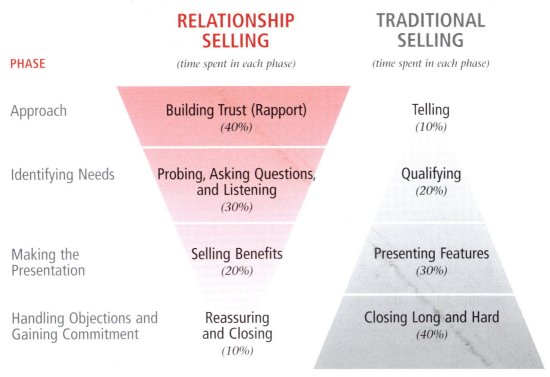

You are selling memberships, but that is really not what customers are buying – customers are trying to improve their health and feel better about themselves. By demonstrating how you can help customers achieve their goals, you distinguish yourself from competitors. Selling is still about relationships, and people buy from people they like. Order-takers will vanish, but creative salespeople who know that selling is about building long-term relationships will flourish.

You are a solutions provider.

SALES CYCLE FRAMEWORK FOR RELATIONSHIP SELLING

A better understanding of the complete selling situation and the problems it generates may be gained by breaking the sale into its basic tasks. These eight steps are presented in a logical sequence, but they are *not necessarily chronological* and the order of the steps will vary. The ebb and flow of a sales interview defies attempts to package it into nice, neat compartments. Every selling situation has a beginning, an end, and a number of identifiable points in between.

Certain predictable tasks must be performed, such as identifying prospects and determining needs. These tasks may be called the *steps* in a sale or the *selling cycle*. When organized into a prescribed sequence they comprise an overall structure rather than a lock-step approach to selling. The eight basics of successful selling described in Figure 2.2 are the focus of chapters 7 through 14. These steps represent your guide to a successful sales career in the health and fitness industry.

Phase One

Identify Qualified Prospects. Prospecting is the process of searching for someone with a *need* for your club's services, the *ability* to pay for it, and the *authority* to make the decision to join. One of the first steps in the process of finding these qualified prospects is to talk to current members to see who might need additional personal training or nutritional help, and then get names and phone numbers of friends who may be interested in membership. At the same time, survey your territory to identify new leads that might be interested in joining your club.

Plan Preapproach Activities. After you identify qualified prospects, establish a definite purpose for each sales call. To accomplish this, you must make an evaluation of your potential customers' needs to determine how to best present your club. This equips you to interact with the customer and then develop an action plan and call schedule to set appointments.

Phase Two

Approach the Prospect. Treat prospects as individuals and not as carbon copies of everyone else. What happens during the opening moments of the face-to-face encounter affects the success of the whole presentation. Some people simply do not thaw out immediately, and you must find ice-breakers that help the prospect feel at ease with you. This is why you should spend time finding the prospect's comfort level. Most first-time meetings between you and a prospect produce an *egocentric predicament* arising from your fear of being rejected and the prospect's

Figure 2.2
A Sales Cycle Framework for Relationship Selling

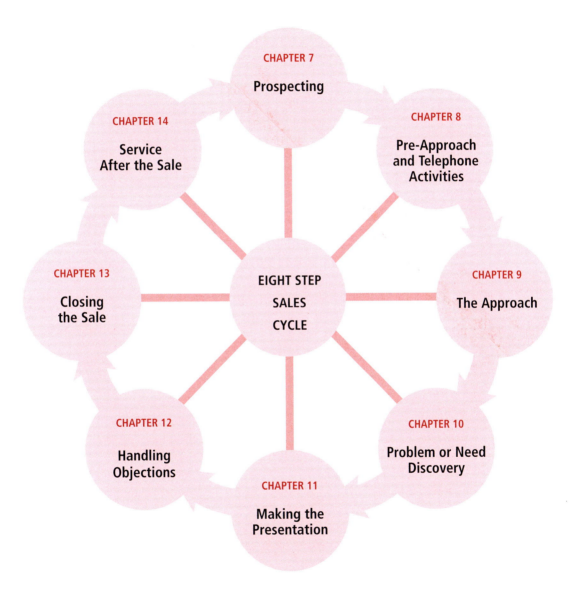

fear of "being sold". By redesigning your approach to selling, you can calm the prospect's fear of joining and reduce your own fear of selling.

Discover Needs. During this step of the sales encounter, you and your potential members discover whether they need or want what your club can provide. Because the success of the whole process rests on this basic discovery, the relationship salesperson spends whatever time is necessary and asks questions to get to know the prospect's fitness requirements. For this reason, one of your primary goals in every sales situation should be to create an atmosphere within which an act of trust can occur—to make a friend rather than a sale, a customer who has confidence in the integrity and ability of the salesperson, and confidence in the club and its services. *You don't talk prospects into a membership; you listen them into a membership.*

Make the Presentation. Your evaluation of the prospect's situation should lead you naturally into the presentation of club benefits that fit the needs the potential member expressed. Every health club has both features and benefits. A feature is any fact about the club, tangible or intangible. For example, a feature of a particular health club may be group aerobics classes. However, prospects want to know about benefits rather than features. This feature is meaningless unless it satisfies some need or provides some benefit to the prospective member. The benefits of group classes might be explained in terms of cardiovascular health or the motivation that comes from group exercise.

Even better than showcasing the value of the club is to allow prospects to assess that value by discovering for themselves the benefits of membership. The relationship salesperson is customer-oriented. A prospect does not join without being certain that what you are saying is true. *No one likes to be sold.* They like to see the value of what is being presented, and then they make their own buying decisions based on their own assessment of whether or not your club can satisfy their needs.

Handle Objections and Gain Commitment. This part of the overall process helps to avoid misunderstandings by bringing any that exist out into the open so they can be handled. Each clarification and confirmation adds weight to the case in favor of a positive decision. As shown in Figure 2.3, when the scale of decision tips far enough toward the positive side, the prospect can, and does, say yes. When that happens, everyone wins—the client, you, and your club. Relationship selling is a matter of presenting positive benefits that respond to a need, use, and value. Selling in this manner reduces your need to deal with resistance, answer objections, or haggle over membership prices. Since the client has been an active participant throughout, the commitment and close should be the natural conclusion to a successful club presentation.

Figure 2.3

The Scale of Decision

Selling positive benefits tips the scale

Phase Three

Service After the Sale. The final phase of relationship selling is service after the sale. After all, one of the purposes of a club is to create and keep a member. Service, service, and more service is what counts and gives you a competitive edge. Plenty of satisfied members do not renew their memberships unless you create some kind of trust-bond relationship.

Ultimately, you should look at customer satisfaction as an economic asset just like any other asset of the club. Creating customer satisfaction is an income-producing endeavor. Too many salespeople perform service mechanically, without thinking of the impact their actions have on customers. Members must sense that you truly care about them. Service after the sale is your way of expressing appreciation for their business. Service makes the difference and is as important as the quality of your facilities. For example, show that you genuinely care by offering to take a new member through a weight training session to get them started.

CONTINUOUS QUALITY IMPROVEMENT

There has been so much written on Total Quality Management that some have dismissed it as merely a theory that is discussed because it sounds good. But to ignore the underlying principles of TQM would not be sensible. TQM is an essential building block for relationship selling, and the principles have practical implications for you.

How does TQM fit into relationship selling in the health and fitness industry? Total Quality Management has a customer orientation. It is an *outside-in* approach to business. The center of all discussions is the customer; every one *inside* and *outside* the club is a customer. Continuous quality improvement is a philosophy, an overall style of management that focuses on customer satisfaction. Federal Express Chief Executive Officer Fred Smith states that, "Employee satisfaction is a prerequisite to customer satisfaction." Therefore, TQM not only focuses on fostering healthy relationships with members, but also on building connections within your club.

The list below highlights the main points of TQM that deal directly with fostering relationships and building lasting associations. While there are variations in the language and scope of TQM programs, it is possible to target these five principles that are especially relevant in the practice of relationship selling:

1. **Listen and learn** from your members and your co-workers.

2. **Continuously improve** partnerships with members and co-workers.

3. **Build teamwork** by establishing trust and mutual respect.

4. **Do it right the first time** to ensure member satisfaction.

5. **Improve communication** in your club to enhance the use of its resources.

Service Quality: A Team Effort

What does a health club have to do to provide exceptional service quality and how does the fitness consultant fit into the process? First, everyone in your club must think in terms of the whole process rather than their own tasks. The goal is to develop a member, and that's a *process* in which the sales rep is only one player. The process includes nutritionalists, trainers, and other fitness consultants. So it's not left to you to solve a customer's problem; the whole club gets behind the effort. Building customer relationships is everybody's responsibility.

It is important to focus on how you relate to other employees, because this can make a difference in the way members are treated. It pays to be liked and appreciated by staff people, especially those at the front desk and the personal trainers. Take a lesson from Mark Twain, who said, "I can live for two months on a good compliment." Take a moment from time to time to compliment and thank your co-workers for the great job they are doing.

TQM is established today thanks to the pioneering work of W. Edwards Deming. One of Deming's most important lessons is his "85-15" rule. When things go wrong there is an 85 percent chance the system is at fault. Only about 15 percent of the time can the individual salesperson be blamed. TQM means the gym's culture is defined by and supports the constant attainment of customer satisfaction, through an integrated system of tools, techniques, and training. Prospects and members notice and think about everyone they come in contact with during and after the presentation. The relationship between perceived effort and customer service is a powerful one. When you and the customer interact, the quality of the interaction itself is an important part of the relationship. Figure 2.4 shows the dynamics of this interaction. Service quality has two dimensions: (1) the process of delivering the gym's services and (2) the actual outcome.

Most business success stories involve taking an old idea or product and doing a better job with it than the next company. Wal-Mart didn't invent discount selling; Sam Walton just did it better. And the executives who now run Wal-Mart are improving the way they buy and stock merchandise to drive their costs and prices even lower. Then there is Starbucks! Coffee shops have been around for a long time, but no one before Starbucks had figured out how to organize and run several thousand of them. The overall point is this: You can get a lot out of the services your club provides if you change the processes around it, or change the process by which it is presented.

Chapter 2 — Relationship Selling

Figure 2.4

The Service Quality Interaction

The $332,000 Customer: Why It Pays to Go the Extra Mile

Tom Peters, author of *A Passion for Excellence*, says, "A customer is not a transaction; a customer is a relationship." The missing link in service often is intense awareness of the customer's point of view. The process of handling the problem is as important to customers as the solution of the problem itself. The logical inference is that every gym better organize its operations to answer every member's implied question: "What are you going to do for me today?"

Peters uses the example of Dallas car dealer Carl Sewell, who has written a book called *The $332,000 Customer* because a loyal lifetime Cadillac customer buys that much from him. Peters goes on to suggest that each happy lifetime customer generates four or five more happy lifetime customers for you. So in fact, one Cadillac customer is roughly a $1,500,000 customer. Two investments Sewell has made illustrate his understanding of the value he places on customer satisfaction. Number one, he bought a street sweeper to keep the front of his dealership extra clean. First impressions count for everything, and people judge his dealership by the cleanliness of everything including the road in front of it. Number two, he convinced an upscale local restaurant to open a branch in his service bay. When it's a simple repair, a lot of his customers come in and enjoy a hot meal while the work is being done.

Figure 2.5 illustrates the kind of behavior wanted in a quality-driven health club and the kind that exists in the typical club. To move from left to right, use the 12 essential elements of TQM and your commitment to customer satisfaction to guide

Figure 2.5

Culture Changes in a Health Club

Traditional Mangement Model	Total Quality Management Model
Focus on club features	Focus on service
Club knows best	Customer knows best
Transactions	Relationships
Individual performance	Team performance
Firefighting management	Continuous improvement
Blame/punishment	Support/reward
Short-term (year or less)	Long-term (years)
Intolerant of errors	Allows mistakes
Autocratic leadership	Participative leadership
Bureaucratic	Entrepreneurial
Top-down decisions	Consensus decisions
Inward-focused	Outward (customer)-focused

you. Some salespeople will read this and say, "This is nothing new; it is simply common sense." They are right, of course, but it has taken many years for men such as W. Edwards Deming, Philip Crosby, Joseph Juran, and Genichi Taguchi to refine and teach this philosophy.

TEAM SELLING

Team Selling is a cooperative action by two or more fitness professionals directed to selling memberships. The sales team often consists of at least one fitness consultant, supported by the desk staff, trainers, and management, a combination that utilizes the relationship expertise of the salesperson as well as the competency of other personnel throughout the club. The concept of team selling balances perfectly with the principles behind TQM because team sales builds lasting relationships, breaks down

Chapter 2 — Relationship Selling   28

walls, and opens communication through teamwork. That's why two heads really are better than one.

The team approach gains an advantage over *one-on-one* selling, because it utilizes the strengths of each individual on the team. Some professional salespeople may lack the patience and attention to detail that are required to eventually guide a hesitant prospect to join. Yet, your manager or another fitness consultant involved on the team may possess these very characteristics if they are more detail-oriented by nature. Similarly, a personality that appears too abrupt in the eyes of a prospective member may be offset by an amiable personality who can energize the prospect with a sense of confidence.

Benefits of Team Selling

A healthy team attitude begins with a solid commitment to help team members win. There is no room for prima donnas within the team. The only person who is allowed to be the prima donna is the customer. One of the primary benefits of team selling is that it enables a gym to improve its relationship with members, by allowing direct communication between the prospect and fitness experts before the sale is made. Thus, you can more accurately define needs, and prospects can have questions answered by an individual who has an intimate knowledge of the health and fitness industry. This creates an aura of authority and trustworthiness for the club and for you.

The Roles of Each Team Member

When giving a club presentation, be sure to involve the appropriate club employees at the right time. For example, if a prospect has a lot of questions about personal training, get a trainer involved in the presentation. If you are finding a close particularly difficult, your manager may want to perform a *takeover*, commonly known in the industry as a *TO*. This allows you to watch your manager to see where you can improve for future presentations. The important thing to remember is to find a combination that is right for you.

Take a lesson from major-league baseball managers. A manager has starting pitchers (openers) and relief pitchers (closers) on his ball club. Many of baseball's best starting pitchers average six or seven strong innings each time out. The relief pitcher then comes in and shuts down the opposing team and saves the game for the starter. Neither player is complete on his own. Together, however, they produce a winning performance.

THE OFFICIAL HANDBOOK FOR HEALTH CLUB SALES

Relationship Selling
REFOCUS

- The traditional role of selling has evolved from the art of persuasion to the psychology of relationship selling.

- The relationship cycle of selling begins with approaching the prospect, discovering needs, presenting your gym as the solution, overcoming objections, and gaining commitment. Service after the sale completes the cycle.

- The purpose of the relationship approach to selling is to discover the needs or problems of the prospect. You become a solutions provider! It is customer-oriented and requires extensive knowledge of the prospect.

- Build relationships through customer-oriented continuous quality improvement. This is an outside-in approach, encouraging the mind-set that every one inside and outside the company is a customer.

- Team selling fosters relationships through encouraging a sharing of ideas, resources, capabilities, and responsibilities.

Chapter 2 — Relationship Selling

Part II

Cultivating an Ethical Climate and Developing Communication Skills

FitnessInsurance.com • 800-881-7130 • a division of Jewell Insurance Associates
8480 E. Orchard Rd., Ste. 5500 • Greenwood Village, Co 80111

INSURING FITNESS CENTERS SINCE 1982

You face risks and exposures that most agents just don't have the experience to recognize. Don't find out the hard way.

Specializing in insurance for:

- Health Clubs • Spas • Equipment Manufacturing
- Supplement Manufacturing & Distribution

Coverages include:

- Professional Liability • Workers' Comp • Umbrellas
- Replacement Cost Property • Bonds • Product Liability
- Supplement Manufacturing/Distribution Liability
- Employment Practices Liability • Tanning Liability

endorsed vendor:

FITNESS INSURANCE · COM
a real understanding of the fitness industry

Chapter 3

Ethical Issues In Fitness Sales

FOCAL POINTS

- •Principles upon which to base ethical behavior.

- • Influences on ethical behavior.

- • Your role in the ethical position of your club.

- • Examining your personal ethics.

THE ETHICAL DILEMMA

Michael Beem feels as though he is being torn apart. He is a personal trainer at a local health and fitness club. One of his single female clients has shown a real interest in dating him and he would like to ask her out. He knows that the club policy strictly prohibits dating members, but he thinks he can go out with her and no one would ever know. After all, some of his co-workers are doing the same thing, and their manager has no idea this is going on.

Michael is facing a situation that falls in the category of ethical considerations. Because fitness consultants are relatively free and independent operators, they may encounter more ethical dilemmas than many other business people. For this reason, you must be clear on your own ethical standards before getting caught up in something that escalates beyond your control.

Today's renewed interest in ethics can be used by sales professionals to their advantage. We have this heightened interest in ethical issues due to the shocking, unethical, and immoral activities of a variety of business and government leaders and other public figures. It is not organizations, institutions, or clubs however, that are unethical; individual people are unethical. Ethics is a personal matter. The ethics of a business, government, or other organization is merely a reflection of the combined value systems of its members.

Some say that business ethics is an *oxymoron*, a contradiction in terms. They suggest that business has no ethics or that ethics is something that people worry about on Sunday morning and not when they are out selling in the real world. This thinking is ludicrous! The notion that honest salespeople finish last is poisonous; in addition, it is untrue. Unethical behavior is ultimately self-destructive; it generates more unethical conduct until a person hits rock bottom financially, spiritually, and morally.

The Origin of Ethics

A *legal* standard is enforced by laws and statutes, but an *ethical* standard is an outgrowth of the customs and attitudes of a society. Most of us have a shared idea of what we mean by ethics, but defining it in a way that everyone would accept is hard. Essentially, ethics is a systematic effort to judge human behavior as right or wrong in terms of two major criteria: truth and justice.

The root of the word *ethics* derives from the Greek word *ethos*, which means the character or sentiment of the community. A society cannot exist unless people agree fundamentally on what is right and wrong, just and unjust. The three most important value-forming institutions in America are family, church, and school. Many people believe that the decreasing strength and changing roles of these three institutions have produced a society with lower ethical standards than those of its earlier history.

Why Behave Ethically? Guidelines for Ethical Behavior

Today we embrace three basic guidelines: Universal nature, truth telling, and responsibility for one's actions. Without them, the free enterprise system itself would be threatened and any kind of business exchange would be difficult. Our society would disintegrate into a "dog-eat-dog" environment.

Universal Nature. The universal nature guideline is a derivation of the *Golden Rule*. We want others to play by the same basic rules by which we would play in a similar situation. This guideline sets up a basic level of trust between people and makes life predictable.

Truth Telling. A fitness consultant needs to believe that what others say is true. The idea of honesty may originate in a set of rules we have been taught, but truth telling makes sense on purely logical grounds as well. Trust facilitates cooperation, member commitment, and the maintenance of long-term relationships.

Responsibility for Your Actions. President Harry S. Truman kept a sign on his desk stating, "The buck stops here." He reminded himself that he had no one to blame when things went wrong. Individuals may choose to live by this attitude and accept personal responsibility for their actions, or they may attempt to follow the impulse of the moment and blame someone else for the consequences. If we demonstrated a higher level of trust and credibility based on universal willingness to accept responsibility for personal actions, our system would work more efficiently and in a less suspicious atmosphere.

INFLUENCES ON A FITNESS CONSULTANT'S ETHICS

Although individual salespeople each have a basic value system and may know what is right and wrong, they encounter many new influences and experience many new pressures on the job. Nothing creates more direction for decision-making, or a better balance for judgment than ethical guidelines. Knowing in advance what can be expected and having a feel for how to balance and integrate them into a personal code of ethics make handling ethical decisions easier.

Club Code of Ethics

Many athletic clubs have codes of ethics and adhere to the code as part of their culture. Clubs may also have ethics training for new employees. The government has also increased its role in ethical issues. Driven by government actions and fear of retribution, fitness clubs are paying more attention than ever to the behavior of their employees. Ethics is a monetary issue as well! Typical issues covered in club ethics programs include:

1. Using expense accounts for external prospecting.

2. Taking product and not paying for it (protein bars, drinks, etc.)

3. Dealing with a prospect's unethical demands.

4. Letting your friends and family work out for free.

Chapter 3 — Ethical Issues in Fitness Sales   **36**

5. Giving away complimentary memberships that are not yours to give away or you are not authorized to give.

6. Dating members and co-workers.

Implementing a code of conduct statement communicates to your members that you and your club have high moral standards. These guidelines can only be effective if sales managers are reinforcing them on a daily basis—observing new fitness consultants give club tours, guiding them through the sales process, and engaging them in open, honest dialogue.

Managers as Role Models

The likelihood that unacceptable selling practices will occur is affected by how your managers behave. If a club manager gives the impression that you must do *anything* possible to get more memberships, you may assume that dealing unethically is acceptable in order to succeed. Often, a club's culture influences how you behave toward your members. Sales managers must emphasize ethical selling behavior in words and actions. The club's top directors must ensure that the managers do not put excessive pressure on their salespeople. If the club owner comes around with a pep talk on moral behavior but proceeds to use underhanded methods of doing business, it is possible to get a mixed message.

"As a manager the important thing is not what happens when you are there, but what happens when you are not there."

— Dr. Kenneth Blanchard

Examples Set by Colleagues

You may sometimes discover that colleagues are acting unethically. Imagine that you and another consultant decide to get a protein bar for the road before leaving work, and your colleague doesn't pay for his, saying it doesn't matter because the club will never notice. As an observer, do you also skip paying, rebuke him, report him (called *blowing the whistle*), or ignore it?

Groupthink refers to the pressure exerted on fitness consultants to be part of the group and not to buck the system—to be team players, no matter what. Being a team player is good if the team has ethical goals and plays by ethical rules, but if the group's thinking contradicts your own personal code of ethics, you must weigh your options carefully.

The Bottom Line

Bottom line profit is one of the most powerful influences on your own income and that of your club. Contrary to popular mythology, maximizing profits is a gym's second priority—not its first. The first is ensuring its survival. Its survival will surely be compromised if fitness consultants take casual views of the legal and ethical implications of their behavior. The club's short-term profits may be maximized by unethical behavior, but the club's very existence could be threatened if it were hit with huge fines or negative publicity. Although short-term profits are important for both the club and its salespeople, long-term success and a good name must always be the first priority.

DEVELOPING A PERSONAL CODE OF ETHICS

Clearly many competing forces that influence your decisions have an ethical dimension. Situations often arise in which a clear right or wrong answer is not readily apparent and discretion in behavior is up to you. Because the influences that come to bear upon you do not always agree and because conflicting demands are numerous, you must develop a personal code of ethics.

Responsibility to Self

In the final analysis, the still, small voice of conscience is the arbiter of conflicting ethical claims. It provides the ability to say that you have made the best decision under the circumstances and take full responsibility for it. If you have personal integrity, then you cannot be dishonest with others—competitors, colleagues, prospects, or members.

Responsibility to the Club

Fitness consultants sometimes rationalize that cheating here or there in dealing with the club would not hurt. After all, the club makes lots of money and what you do would never be noticed. Several areas particularly lend themselves to temptations to be less than ethical.

Accuracy in Accounts. Padding accounts used for club related expenses, advertising, and prospecting can be relatively easy to do. A fitness consultant can take

Chapter 3 — Ethical Issues in Fitness Sales **38**

product without paying for it or pocket a cash payment from a member. As a practical matter, these actions unnecessarily increase the costs to the club and may put it at a competitive disadvantage.

Honesty in Using Time and Resources. The temptation to use the Internet, talk on the phone to friends, and stand around chatting with members when you are supposed to be out prospecting are examples of ways a fitness consultant may misuse time. No time card is punched, and slipping in personal time may be quite easy. This ultimately hurts both you and your club because fewer membership sales are made. It is estimated that losses of goods and cash to worker theft exceeds $120 billion a year. Misusing resources for your own profit hurts the club.

Representing the Club. You are the spokesperson for your gym and for that reason must accurately represent its services and deliver the kind of follow-up that the club promises. Exaggerating the features of your facilities or failing to point out any risks that might be associated with its use is unethical and can be disastrous to a long-term relationship with a member. In some instances, it is also illegal, with the potential for causing both you and the club serious legal consequences.

Responsibility to Competitors

Being honest and refraining from taking unfair advantage are the basic guidelines when dealing with competitors. Making untrue or derogatory comments about competitors is poor business. Some salespeople go so far as to use sabotage, espionage, and dirty tricks to gain unfair advantage over a competitor. These tactics include such schemes as planting "spies" in a club to hear a competitor's sales presentation. Persuading a member to fake interest in joining a competitor's gym to see what deals they can give is another unfair tactic sometimes practiced. Instead, your club should want to gain members fairly by providing a quality atmosphere and superior service.

Responsibility to Members

As a fitness consultant, your responsibility is to give prospects and members what they want by showing them the benefits of exercise such as looking good and feeling good. This gets them excited and ready to join. But you also have to give them some facts that will reassure them about their decision to join, such as the benefits to overall health, lowered risk of disease, better sleeping habits, and the ability to cope with stress.

So, what do your members want and expect from you and your club? That is simple. They want to:

- Look good
- Feel good
- Live longer
- Have sex appeal
- Enjoy a social experience
- Be listened to

Remember, your prospects and members DO NOT want to be:

- Pressured
- Stressed
- Isolated
- Threatened

Dating Co-Workers and Members. Because of the age, egos, and vanity of a large number of the individuals in the health and fitness industry, there is a lot of dating and relationships that develop that, if not done properly, can hurt the reputation of you and more importantly your club. Finding out the rules of behavior within your own club is important in determining what is and is not an ethical policy for dating members and co-workers.

ETHICS AND JOB TENURE

You want to be affiliated with a club where you can feel good about yourself. Disagreements or issues of unethical behavior on the part of the club may, however, emerge during your employment. Deciding how to handle conflicts involving ethics can be stressful because your decision may mean you could soon be looking for another job. Weigh the options carefully and determine who is being helped and who is being hurt. Are there any alternative, creative options that minimize risk and allow career and conscience to be reconciled?

Whistle-Blowing

In the pursuit of the goals of productivity and increased membership sales, many consultants fail to preserve individual and community values. In some clubs, individuals have been reduced to a cog in the corporate wheel, a capital investment, a club property. This attitude can make fitness consultants feel unimportant and fear that their ideas and suggestions are not valid. This reaction is particularly true if they attempt to pass on valuable information to superiors and are rebuffed.

Chapter 3 — Ethical Issues in Fitness Sales

Consider the following scenario:

Sheila knows that when some of the other sales reps at her club take cash payments from members, they pocket the money instead of putting it in the cash drawer. No one has ever been caught. A member just paid for some supplements in cash and the fitness consultant who took the money did not put it in the cash drawer. Sheila mentioned that these kinds of activities have been going on to a manager, but he did not seem to show any concern and did not confront the co-worker in question.

What should someone like Sheila do? She has a number of options:

- File a memo stating that she was ignored when she brought up the issue.
- Blow the whistle on the other fitness consultant.
- Ignore the whole situation and continue selling memberships.
- Look for another job.

On the surface, the wiser course appears to be to keep quiet and let the problem resolve itself. After all, Sheila wasn't doing anything wrong. Sometimes the best policy is to keep quiet until solid evidence can be accumulated or until the co-conspirators are identified, but silence as a long-term strategy is indefensible. "The greatest good to the greatest number" is often a sound rule to go by in business. Therefore, the values of fairness and ethical behavior must be given higher priority than saving the club and some of its sales in the short term.

Treatment of the Salesperson as a Resource, Not Rubbish

A club may treat its fitness salespeople as partners joined with it in a common mission or simply regard them as cannon fodder out in the field. You are an extremely valuable resource and deserve to be treated fairly, informed of decisions affecting you, and protected from situations in which you might be under pressure to make unethical decisions. If you know that your ideas are important and your judgment valued, you feel ownership in the club and want to do a better job overall. Here are some measures that clubs can take to prevent unethical behavior and promote a positive environment among salespeople.

- Avoid setting up incentive systems in a way that makes fudging the membership numbers tempting.

- Be sure that managers are accessible to salespeople in order to get early warnings on troublesome developments.

- Set up appropriate controls not only on financial accounts but also in member complaints, salesperson dissatisfaction, and expense accounts.

- Set sales goals that are motivating but not impossible to achieve.

Another decision you face is that concerning prospecting territory. Obviously, the prime prospecting territory is in a 5 to 10-mile radius of your gym. Since all of the fitness consultants of the club will be cultivating members in the same basic area, the key is to keep open lines of communication among the other fitness consultants so as not to interfere with leads they have already established.

SEXUAL HARASSMENT

A number of prominent sexual harassment cases have made the news in recent years. In today's legal environment, any institution's failure to recognize the consequences of workplace sexual harassment can be a capital blunder. For employees in clubs lacking sound policies, the negative impact from sexual harassment—including liability, embarrassment and lost productivity—can be extensive. Title VII of The Civil Rights Act of 1964 strictly prohibits sexual harassment. The Equal Employment Opportunity Commission (EEOC) defines sexual harassment this way:

> *"Unwelcome sexual advances, requests for sexual favors, and other verbal or physical conduct of a sexual nature constitutes sexual harassment when submission to or rejection of the conduct explicitly or implicitly affects an individual's employment, unreasonably interferes with an individual's work performance or creates an intimidating, hostile or offensive work environment."*

If you truly feel that you have been the victim of sexual harrassment, the best course of action is to immediately report it to your superior or the superior of the offender. Certain rules should apply to every sexual harassment investigation:

1. **Act Promptly** – Don't assume "time will heal all wounds." By failing to act with dispatch, you may give up the defense that you vigorously enforced the club's sexual harassment policies.

Chapter 3 — Ethical Issues in Fitness Sales

2. **Take all complaints seriously** – Embarrassment or fear of reprisal often causes a person to understate the incident. Do not ignore complaints coming after broken relationships between co-workers.

3. **Involve Management** – It is important to get management involved as soon as you hear about the incident. Record all interviews. Companies have successfully used evidence gathered during their investigations to support their action or inaction against the accused. Prompt action is imperative.

4. **Conduct Interviews in Private** – Employees are more candid in private. If bystanders overhear, parties may claim you negligently publicized the incident and invaded their privacy.

5. **Maintain Confidentiality** – Discuss the investigation and its results only with management. You may lose business if you over-publicize.

ETHICS AS GOOD BUSINESS

Unethical behavior may sometimes appear to be an attractive alternative. After all, for every inside trader, fraudulent salesperson, or immoral politician who gets caught, perhaps hundreds get away with unethical behaviors. However, the recent bumper crop of ethical scandals in corporate America has brought with it a renewed concern for ethics.

Ethics is receiving more attention in the health and fitness industry because of an awareness on the part of clubs of the enormous costs of unethical activity—in a loss of memberships and in damage to their public image. In short, health clubs are paying attention to ethics because it happens to be good business strategy.

If you are honest in relationships with superiors, prospects, members, and competitors alike, you will become a trusted and valued individual. The key to making more membership sales is to build up these kinds of relationships and maintain them. A well-defined personal code of ethics as part of one's character and as a basis for behavior is an invaluable asset.

Checkpoints in Ethical Decision Making

When faced with an ethical conflict, a standard set of questions to ask yourself is helpful. Use the five questions suggested on the next page to guide your thinking.

THE OFFICIAL HANDBOOK FOR HEALTH CLUB SALES

A FIVE-QUESTION ETHICS CHECKLIST

1. Is it legal? Look at the law and other standards.

2. Is it fair to all concerned?

3. Would I want someone else to act this way toward me?

4. How would I explain my actions to someone else?

5. How will it make me feel about myself?

These questions first require careful evaluation regarding existing standards and personal liability. Next, the questions are designed to activate your sense of fairness and rationality. Last, realize that your personal feelings are important because negative feelings adversely affect positive performance. If your truthful answer to any one of these five questions damages your self-image or causes you to be troubled by your conscience, then you should probably avoid the action in question.

There is no pillow as soft as a clear conscience.

Ethical Issues in Fitness Sales
REFOCUS

- It is essential that you develop your own personal code of ethics, but you must also be aware of the ethical obligations your club sets forth.

- Fitness consultants who find themselves in situations in which club violations are evident must make difficult choices about whether to blow the whistle or settle on another strategy that could include finding another job.

- Ethics is a smart business decision because fitness consultants who are honest in relationships with employers, members, and competitors become trusted and respected professionals.

- When faced with an ethical conflict, use a standard checklist of principled questions to guide your thinking.

Qualities of High Sales Performers

1. Exchange information. Ask a variety of questions that help the customer to analyze, evaluate, or express feelings and become a valuable information resource to the customer.

2. Know when to close. Advocate your products only after you have identified an important need in the customer's mind and involved the customer in developing the solution.

3. Sell to people, not organizations, and demonstrate a strong commitment to meeting customer needs. You are helping the customers personally, and the customer's company.

4. Be genuinely interested in your prospects' needs, even while actively promoting your company and its products or services.

5. Listen to what your customers have to say. If you let them talk, they will reveal their needs. Remember, if the customer says it, he believes it.

6. Become a valuable resource for your company. Act as an information feedback source, able to directly provide expertise to your sales manager.

7. Regularly establish trust within your own organization by sharing information, encouraging participation in decisions, and recognizing the contributions of the internal staff to your success as a salesperson.

8. Engage in behavior such as maintaining eye contact, showing enthusiasm, asking questions about customers' needs, and being prepared with effective responses to buyers' objections.

INTRODUCING A REVOLUTION IN CLUB MANAGEMENT
iFitness Solutions offers complete back-office services that save you money

Club Management Software

Billing and Transaction Processing

Member Retention and Communication

Full-Service Accounts Receivable management

Accounting and Payroll Integration

Website Design and Hosting

Marketing

800-506-1673 | www.ifitness.net

Chapter 4

Purchase Behavior and Communication

- **Influences on the membership purchase decision process.**

- **The value of effective communication.**

- **Sending and receiving a successful message.**

- **Overcoming communication barriers.**

- **The voice as a communication tool.**

- **Body language and proxemics.**

CAUTION: SMALL WORDS AT WORK

When asked to explain Britain's wartime policy to Parliament, Prime Minister Winston Churchill said: "It is to wage war, by sea, land and air, with all out might and with all the strength that God can give us." As Neil Armstrong set his foot down on the moon he simply said, "That's one small step for man, one giant leap for mankind."

Small words are not only more understandable and exact than large words, they also add elegance to your club presentations. Realize and appreciate the persuasive power of a well-written and delivered sales presentation. If you must choose between a large word and a small word, select the small word everytime. Take a lesson from your local highway department. Place a sign at the boundaries of your speech that reads:

Caution—Small Words at Work.

Chapter 4 — Purchase Behavior and Communication   48

WHY PROSPECTS JOIN

Consumer behavior is the set of actions that make up an individual's consideration, purchase, and use of a membership. The term *consumer behavior* includes both the purchase and the use of your club. Your role is vital in this process of matching the offerings to the needs of the prospective member. However, this process does not end with the sale. You must be equally concerned with member satisfaction after the sale.

Understanding the Purchase Decision Process

The model presented in Figure 4.1 provides a useful tool for examining the buying process. It presents a view of the buyer as someone observed, not in a single act, but in a complex problem-solving process.

To understand why an individual makes a decision to join, look at events preceding and following the membership purchase act itself. A buyer generally passes through five stages: (1) problem recognition, (2) search for alternatives, (3) evaluation of alternatives, (4) the purchase decision, and (5) postpurchase evaluation.

Problem Recognition. The membership purchase process begins with mental recognition that a health or fitness need exists and must be satisfied. A need is something regarded as necessary, or also simply something the buyer wants or desires such as flatter abs, and therefore perceives as a need. These needs are what drives the health and fitness industry. No one takes action until motivated to do so, and motivation arises from awareness of needs.

Figure 4.1

The Purchase Decision Process

Problem Recognition (Motive Arousal)

⬇

The Search for Alternatives

Internal Search
- Habitual
- Routine

External Search
- Extensive
- Limited

Evaluation of Alternatives

⬇

The Purchase Decision

⬇

Post-Purchase Evaluation

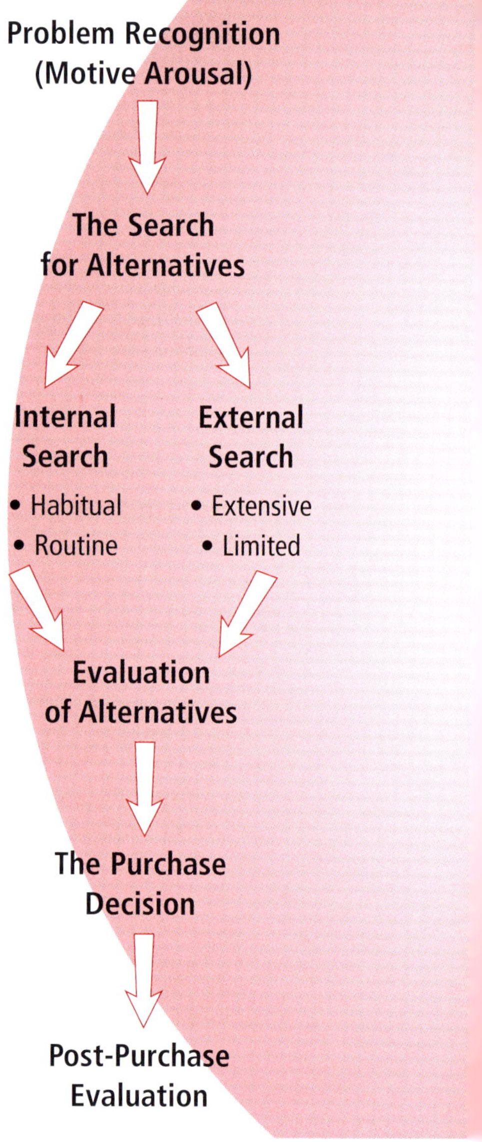

All kinds of needs affect the buying decision. Abraham Maslow defined five levels of needs: *physiological, safety, social, esteem, and self-actualization.* Most prospects you will encounter have come to your club because of a combination of physiological, social, and esteem-based needs. Regardless of the kind of need, some buyers are not consciously aware of the nature of their needs until you bring them out into the open.

Search for Alternatives. After recognizing an unsatisfied need or desire to look better, the prospective member begins to search for information concerning the available alternatives in their area. The search may involve both internal and external sources. The internal search makes use of the buyer's previous experience with other health clubs, prior attitudes, and occurs largely without conscious effort. The external search process involves added dynamics. It may require an information search by going to other clubs in the area or getting recommendations from friends or co-workers.

Evaluation of Alternatives. The search process provides the buyer with knowledge of various health clubs. All individual consumers have specific criteria to use for making a decision—*personal mental rules for matching alternatives with motives.* These criteria are learned by actual experience with health clubs or derived from information obtained from commercial or social sources.

The implications for the fitness consultant are important here. If you can determine the buyer's *choice criteria*, you can tailor the presentation to focus on specific benefits that differentiate your club from the competition. Once you have matched the prospect's buying motives with what your facilities have to offer, the determinant attributes come into play: membership price, club reputation, service and training capabilities, or the look and feel of the gym.

Purchase Decision. After evaluating the alternatives in the search process, the buyer is ready to make the purchase decision—actually a whole set of decisions. Buyers want to minimize the risk and simplify the decision to join. The professional fitness consultant knows this and assists the prospective member in making the decision. Your role in helping prospects reach a satisfactory purchasing decision is what makes professional relationship selling so rewarding and fulfilling.

Postpurchase Evaluation. The purchase decision continues after the sale of the membership has been made. In the health and fitness industry, this evaluation part of the process may continue for several weeks as the new member becomes more familiar with your club and its staff. Sometimes a new member experiences postpurchase anxiety or *buyer's remorse.* The magnitude of the anxiety depends upon the importance of the decision and how determined that individual is to getting or staying in shape. You can help lessen this feeling by providing exceptional member services and follow-up on the gym floor, which is discussed in Chapter 14.

Chapter 4 — Purchase Behavior and Communication

INFLUENCES ON THE DECISION MAKING PROCESS

Buying motives cannot be directly observed, but can be inferred from observing behavior. Many factors influence buying behavior. Figure 4.2 illustrates some of the psychological and sociocultural influences that affect a buyer's purchase decision. You must understand the significance of the impact of these factors at the various stages of the decision-making process.

1. Behavioral concepts such as perception and the self-image impact *problem recognition*.

2. Psychological factors like the mood-of-the-moment, attitudes, and perception, as well as sociocultural factors including the physical environment and culture, influence *purchase decisions*.

You can make positive use of these factors by becoming proficient in the art of communication—that is, the sending and receiving of messages in a manner that results in understanding and productive discussion.

Psychological Influences: It's All in Your Head

Several psychological factors affect a prospect's membership buying decision. You must be aware of these factors and understand the role they play in the process.

Perception. Individual behavior is an organized and meaningful response to the world as that particular person sees it. We perceive situations according to our own personal needs, values, expectations, past experience, and training. Figure 4.3 illustrates the difference in individual perceptions. How many squares do you see? *There are 40 squares.* Can you find them all? If you didn't see that many, you may be exercising selective perception. Prospects often perceive not what you

Figure 4.2

Influences on the Buyer's Purchase Decision Process

Psychological Influences
- Perception
- Mood of the moment
- Attitudes
- Self-image

Sociocultural Influences
- Culture
- Physical environment
- Social class

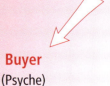

Buyer
(Psyche)

think is most important but what they select as important to themselves.

Mood of the Moment. Perception is also influenced by an individual's psychological state or mood of the moment. On some days a minor mishap may be laughed off, but if nothing has gone right all day, the very same situation may be perceived in such a way that you become infuriated.

Attitude. Attitudes are merely habits of thought and habitual patterns of response to experiences. Because they have been used so often, they have become automatic and are used to save the time that would be required to think about a situation and make a decision. For example, some prospects operate from an attitude that the exercise routine or methods they have used in the past are obviously the way to do things in the future. Their attitude is that change is bad. Any attitude on the part of a prospect that makes the purchase decision more difficult can become a barrier that must be overcome before a sale can be made.

Self-Image. *Self-image* is an individual's unique and personal self-appraisal at a given moment in time. This is a crucial aspect for every potential member. People want to look good so they will feel better about themselves. This affects what they perceive as reality and, as a result, how communication proceeds. In choosing how to communicate, even more important than what is true is what the person believes is true.

Every behavior can be explained if the self-image of the individual is understood. In one sense we are all self-centered, and we act in keeping with what we consider best for us at the moment. If you wish to communicate effectively, you must learn to recognize these important dimensions of the prospect's self-image:

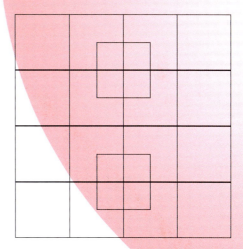

Figure 4.3

How many squares do you see in the figure?

You may not see what others see.

Chapter 4 — Purchase Behavior and Communication   52

1. *Physical.*
   People picture themselves as weak or strong, attractive or unattractive, lean or fat. They buy products that fit their self-image or that promise to change it to fit a desired goal.

2. *Social.*
   Individuals see themselves as liked or disliked, accepted or rejected, loved or unwanted, successful or unsuccessful.

3. *Moral.*
   Internalized values give people a picture of themselves as loyal or disloyal, honest or dishonest, straightforward or devious.

THE COMMUNICATION AGENDA

Success in relationship selling depends upon accurate communication—the useful exchange of information between you and the prospective member. Communication can be viewed as the verbal and nonverbal passing of information between you, the *source*, and your prospect, the *receiver*. However, for effective communication to take place, you each must understand the *intended* message. Thus, the goal of communication is a mutual understanding. Figure 4.4 shows the channel through which communication must flow in a selling situation. At each intersection the potential exists for both problems and opportunities. Although the model considers communication from your perspective, in any successful relationship both parties participate meaningfully in an active two-way process.

Encoding the Message: How To Get Your Point Across

Encoding is the process in which you convert an idea or concept into symbols the buyer can clearly understand. You know what you are trying to say; the real challenge is getting your point across. This requires the proper mix of symbols to express your meaning correctly. The most common symbols used in delivering a message are words, pictures, numbers, sounds, physical touch, smell, body movement, and taste. The club environment itself helps create your message through the sound of the equipment, music, voices, and the overall club atmosphere. You, as the source, must encode your message, organize it, and then put it into a presentation format the prospect will understand, accept, and believe.

Communication is successful if the symbols you choose make it possible for the listener to understand you. The real challenge in communication is to transfer your thoughts, ideas, and intentions without distortion or omission. Because communication is affected by the assumptions and the needs of both parties – as well as by outside

Figure 4.4

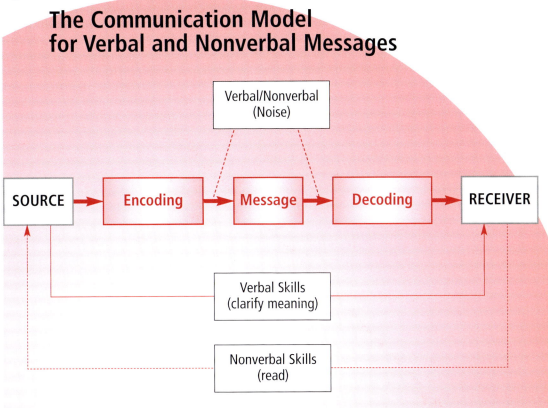

factors such as time pressures, interruptions, and the environment – communication is often far from perfect.

The Message Itself: So Much More Than Words

The actual message is a blend of symbols that you use to influence a change in a prospect's attitude or behavior. The message itself involves both verbal and nonverbal elements. In his book *Silent Messages*, Albert Mehrabian points out that *words* convey only seven percent of feelings and emotions, *tone of voice* conveys 38 percent, and *visual communication* conveys the remaining 55 percent. Nonverbal elements in the presentation make up the majority of the total impact. If verbal and nonverbal messages conflict, the listener relies on the nonverbal message. Figure 4.5 illustrates the contribution of various factors to the messages we deliver to others and the amount of control we maintain over each one. The factors most easily controlled are those that have the least effect, and those with the biggest impact are the most difficult to control because they happen automatically.

Research suggests that if the first thirty seconds of communication result in a negative impression, you have to spend the next four minutes just to overcome that impression before any real communication can begin.

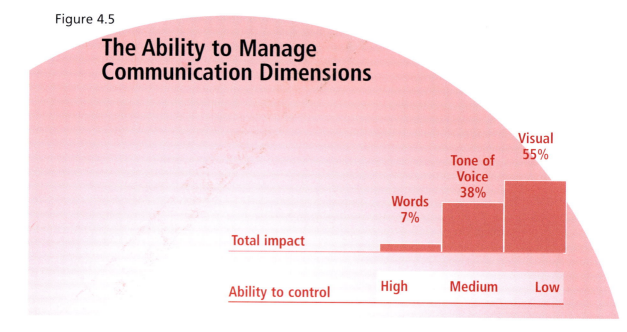

Figure 4.5

Evaluating the Prospect's Decoding: Did They Get It?

Decoding is the mental process by which a prospect figures out the meaning of your message. It is the way in which your prospect attempts to translate the symbols used in your presenation into something that relates to their needs. If the message was obviously both understood as it was intended and also accepted, there is no problem. At this step in the process, either real communication or misunderstanding will occur. Your prospects listen to your message, then make their own conclusions. If the prospect fails to understand the message, the result is called *noise*, and this means a breakdown in communication has occurred. This results when there are barriers to effective communicaton, which are discussed in the following section.

Watch Out for These Barriers to Effective Communication

Seldom does the prospective member interpret exactly the same meaning that you intended. As mentioned above, when the result of decoding is different from what you encoded, noise exists. *Anything that interferes with or distorts understanding of the intended message is called noise.* Noise can take many forms and may affect any or all parts of the communication process. There are logical reasons why your message may not be understood or accepted. Some reasons for such miscommunication are:

Words. All language is a code. Even if you and your prospect use the same words, you are probably putting out different meanings. Words only represent ideas. Noise is created when words are inappropriate: for example, the use of casual profanity that may offend the listener, language that seems to imply the listener is ignorant concerning health and fitness, language that assumes too much knowledge on the listener's part, or language that obscures the real meaning.

Distractions. Any element that may focus the prospect's attention on something other than the message is a distraction. Some typical distractions are inappropriate dress, an uncomfortable temperature in the club, excessively loud overhead music that makes listening difficult, or a nagging personal problem occupying the prospect's mind.

Timing. If a prospect has some reason for not wanting to listen, no amount of communication skill on your part is enough. The prospect may be feeling under the weather, preoccupied with an unpleasant disciplinary task or may be feeling intimidated by the other members in the club at the time. Some prospects need time to *warm up* before getting down to business, especially if this is the first time they have considered joining a health club; others want to get right to the gym tour and skip the small talk.

Interruptions. Phone calls, people walking up to you on the gym floor to ask questions, and emergencies represent the kinds of interruptions that hurt the impact of the message.

Technical Erudition. Information overload often complicates a message. An unconscious desire to appear personally knowledgeable about fitness often results in talking too much, poor organization of features and benefits, or wrongly assuming that the prospect has adequate knowledge of health and fitness. As a result, the prospect may fail to see a need for the gym and its services. Don't assume that every prospective member knows what circuit training or free weights are or even that they know how to work a treadmill, and avoid the use of technical terms and jargon without clarification.

Poor Listening Habits. If the prospect is a poor listener, you are faced with a monumental challenge in designing a message and delivering it in an effective and successful manner. On the other hand, the fitness consultant who is a poor listener never picks up the prospect's cues that are keys to molding the message for quick acceptance.

Making Use of Feedback

The buyer will draw conclusions from the messages received and react accordingly. This *feedback* is crucial to your success. During face-to-face communication, verbal and nonverbal feedback is immediate and quite revealing. Become skilled in receiving feedback and you can adapt your sales presentation to fit each individual's requirements. Use the feedback that passes back and forth from the prospect to you, and this will bring you closer to an exact understanding of what is being said by each. In this manner, the noise is filtered out so that the result is clear communication.

USING YOUR VOICE AS A SELLING TOOL

The first impression you make is often based on your voice. When you call to set up an appointment, your voice is all you have for communicating. A voice that is pleasing and confident is a great asset. Your voice and how you use it play an important part in your success. Several basic components of verbal communication deserve your attention.

Clarity or Articulation. Do you recall the device Professor Higgins used in *My Fair Lady* to help Eliza Dolittle improve her speech? He had her talk with marbles in her mouth. To be understood at all, she was forced to form her words very carefully. As a result, her articulation improved. When you speak, do people hear separate words and syllables or *doyourwordsallruntogether?* A fitness consultant with poor articulation leaves prospects confused and bewildered.

Volume. The volume of your voice will vary during conversation. The same is true during a sales presentation. Stressing a benefit may call for increased volume. Lowering your voice, sometimes almost to a whisper, may produce quite a dramatic effect; it causes the prospect to lean forward (a body position that signals agreement or approval) to avoid missing your words. Variation in volume enhances the message if it is not overdone.

Silence. Silence is a powerful selling tool. Use it to give the prospect time to absorb the full impact of what you have said. Slight pauses between major points in the presentation suggest that you are thoughtful, intelligent, and analytical. Pauses also give the prospect an opportunity to comment, ask a question, or think about how the idea you have presented can be applied. Avoid becoming so enamored with the sound of your own voice that you must talk all the time.

Rhythm. The rhythmic pattern of your speech comes from your basic personality style and your emotions of the moment. Some voices seem to flow in long, continuous sentences, and others come in short, choppy chunks. Just as the rhythm in music changes to indicate that something new is happening, the same happens in speech patterns. Be alert to any changes in your own or the prospect's speech. Changes are even more revealing than initial patterns. If the prospect suddenly shifts to a more drawn out rhythm, for example, the message may be "Let me think more about that" or "I don't believe what you are saying."

Rate of Speech. The tempo of your delivery should be comfortable for you as a speaker and for your listener. Speaking too rapidly may cause you to lose a prospect who customarily speaks more slowly and feels that your fast pace is pushing for a decision without allowing time for thought. Speaking too slowly may make the prospect want to push your fast-forward button. A moderate pace allows you to enunciate clearly, establish natural rhythmic patterns, and speed up or slow down for proper emphasis of some point.

SELLING WITHOUT WORDS

Different people have different levels of competence in nonverbal communication skills, and some professions require more skill than others. The success of a professional gambler depends on the ability to exercise strict control of nonverbal messages to disguise a bluff. A mime depends exclusively on nonverbal skills to deliver a message. However, you must possess skill in both verbal and nonverbal communication. Two particularly important components of nonverbal communication to understand are body language and *proxemics* (use of space).

Body Language

Body language can be portrayed as messages sent without using words. The essential elements of body language include shifts in posture or stance (body angle), facial expressions, eye movements, and arm, hand, and leg movements. It includes every movement from the subtle raising of an eyebrow to the obvious leaning forward of an interested listener.

Through body language, prospects express their emotions, desires, and attitudes. As a result, body language is a valuable tool for you to use in discovering what the prospect is really saying. When you can *read* the prospect's body language and, in addition, control your own body signals to add impact to your words, you are likely to be understood.

Understanding the Language of Gestures. Important signals involve body angle, position of hands, arms, and legs, and the face—especially the eyes and lips. All of these should be observed as a cluster of gestures that together state a message. A prospect sitting with arms crossed may be communicating doubt or rejection or may simply be sitting comfortably. In this case, you must also observe whether the legs are crossed, the body withdrawn, eyes glancing sideways, and an eyebrow raised. All these signs taken together surely suggest doubt or rejection, but one of them in isolation is inconclusive.

Body Signals. A hunched figure, rigid posture, restless stance, or nervous pacing may contradict what a person says verbally. Prospects allow you to sit closer if they feel comfortable and lean toward you if they like what you are saying and are intent on listening. A recent study used videotape to study the behavior of successful and unsuccessful salespeople. One mannerism difference noted was the relative calmness of professional salespeople in comparison to those who were less successful. Their body movements were smooth, unhurried, and without jerky motions, particularly when handing a contract or a pen across the table. Every movement was gradual. Less successful salespeople exhibited jumpy, nervous movements that were picked up— perhaps unconsciously—by prospects.

Look for the prospect's changes in body posture and gestures. For example, one who is ready to buy shows signs of relaxation—nodding in agreement, mirroring your movements, moving to the front of the chair, extending the palm of the hand outward toward you, and uncrossing legs. Your posture and gestures also communicate your feelings to the prospect. If you sit in an open, relaxed position, you are likely to be more persuasive and better accepted than if you sit in a tight, closed posture.

Hand Movements. Rubbing the back of the neck may indicate frustration, but it can also indicate that the prospect has a sore or stiff neck from painting the bathroom ceiling over the weekend. Next time you are speaking with a prospective member, notice their hand movements and read their hands as indicators of what they are really feeling. People can say so much with simple unthinking hand motions. If you begin to notice that you are also making involuntary hand gestures, focus your hand gestures toward your club presentation rather than let them give away what you are feeling!

Evaluate the following hand gestures in the context of other nonverbal clues:

THE OFFICIAL HANDBOOK FOR HEALTH CLUB SALES

1. *Other gestures of hand and head.*
   Tugging at the ear suggests the desire to interrupt. Pinching the bridge of the nose and closing the eyes suggests that the matter is being given serious thought.

2. *Posture.*
   Leaning back in the chair with both hands behind the head communicates a sense of superiority.

3. *Involuntary gestures.*
   Involuntary hand gestures that contradict a facial expression are likely to reveal true feelings. Tightly clasped hands or fists indicate tenseness.

4. *Steepling of the hands*
   Fingertips together forming what looks like a church steeple commonly indicates smugness, self-confidence, or perhaps superiority.

Facial Expressions. Eyebrows, eyelids, eyes, lips, jaw, mouth, and facial muscles all work together to communicate feelings and emotions. Research attributes as much as 70 percent of nonverbal message sending to the muscles of the face.

The face is a highly reliable indicator of attitude. A person may avoid eye contact when trying to cover up true feelings. Increased eye contact signals honesty and interest. Be sure to maintain eye contact at critical moments of the presentation. For example, when describing how to operate a particular piece of equipment, direct the prospect's eyes to the machine itself, but when stressing the benefits of using the equipment, maintain eye contact. Proper eye contact makes a positive statement that words alone cannot.

Suspicion and anger are shown by signs of tightness around the cheeks or along the jaw line. Muscle movement at the back of the jaw line just below the ears indicates an angry gritting of the teeth. A sudden flush of facial redness may warn that the situation has taken a bad turn; embarrassment or hostility may be radiating under an apparently calm exterior.

An isolated gesture or posture is seldom a reliable indicator of attitude or feelings. Obviously, you have to take a look at the buyer in the context of the whole situation. Buyers may fold their arms just to be more comfortable. Generally, if there is an objection then the whole body will become more rigid. And you will see signals: Skin texture will tighten up; voice tone will change. They may even have frustrated looks on their faces. When a cluster of gestures is consistent with verbal messages, accepting their validity is relatively safe.

Chapter 4 — Purchase Behavior and Communication

Proxemics

Proxemics is the distance individuals prefer to maintain between themselves and others. Most people seem to consider observing desired distance a matter of courtesy. Violating distance puts you at risk for closing down the communication process. Highly successful salespeople tend to move closer to clients when closing a sale. Their skill in reading the individual prospect allows them to move as close as possible without causing discomfort for the prospect. The difference between how successful and unsuccessful fitness consultants use physical closeness can be observed in the prospect's reaction. Carefully test for the existence of comfort barriers; then place yourself just outside those barriers.

Figure 4.6 shows the four basic zones or ranges that apply in the typical sales situation. Generally speaking, the intimate zone is about two feet (hence the expression, *to keep someone at arm's length*). Enter this range only if invited. To move inside the intimate zone, except for a handshake, is not a good idea. Beyond that, we all have a personal zone which is an envelope around us extending from two to four feet. Move into the buyer's personal zone only after invitation, which typically occurs after a satisfying professional relationship has been established. The outer shell is the social zone, which extends up to 12 feet.

Figure 4.6

How to Use Space

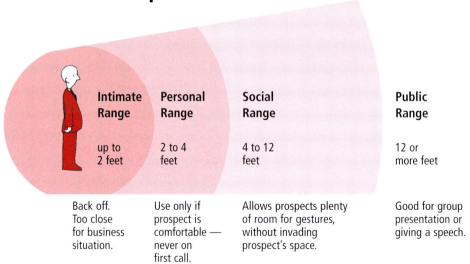

THE OFFICIAL HANDBOOK FOR HEALTH CLUB SALES

Purchase Behavior and Communication
REFOCUS

- The consumer's purchase decision process involves five stages:
    1. Problem recognition
    2. Search for alternatives
    3. Evaluation of alternatives
    4. The purchase decision
    5. Post-purchase evaluation

- Fitness consultants are successful in closing the sale when they discover the membership buying motives of the prospect, present benefits of the product that relate to those motives, and are sensitive to psychological influences.

- Communication is the vehicle for designing your message in a manner that the prospective member comprehends, accepts, and believes.

- Understanding body language and how prospects use their space adds to your ability to communicate with the prospect.

- Remember, we send the majority of our messages in our daily communication through nonverbal means. We cannot not communicate!

Chapter 4 — Purchase Behavior and Communication

Innovative Fitness Systems offers all you need, all in one spot. In addition to facility design, we select, layout, deliver, install and service everything from strength equipment to cardio equipment, group exercise equipment to flooring, lockers to tanning beds, saunas to AV systems and much more. Everything you could possibly need inside your facility is right at your fingertips, provided by fitness professionals with over 16 years experience in the industry and top-tier customers ranging from World Gym and Gold's Gym to the Fairfax County Police and Maryland National Park. Call us today and get us started on a turnkey solution for *your* fitness center.

Innovative Fitness Systems

301-805-9872

Chapter 5

Finding Your Selling Style

FOCAL POINTS

- The various behavioral styles.
- Your own favorite style.
- Dealing with people from each style.
- The concept of versatility.
- Gender issues in health and fitness sales.

A DIFFERENCE IN SOCIAL STYLE

Six weeks into her new job as a fitness consult-ant, Jolene Reynolds realized that something was very wrong. Not the work itself—Jolene loved prospect-ing for potential members and helping current members out on the gym floor. The job was fine. It was the sales manager she couldn't stand.

Jolene recently noticed that some of the new members seemed to feel neglected, and their trips to the club dropped after a few short weeks, so she developed a new-member motivational program. When she approached her manager with the plan, everything was detailed specifically: The date when fitness consultants would begin the plan, new approaches to use, motivational techniques, mem-bership appreciation parties, costs of the plan, the works. Halfway through Jolene's explanation, the sales manager leaped to his feet and began tossing out ideas right and left. Some were impractical; all would throw the carefully thought-out plan out of whack. When Jolene pointed this out, her manager

Chapter 5 — Finding Your Selling Style   **64**

got miffed and charged out of the office, bellowing over his shoulder, "Now you've got the plan. Make it happen."

"Make what happen?" Jolene pondered. "All I've got to work with is a blast of hot air."

Some call such an incident a personality conflict. Others would say they are not on the same wavelength. They're not seeing eye to eye. Let's call it what it really is—*a difference in social style*. Conflict or miscommunication will exist not simply because of work pressures, but because of social style differences.

Jolene, as you will learn in this chapter, has an *analytical* social style, while her boss has an *expressive* style. Unknowingly, they communicate disrespect to one another. This lack of understanding and knowledge concerning behavioral styles can cause lost sales, frustration, and resentment.

Communication broke down in the situation because Jolene did not recognize that her ideas got her manager thinking, and the sales manager did not stick around to clarify his suggestions. Jolene stopped listening and took the manager's brainstorming personal, seeing it as criticism rather than as development of her original thoughts.

They were like the two old-timers who sat in their rocking chairs reminiscing about days gone by. Both were so hard of hearing that neither ever knew for sure what the other was saying. They just took turns talking, each lost in his own memories, but content that there was someone nearby. For the fitness consultant who wants to succeed in a selling career, however, "being nearby" isn't enough.

Success and Behavioral Styles

Because of the importance of communication in the selling process, successful fitness consultants constantly search for new ways to make their communication more effective. They are eager to learn how they may better anticipate and avoid conflict situations. A membership sale is actually a communication exchange in which two individuals develop a mutually desirable solution to a problem about which both are concerned. The best sales relationships are long-term ones based on mutual trust and credibility. The pertinent question then becomes, "How can I sell so that I demonstrate respect for the customer, build credibility for myself and my club, and set up a benefit for both of us?"

THE SOCIAL STYLES MODEL

In your family and personal life, you have time to learn the ways you can best persuade or get along with various relatives. In the club, you have limited time to evaluate and adjust your persuasive skills. The prospect's manner and social style are often different than yours and you may miss what is being communicated. The most common mistake is not understanding how prospects think and make decisions. The social styles model provides a useful tool for making such an evaluation in the shortest possible time. The better you understand personality types, the more successful you will be in communicating with the various people you meet.

The Four Distinct Social Styles

Each person has a primary communicating style that is blended or fine-tuned by a secondary style. These primary and secondary styles shape others' perceptions of you and filter your perceptions of other people. A second dimension to this model comes into play when you are under stress. At such times, you may shift to a different style of behavior. You may be aware of the shift yet feel unable to prevent it.

We use four basic styles to deal with the world. Each is based upon one of four basic functions of human personality.

1. The driver or *sensing* function of taking in here-and-now sensory information and reacting to it.

2. The expressive or *intuitive* function of imagination and abstract thought.

3. The amiable or *feeling* function of personal and emotional reactions to experience.

4. The analytical or *thinking* function of organizing and analyzing information in a logical fashion.

Everyone uses each of the four functions, but the frequency of use differs among individuals. These styles can be observed even in young children. Behavior patterns, psychologist Carl Jung claimed, are genetically determined and are seen in infants during their first days of life. Like adults, young children process experiences according to their own individual styles.

Chapter 5 — Finding Your Selling Style   **66**

Basic Concepts

Three basic concepts underlie the behavioral styles communication model presented in this chapter:

1. Everyone uses a *blend* of the driver, expressive, amiable, and analytical styles, although each person has a favorite style that is used more often than others. A *style* is an overall approach used to send and receive messages. It consists of verbal, nonverbal, and behavioral elements.

2. Every person operates the majority of the time from a favorite style. This is the *primary style*, which you can identify by observing behavioral clues such as their use of time, manner of speech, typical reaction to other people, and approach to reaching a certain level of fitness.

3. People respond favorably to a style that is *similar* or *complementary* to their own. When your style is too different from that of the prospective member, the resulting conflict can be disastrous to the outcome of the presentation. *What* is said is often much less important than *how* it is said.

Behavioral Styles in Selling

Your choice of style affects what you do and say. It also affects what prospects hear and believe during your presentation. Understanding the strengths and liabilities of your primary communicating style and learning to be *versatile* in your style can help you sell to more prospects more often. The objective of this chapter then is to help you learn how to manage your daily interactions with members and prospects more productively.

Figure 5.1 illustrates that your most damaging weaknesses (-) are merely exaggerations or over-extensions of your strengths (+). Your behavior responds to circumstances like the volume dial of a radio. When the volume is just right, the music is pleasing. Similarly, when a behavioral style is used in moderation it is seen as a strength; when overused (that is, when the volume is too high), it becomes a weakness and leads to ineffective communication. Professional selling is all about managing relationships. Remember that a customer is not a transaction, a customer is a relationship! Most of us don't even think about working on relationships in our daily lives. On the other hand, relationship salespeople take time to think about and understand those around them.

Figure 5.1

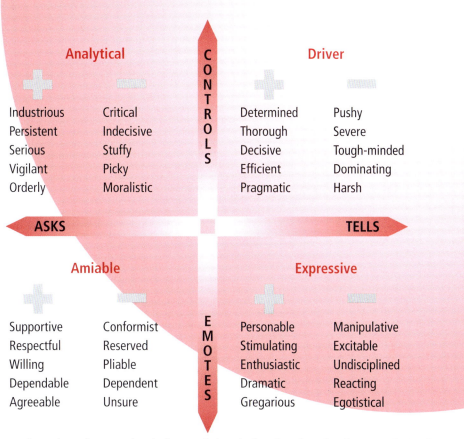

Remember that the emphasis in studying behavioral style characteristics is on *surface behavior*, not on in-depth personality analysis. Human behavior is predictable because ninety percent of our actions are controlled by habits and attitudes. Social styles do not reveal a person's complete personality, but rather, they describe two basic attributes or characteristics of behavior: *assertiveness* and *responsiveness*.

Attributes of Behavior

When you meet someone for the first time, your mind subconsciously reacts to two main characteristics: assertiveness and responsiveness. *Assertiveness* represents the effort a person makes to influence or control the thoughts and actions

Chapter 5 — Finding Your Selling Style

of others. *Responsiveness* is the willingness with which a person outwardly shares feelings or emotions and develops relationships.

Assertiveness and responsiveness levels vary from one individual to another. Several basic terms provide a thumbnail sketch of the characteristics of each dimension:

Low in Responsiveness
- formal and proper
- fact-oriented
- guarded, cool, and aloof
- disciplined about time
- seldom makes gestures
- controlled body language

High in Responsiveness
- relaxed and warm
- open and approachable
- dramatic and animated
- flexible about time
- oriented toward relationships and feelings

Low in Assertiveness
- introverted
- supportive, a team player
- easygoing
- avoids taking risks
- good listener
- reserved in their opinions

High in Assertiveness
- risk-taker
- swift in decision-making
- willing to confront others
- very competitive
- take-charge attitude
- readily expresses opinions

Recognizing Social Styles

Combining the assertiveness and responsiveness characteristics makes it possible to develop a map of what others are doing or saying. Figure 5.2 shows the relationships among the four social styles. The horizontal axis is the range from the least to most assertive. Assertive people take a stand and make their position clear to others. Because they are ambitious, competitive, and quick to take action and express strong opinions, they are located on the *telling* end of the social style axis. Nonassertive individuals are seen as cooperative, silent, and slow to act, and

Figure 5.2

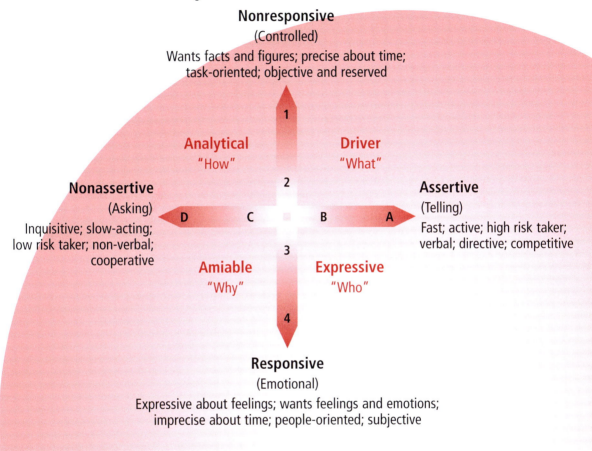

they are located at the *asking* end of the axis. The least assertive individuals are in quartile D, and the most assertive in quartile A, with quartiles B and C representing intermediate levels of assertiveness.

The vertical axis indicates the range from least to most responsive. Nonresponsive individuals, those in quartile 1, are largely indifferent to the feelings of others, reserved, and no-nonsense in attitude. The responsive individuals found in quartile 4 are strongly people-oriented, concerned about relationships, and subjective. Those in quartiles 2 and 3 display intermediate levels of responsiveness.

IDENTIFYING THE FOUR BEHAVIORAL STYLES

Identifying the levels of assertiveness and responsiveness a person demonstrates is not a precise method of complete personality evaluation. With study and practice, however, you can become seventy to eighty percent effective in using your observations to predict habitual behavioral patterns and be prepared to use your knowledge to improve the communication environment. The four styles are linked to distinctive and unique habits of interactive behavior. The name given to each style reflects general characteristics rather than full, specific details. Keep in mind that no *one* style is preferred over another. Each has its own strengths and weaknesses, and successful individuals as well as failures are found in each style group, as are those of different ethnic groups, ages, and gender.

Drivers

Drivers tell and control, are high in assertiveness, and low in responsiveness. They control others by telling them what to do and control themselves by remaining objective. They are task-oriented and combine personal power and emotional control in relationships with others. *They are control specialists.*

Drivers exhibit minimum concern for the feelings of others. A sales manager for a health club in California was heard to say, "My desk attendant used to drive me crazy. I'd ask her how her weekend went and she'd actually tell me. In detail! All I wanted to hear was fine or not so hot." Now those are the words of a true *driver*. They consider *yes-people* to be weak. Stand up to drivers. Sell to them by showing them what your club can do for them. Drivers' feelings are not easily hurt because they do not take things personally.

Drivers tend to be intense, competitive, fast-paced, and goal-oriented. They pride themselves on the ability to get things done. They like to *make things happen*. Convince them that your club is what they need to reach their fitness goals and that it will provide all the benefits you promise. They are more impressed by what they see and hear than by what others say about you or your offering.

At their best, drivers are human dynamos. Resourceful, organized, and pragmatic, they impose high standards on themselves and others. As a result, they may be seen as impatient or tireless. At their worst, they appear to give inadequate consideration to the long-range consequences of their actions.

Under stress, drivers can seem anti-intellectual and may defensively overreact to any opinions differing from their own, especially to those that seem to resist action. When selling to drivers, be prepared and organized, fast paced and to the point. Remain professional and businesslike. Study their goals and propose solutions that are clearly related to those goals. Suggest several options and allow them to choose.

> **Customize Your Selling Style to Hit a Hole-in-One with the Driver**
>
> Drivers do not care about developing a personal relationship with you. They are impatient and need to be in control. Therefore,
>
> 1. Spend little time attempting to relate to them on a personal level and keep your pre-tour questioning short and direct to discover their fitness needs or concerns.
> 2. Move fast and isolate the most visible benefits by producing concrete evidence.
> 3. Do not make a lengthy presentation citing all the benefits. Be brief and stress the bottom line based on their fitness needs.
> 4. Ask questions to involve them, get them to talk, and allow them to lead. Asking questions helps you to maintain control of the presentation.
> 5. They will test you to see what you are made of; so be willing to joust with them. If you challenge them, challenge the concepts rather than the person.
> 6. Answer objections immediately, and never try to bluff.
> 7. Present several alternatives from which they may select their own solution. Avoid telling them what is best.
> 8. An action close stressing an immediate opportunity works well.

Expressives

Expressives tell and emote. Like drivers, they are highly assertive, but they are also high in emotional responsiveness. They attempt to tell people what to do, but place more emphasis on their relationships with people than they do on the task itself. *They are social specialists.*

Expressives temper assertiveness with concern for the feelings of others. You must compliment them. They desire success, but are recognition motivated. Show them how to win. Let them talk and they often sell themselves. Give them names of current and active members, especially if it is someone they know. Testimonials from well-known people or people they respect are important.

Chapter 5 — Finding Your Selling Style

Expressives pride themselves on originality, foresight, and the ability to see the big picture. At their best, expressives often see new possibilities and present fresh ideas and approaches to problems. At their worst, they seem to base decisions on opinions, hunches, or intuition rather than on facts. Under stress, expressives run the risk of seeming detached. They may spend time defending their ideas instead of trying to make them work in practical manner.

The expressive's love of risk-taking makes it easier for them to take a chance on your club. Refer to the club as a "sure bet" for getting healthier. Emphasize the importance of risk-taking to making progress and meeting goals, and show the expressive your health club's payoff potential. When you have a qualified expressive whose needs fit what your club offers, you should not have to do much persuading. Remember, expressives are intuition-driven.

Developing A Presentation Strategy For The Expressive

Expressives are visionaries and dreamers. Therefore,

1. Plan to show them how they can personally win and how their health and fitness levels will be met.
2. Open with innovative ideas for them to grow and win with through your offering.
3. Ask open-end questions that allow them to talk at length about "their" fitness goals. Then relate your benefits to their goals.
4. Never argue or back them into a corner.
5. Ask if they want you to respond to their stated concerns. Often they respond, "No, I just wanted you to know how I am thinking."
6. Use testimonials, especially from members they may know because they identify with who else uses the club.

Amiables

Amiables ask and emote, are low in assertiveness, and high in responsiveness. They rely on a personal feeling approach to get things done. *They are support specialists*, combining personal reserve and emotional expression.

Amiables are submissive and willing to go along with the crowd. They need time to get to know you personally, so allow plenty of warmup time. They are undisciplined in the use of time. Agreeable in nature, they are also easily hurt. They want to be liked.

Amiables tend to be perceptive and observant individuals who are concerned with whether they like you, trust you, and can picture a positive long-term relationship with you. They are highly people-oriented and resent doing business with anyone who makes them uncomfortable or is unresponsive to their feelings. Before they consent to join your club, they must be convinced that you personally believe in it.

Amiables at their best are truly perceptive and aware, skilled in communication, and empathetic listeners. At their worst, they seem more concerned with the process of interaction than with the content of the matter at hand. They appear to be flying by the seat of their pants instead of relying in any measure on logic and thought. They seem to regard their own emotions as facts and act on the basis of their feelings. They may be criticized for being defensive, over-reactive, and too subjective.

To sell effectively to amiables, you have to show them you're a team player. Build rapport by proving you are there to help them set goals and get in shape, then work side-by-side with them to accomplish the goals they've set. To minimize the amiable's insecurities, talk about the needs your club can satisfy and how meeting those needs will help them gain control over their health and well-being, as well as give them more confidence in their personal and family life.

A Presentation Strategy for the Amiable

Amiables must be convinced that you are authentic and have their best interests at heart. They have a difficult time saying yes. Therefore,

1. Plan to approach with as much personal information as possible.
2. Avoid a rigid or canned approach and presentation.
3. Make an informal presentation with more visuals and testimonial information integrated.
4. Use empathy and show that you understand and accept their feelings.
5. Spend some time relating. Use their first name often.
6. Be open and candid. Develop a personal relationship with them.
7. Offer them personal assurances that if they work hard, they will achieve their goals.
8. Avoid asking directly for their business. Instead, assume that they are favorably disposed to your proposition and suggest an easy next step.
9. Be prepared to use third-party references and case histories that link them to current members.

Chapter 5 — Finding Your Selling Style

Analyticals

Analyticals ask and control, and are low in both assertiveness and responsiveness. They are highly task-oriented but soften that style with low assertiveness. They ask rather than direct. *They are technical specialists*, combining personal reserve and emotional control.

Analyticals are highly logical, organized, and unsentimental. They tend to be fact-oriented. Their contribution is their ability to solve difficult problems and make sound, rational decisions based on evidence and intelligent inferences rather than on imagination or gut feelings. They take a logical, ordered approach to responsibilities. The more supporting data you can provide which shows why your club is right for them, the more likely they are to join. They have little interest in your opinions and more in your ability to assemble and organize supportive data for showing them proof of what the club has to offer.

At their best, analyticals appear to be a consistent force for progress. They are top-flight planners and doers. They can cut through untested ideas and emotional fervor to find the core truth. They are effective organizers for research and planning. They are valuable in executing logical, painstaking, and profitable projects.

Customize Your Presentation for the Analytical

Analyticals are data and fact-oriented and slow to make decisions. They are naturally suspicious and extremely cautious. They read and study everything. Therefore,

1. Get to know their fitness concerns quickly and thoroughly.
2. Use a logic-based, low-key style of relating.
3. Be sure prospects understand the structure of how you will present the club features and solicit feedback at each step of the club tour.
4. Make use of your environment by getting them involved hands on—allow them to participate by testing the machines, lifting some of the weights, or trying out a piece of the cardio equipment.
5. Present information in a controlled, professional, highly organized fashion.
6. Point out the pros and cons of your gym. They will be thinking about them.
7. Present a detailed summary of major points and use the summary as a close.
8. Avoid saying, "Well, in my opinion. . ." They don't care about your opinions, just facts or physical evidence that you can show them.

At their worst, analyticals are overly cautious and conservative. They emphasize deliberation over action. They may become so involved in evaluating all the various details of a situation that others may regard them as indecisive stumbling blocks to innovative action. Under stress, analyticals can become rigid and insecure. They may fear taking risks. They seem more concerned with being right than with seizing opportunities.

When you first meet analyticals, be well prepared and equipped to answer all questions. Be cordial, but move quickly to the club tour. Study their fitness needs logically. Ask lots of questions that show a clear direction and pay close attention to their answers.

VERSATILITY AS A COMMUNICATION TOOL

When people of different styles meet and behave strictly according to the characteristics of their own personal styles, conflict often results. When such a situation occurs, the only way to avoid an escalation in miscommunication or a conflict is for one of the two people involved to engage in some style flexibility. In an ideal situation, both are willing to move part way, but you must be capable of making most or all of any necessary temporary adjustment. This willingness to try behaviors not necessarily characteristic of your style is called *behavioral flexibility or versatility.*

Versatility is the ability to adjust your personal pace and priorities so you can relate effectively with someone who is another style. Your own personal style does not change, but rather techniques are applied that work in that particular situation. For example, when meeting with an analytical, the expressive fitness consultant can incorporate versatility by talking less, listening more, and focusing on facts.

Versatility should never be equated with either insincerity or mere imitation of the prospect's style. Versatile salespeople seek a reasonable compromise. They do not become so highly changeable that their pace and priority needs are constantly set aside for those of a prospective member, yet prospects' preferences in pace and priorities must be recognized and given the importance that seems right to them.

The Interaction of Styles

The dimensions of assertiveness and responsiveness also operate in people's pace and their priorities. *Pace* is the speed at which a person prefers to move. Those who are low in assertiveness (analyticals and amiables) prefer a slow pace;

those high in assertiveness (drivers and expressives) prefer a fast pace in conversation, deliberation, and problem solving.

Priorities are what a person considers important and tend to be related to the dimension of responsiveness. Those who are low in responsiveness put tasks at the top of their priority list, and those who are high in responsiveness put relationships in first place. These conflicts may be summarized as follows:

The Interaction of Styles

Style	Shared Dimension	Source of Conflict	Area of Agreement
Analytical — Amiable	Low Assertiveness	Priorities	Pace
Driver — Expressive	High Assertiveness	Priorities	Pace
Analytical — Driver	Low Responsiveness	Pace	Priorities
Amiable — Expressive	High Responsiveness	Pace	Priorities
Analytical — Expressive	None	Both	None
Amiable — Driver	None	Both	None

Conflicts that involve only priorities or only pace can be handled with relative ease; real trouble results when the styles of two people conflict in both pace and priorities. If you deal with every prospect or member in the same way, you will close a small percentage of all your contacts, because you will only close one personality style. But if you learn how to effectively work with all four personality styles, you can significantly increase your closing ratio.

Fitness consultants who do not adjust their behavior to meet the style needs of prospective members face deteriorating situations. For example, an expressive salesperson's questions may be interpreted as a personal challenge or attack by an analytical prospect. If the analytical prospect responds to the questions merely to save face, the expressive salesperson then tends to talk more, move faster, and push the analytical into still greater conflict.

To avoid distrust and ultimately a breakdown in communication, you must meet the needs of your prospects, especially their behavioral style needs. Treat them as they want to be treated, and move according to the pace and priority they desire.

Identifying Pace and Priority

How do you go about determining someone's pace and priorities? Ask yourself these three questions and observe the answers:

1. How fast does the person make decisions and get things done?

2. How *competitive* is the person?
   – Is the person competitive in a conversation?
   – Does the person fight for air time in a discussion?

3. How much *feeling* is displayed in a verbal and nonverbal communication?
   – How often does the person smile?
   – Do they gesture broadly?

Your goal is to identify pace and priorities accurately and respond in an appropriate manner. How can you find out your prospect's information preferences? Use one of these statements to assist you:

1. *"Ordinarily I have an organized presentation of the club and get right to it, but today I think I should get to know you better to see how our club can be a fit for your lifestyle. What would you like me to do?"*

2. *"I am prepared to get right into my presentation or if you prefer we can chat a bit so that I can learn about you and your fitness goals or concerns. Which do you prefer?"*

3. *"There are a lot of ways I can start explaining how our club would benefit you based on the concerns you were kind enough to share with me over the phone yesterday. Would you prefer I start with the end in mind and then work backwards, or would you like to hear the step-by-step details first?"*

The expressive and amiable styles would respond to these statements indicating a desire to chat and get to know one another. While the driver and analytical styles would want you to begin your presentation.

Chapter 5 — Finding Your Selling Style

GENDER STYLE DIFFERENCES

While it is essential to recognize and adjust to different social styles, it is also necessary to recognize the difference that gender makes on our communication in the health and fitness industry. That is why we must be sensitive to gender issues and adjust to them just as we do for social style differences. If not handled correctly, these seemingly insignificant differences can break down communication lines and hurt relationships, and this ultimately hurts your club and your income!

One way to ensure effective cross-gender communication is to *emphasize* and *encourage* male and female distinctions and how both genders have much to contribute to the club and its members. By emphasizing the differences in a positive manner, the different viewpoints can be highly productive. Both men and women bring to the table different perspectives, experiences, and communication skills, and they interpret language in very distinct ways. Ultimately, however, they use these distinctly different styles and patterns of speech to deliver roughly the same message.

It is ironic that early stereotyping itself may have fostered the development of communication styles that manifest themselves among men and women today. Research clearly shows that men tend to be more assertive while women tend to be more attentive listeners.

Boys learn the art of playing the game early. They learn about power and hierarchical order. When boys grow up, conversations for men become negotiations of power and achievement. Women have their own distinctive character and essence. By the time girls become women, they approach the world as a network of connections. Women weave webs of relationships; conversations are negotiations for closeness and intimacy.

Relating to the Opposite Sex. Whether or not you have experienced how gender differences hinder relationships in selling when handled improperly, it is clear that the unequal treatment of employees by management hinders the success of any club. A key question to ask is whether gender differences, in and of themselves, create diverse ways of thinking or different behavioral relationships. If so, what are some things to be aware of when you're selling to someone of the opposite sex? When men and women find themselves sitting across from one another to discuss membership, they must learn to adjust their styles. During the presentation they should use the strengths unique to their gender.

Remember that nothing can kill a membership sale more quickly than acting on stereotypes or generalities, regardless of gender.

Exhibit 5.1 provides some suggestions for dealing with gender differences. You must be prepared to communicate effectively with your male and female sales managers, fellow sales reps, as well as the men and women that come in for club tours. No one can make a sweeping statement about how all women or all men like to sell or be sold. In any selling situation it's vital to communicate in a way that substantiates what's meaningful to that individual, and gender may help determine what a person feels is important. Subtle, gender-based changes to your presentation may give you the edge you're looking for to boost sales.

Exhibit 5.1

Dealing With Gender Differences During your Club Presentation

Point out aspects of the club... carefully

Not all men use free weights and not all women use only machine resistance training. Undoubtedly, in your club you have seen an increase in women's awareness of the benefits of free weights and weight training. Never tailor your presentation so you exclude an aspect of the club in which the prospect may be interested.

Stop interrupting

Tension or nervousness caused by gender differences can often cause people to interrupt each other. This is a good way to lose the membership. Learn to listen. Then answer in a confident and clear manner.

Feel the sale

There is more to selling than numbers. Read your prospects. Sometimes they need emotional satisfaction as well as bottom line results.

Control the language

Never use terms such as "honey", "dear", or "sweetie" in a professional situation. This is simply not acceptable.

Practice your humor

Being funny at the right moment is very important to almost any presentation. However, think about your jokes and make sure they are not offensive or rude.

Watch your language

Avoid "guy" or "girl" talk when presenting to mixed genders. For example, women should avoid using descriptive words such as "cute" or "adorable" and men should keep away from the use of overtly masculine phrases and terms.

Chapter 5 — Finding Your Selling Style

Social Style Summary

	Driver	Expressive	Amiable	Analytical
Backup style	Autocratic	Attacker	Acquiescer	Avoider
Measures personal value by	Results	Applause or approval	Security	Accuracy, "being right"
For growth, needs to	Listen	Check	Initiate	Decide
Needs climate that	Allows to build own structure	Inspires to reach goals	Suggests	Provides details
Takes time to be	Efficient	Stimulating	Agreeable	Accurate
Support their	Conclusions and actions	Dreams and intuitions	Relationships and feelings	Principles and thinking
Present benefits that tell	What	Who	Why	How
For decisions, give them	Options and probabilities	Testimonials and incentives	Guarantees & assurances	Evidence & service
Their specialty is	Controlling	Socializing	Supporting	Technical

Finding Your Selling Style
REFOCUS

- Knowledge of behavioral styles is a useful tool for gaining insight into the thinking of prospects. The model uses the assertiveness and responsiveness dimensions of behavior to assess an individual's social style.

- Never attempt to adopt a style that is an insincere imitation of the prospect. Take the lead in finding common ground with the prospect. Practice and use psychological reciprocity.

- Recognizing typical behavioral cues makes it possible to classify people quickly into one of four basic personality styles: driver, expressive, amiable, or analytical.

- Versatility is your ability to adjust your own personal pace and priorities to facilitate interaction with a person of another style.

- Gender differences require diverse ways of thinking and using our behavioral relationships. Adjust to different gender styles to enhance communication.

Chapter 5 — Finding Your Selling Style

Part III

Gaining Knowledge, Preparing, and Planning for the Presentation

what are your goals?

No matter what your facility goals are, FreeMotion Fitness™ is dedicated to helping you achieve them. Supplying unparalleled products that boast quality construction and user-friendly features. Competitive financing and hassle-free application. Customer care, committed to providing support. Progressive training and education resources. Whether you are looking for maintenance-free products, financing, customer care or training resources, we have solutions to help you.

 EPIC STRENGTH   NordicTrack   

TOLL FREE 877.363.8449   [+1] 719.533.2900   www.freemotionfitness.com

Total Fitness Systems
6 3/4 x 8 3/4
Black & White
PDF format requested

Chapter 6

Preparation for Success in Fitness Sales

FOCAL POINTS

- **Product knowledge about the health and fitness industry.**
- **Product positioning.**
- **Three types of motivation.**
- **Maintaining self-motivation and exercising initiative.**
- **Setting and achieving goals.**

PREPARING TO SELL

Success in fitness sales involves a combination of the training provided by your club, your own active preparation in learning, your level of fitness, and personal commitment. The more help the club gives, the easier your job is. Because the club's success depends upon your success, your preparation is a major mutual concern. Adequate preparation for success in selling involves the following areas that are considered in this chapter.

1. Fitness knowledge

2. Product knowledge

3. Motivation and goal setting

Product knowledge is critical in any business, and this industry is no different. All sales consultants and trainers must be experts on health and fitness. Thus, there is some fundamental knowledge necessary to answer

Chapter 6 — Preparation for Success in Fitness Sales   86

the prospects and members' basic questions and to give you the ability to take members through their first program.

FITNESS KNOWLEDGE

Newly hired fitness consultants may have some general knowledge of the club or the health and fitness industry and may even have some specific training and nutrition knowledge. However, perhaps you were hired with little or no knowledge of the industry or of the way a health club operates. Obtaining product knowledge for your industry is one of the first prerequisites of success. One of the most important things you must do is get enough knowledge to feel comfortable in your sales presentations and interacting with members on the gym floor.

What do you need to know about fitness? One answer to that question is *everything!* Nevertheless, you cannot delay beginning sales activity until you have had time to learn everything, and you cannot cease to learn about nutrition and exercise once you begin to sell. Gaining knowledge is an ongoing process. The following are the four basic components of fitness that you need to learn and understand if they are not already familiar to you:

1. Muscular Strength and Endurance

2. Cardiovascular Endurance

3. Body Composition

4. Flexibility

You may already know much of the information in the following sections. If that is the case, use this material to refresh your memory so you can provide the best possible service and support to your prospects and members. If this information is new to you, take some time to learn it. It will prove an invaluable resource in your presentations and help you sound like the "authority" on health and fitness to prospective members.

Muscular Strength and Endurance

Improving muscular strength and endurance results in muscles becoming larger, tighter, and shapelier. Muscular strength is the ability to apply force to an external resistance or being able to lift things without fear of injury. Endurance is the ability to lift things repeatedly over a short period of time without undue fatigue.

Muscular endurance strengthens ligaments, tendons, and joints, and most importantly reduces and even prevents low back pain.

Increasing Muscular Strength and Endurance. This is accomplished by subjecting a muscle to some resistance. The resistance should be enough to force the muscle to the point of failure. The muscle remembers this point and prepares itself (becomes stronger) for the next time it is subjected to resistance.

Male and Female Differences. The increased muscle size in males that comes from strength training is due to the male hormone testosterone. This hormone is responsible for male characteristics – large muscles, facial hair, deep voice, and so on. Women have very little of this hormone, so they experience very little, if any large muscular growth. They are, of course, able to strengthen their muscles, tighten, and shape them.

Free Weights. Weight training is by far the best method of increasing your muscular strength. Free weights are a form of weight training that require the involvement of several muscle groups to stabilize, balance, and coordinate the movement of resistance. Because of this, free weights should dominate your training if you are preparing for sports participation, body building, or power lifting.

Weight Resistance Machines. This type of training isolates specific muscles by stabilizing the body in the machine and restricting the movement to a specific range. Machine training is adequate and beneficial for beginners and fitness enthusiasts.

General Weight Training Principles. You can never know too much about fitness to ensure that you can provide the best and most thorough information to your members. Exhibit 6.1 provides common answers when you are asked specific resistance and weight training questions. The following is a list of weight training principles that every fitness consultant needs to know and be able to share with members who need assistance.

- Exercise larger muscle groups first and proceed down to smaller groups.

- Perform exercises in a smooth, controlled manner – no jerking.

- Breathe normally. Never hold your breath while training.

- Use as much of your range of motion as possible to develop full-range strength and flexibility.

- When using machines make sure the rotational axis of the cam of all rotary exercises is in line with the joint axis of the body part that is being moved.

Exhibit 6.1

Common Questions and Answers Concerning Weight Training

Q: What exercises should I do?
A: Select the exercises that train the muscle groups you use most frequently or wish to strengthen. A complete program working all body parts is best.

Q: How often should I work with weights?
A: Exercises should be performed two to three times weekly.

Q: How much resistance should I use?
A: The weights should force your muscles to failure or tax your strength at eight repetitions.

Q: How many repetitions should I do?
A: The ideal point of failure is eight repetitions. Research has found that eight reps is ideal for strength gains. Lower reps (4-6) is for size, and higher reps (10-15) is for endurance.

Q: How many sets should I do?
A: One set performed to failure is adequate for the beginner. Multiple sets are used for advanced or sports related training.

Q: How much time should I give my muscles for recuperation?
A: Resting the muscles is just as important as the actual training. Forty-eight hours is required between training the same muscles.

Cardiovascular Endurance

Cardiovascular endurance is the ability to sustain activity over long periods of time or how efficiently your heart is able to get nutrients and oxygen rich blood to your working muscles. An improved level of cardiovascular endurance is associated with a reduced risk of heart disease.

Resting Heart Rate. The heart rate is a general indicator of cardiovascular fitness. It becomes slower as people become more aerobically fit. The slower an individual's heart

THE OFFICIAL HANDBOOK FOR HEALTH CLUB SALES

rate is at rest, the less the heart has to work, adding minutes, hours, days, and years to your life.

Training. Cardiovascular endurance is improved by doing aerobic activities. Aerobic means using oxygen. Aerobic activities include aerobic dance, jogging, bicycling, stair climbing, swimming, or any activity that involves large muscle groups for extended periods of time. To receive maximum benefit from training, the activity must maintain at least 60 percent of your maximum heart rate for 20 minutes and be done at least three times per week. Your maximum heart rate is computed by subtracting your age from 220. Cardiovascular exercise can be done more than three times per week and can be done on consecutive days. Here are some basic guidelines to follow when doing such activity:

- Each cardio workout session should consist of 5 to 10 minutes of warm-up, followed by 20 to 30 minutes of aerobic training, and a 5-minute cool down.

- The warm-up period gradually increases the heart rate thereby preparing the muscular and circulatory systems for the upcoming training period. This also helps prevent injuries.

- The training period should consist of exercising for at least 20 to 30 minutes in your training zone (60 percent to 80 percent of your maximum heart rate) to produce significant improvement of the cardiovascular system.

- After completing the training period, gradually lower your exercise intensity before suddenly stopping. This cool down period allows the muscular and circulatory systems to return to normal. This also helps to prevent dizziness, fainting, or nausea.

- When your cardiovascular fitness level has been achieved maintaining it can be accomplished by continuing your training at least three times per week.

Body Composition

Body composition refers to the amount of fat and lean body tissue or fat free mass that comprise the body. Though most individuals are concerned with body composition for cosmetic reasons, it is extremely important for good health. The build-up of fat is a contributing factor to many diseases. The body fat chart illustrated in Table 6.1 shows the range of body fat percentages for men and women from excellent to poor.

Table 6.1

BODY FAT CHART

MEN		WOMEN
8% or less	Excellent	15% or less
9%-15%	Good	16%-22%
16%-19%	Average	23%-27%
20%-24%	Fair	28%-33%
24% or more	Poor	33% or more

Lowering and Controlling Body Composition

This is best accomplished by combining a proper diet with aerobic exercise and weight training. Improving body composition means decreasing fat weight while increasing muscle weight. Dieting alone will reduce fat weight, but it will also reduce lean weight, usually by decreasing the amount of muscle tissue. This is counter-productive because muscles are the "engines" of the body and have high-energy requirements twenty-four hours per day. Consequently, anything that lowers muscle mass also lowers metabolic needs and actually works against fat loss.

Aerobic exercise increases the rate of fat loss by burning additional calories and decreases the rate of muscle loss by providing low intensity exercise. Aerobic activity also enhances cardiovascular fitness and should be included in every weight loss or weight control program.

Weight training also increases the rate of fat loss by burning additional calories. However, strength training actually increases muscle weight by providing high intensity exercise. That is, strength training increases muscle mass which automatically increases metabolic needs. Strength training, therefore provides a double reducing effect by using additional calories for exercise and for muscle maintenance and repair.

Flexibility

Flexibilty is the ability to bend and extend your joints through their full range of motion. Good flexibility is critical to improving power, balance, agility coordination, and helps prevent injuries and soreness. Static stretching is the more common and easier to practice method for improving flexibility. Concentrate on relaxing into the stretched position and hold it for a minimum of thirty seconds, preferably a minute or so for each position.

Exhibit 6.2 is a list of fun and informative answers to common myths believed by many novice gym goers and even some seasoned athletes. Use these as an enjoyable way to educate your prospects and help them see the truth behind some commonly misunderstood facts about fitness.

Exhibit 6.2

Common Exercise Myths

Myth: More is better.

Fact: Progress can be made with as little as twenty minutes, three days a week.

Myth: You have to experience soreness when starting a program.
Fact: Pain and soreness when starting out can be avoided if progress is gradual.

Myth: No pain, no gain.

Fact: Progress is made by increasing the amount of weight, resistance, repetitions, or time from workout to workout. In other words, try to increase the intensity of the workout. Take the exercise to the point of failure, not past it.

Myth: Muscle turns to fat if you stop exercising.

Fact: Muscle is muscle and fat is fat. If exercising stops, the muscles weaken and decrease in size (slowing metabolism) and fat cells increase in size

Myth: Weight lifting will cause an individual to lose flexibility.

Fact: Weight lifting exercises and machines performed through a complete range of motion can actually improve flexibility.

Myth: Sit-ups will trim waistline.

Fact: There is no such thing as spot reduction. Sit-ups and other exercises help strengthen and tighten particular areas of the body. Fat stores are used equally from the entire body as energy is required.

Chapter 6 — Preparation for Success in Fitness Sales 92

PRODUCT KNOWLEDGE

The Club Itself

Now that you have some general knowledge pertaining to health and fitness, it is critical that you combine that knowledge with your club's specific features. Fitness information would be useless if you did not learn how to show prospects the ways your club specifically solves areas of fitness needs or concerns. Learn the club's specific features, its benefits, and its acceptance in the marketplace. Detailed product knowledge prepares you to answer any question a prospective member might have and to offer whatever reassurance is necessary in the process of helping the prospect reach a decision to join.

When you know the club and its equipment backward and forward, you can answer detailed, technical questions from veteran fitness enthusiasts to those who are considering a health club for the first time. You seldom tell a prospect all the information you have, but having all the information gives you a whole library from which you can choose the best items for the current situation.

Product knowledge also involves gaining as much information as possible about the club you represent. You need to know something about its history: Who founded it and when, how the present facility layout evolved, its position in the marketplace, and even its past and present performance and growth. Knowledge of the club also includes commonly used tactics and strategies that affect the members—service, membership options, and policies.

Knowledge of the Competition

Knowledge of the competition is often overlooked as an element of product knowledge. Learn about the equipment and features of your major competitors; know their terms, their membership prices, their personal training policies, and their reputation for service. Most prospective members are not weighing the advantages of joining against those of not joining; they are trying to decide *which* club to join.

One of the advantages of studying your competition is that you are reminded of the good points of your own club, its services, and staff. This will help refresh your own presentations, especially if you have been selling memberships for a period of time. Exhibit 6.3 provides an overview of the four possible areas of competitive advantage.

Exhibit 6.3

Differential Competitive Advantage

Product Superiority	Service Superiority	Source Superiority	People Superiority
Location	Training availability	Time established	Personal knowledge and skill
Environment	Individual Trainers	Competitive standing	Integrity and character
Safety	Group Classes	Community image	Standing in community
Appearance	Variety of Casses	Location	Interpersonal skills
Design	Attainability of support on the gym floor	Size	Mutual friends
Type of equipment	Knowledgeable nutrition experts on hand	Financial soundness	Cooperation
Availability of machines		Policies and practices	
Special Features (child care, tanning, etc)			

Product Knowledge Application

Product knowledge is sterile and unproductive unless you can use it and apply it to the needs of a particular prospect or member. Knowing the crucial areas of health and fitness information and how your club can help in those areas enables you to advise a prospect accurately and safely. When you know your club, no prospect will likely ever have an exercise or fitness question that you can't handle. The application of product knowledge to the individual's specific concerns is the key then to unlocking the formula to more memberships and more satisfied members who truly feel they are being helped by you and your expertise.

PRODUCT POSITIONING

The level of competition today is just amazing. There are so many health clubs, and so many fitness consultants trying to get everybody else's business, and they're coming at you from all over. That makes **positioning** – the marketing strategy

Chapter 6 — Preparation for Success in Fitness Sales   94

of differentiating your health club in the mind of a prospect – more important than ever. Once a gym identifies what makes it *unique* in the *eyes of the consumer,* that idea should be the focus of its entire marketing and sales strategy. You must be given that differentiating idea. Exhibit 6.4 gives sales professionals five points to consider that will enable them to go into a sales presentation with this attitude–"*Allow me to explain to you how and why my club and its services are better and different.*"

Exhibit 6.4

Key Points for Developing a Powerful Market Position

- **Find Out** what qualities of your club and its services are most important to your members. Then use the information to create a unique niche for yourself.

- **Put Together** a marketing strategy built around several features that are important to your members and that will set you apart from the competition. And then develop an integrated marketing communication message that reinforces those attributes in the prospective members' minds.

- **Recognize** that focusing on the few attributes that really set you apart means you can't be all things to all people. When you shout, "Hey, everybody," you end up satisfying nobody.

- **Remember** the way you service your members or sell to them can be a powerful difference. You are an industry where the prevailing culture stresses "belly-to-belly" interactions, so remember to add personal, sincere touches to your presentations and the way you interact with members.

- **Keep** an eye on how your competitors are positioning themselves. Be ready to respond to their claims and make sure you maintain a differential competitive advantage.

Positioning was popularized by Jack Trout and Al Ries in their book *Positioning: The Battle for Your Mind.* "Positioning" is the place a product – in this case your health club – occupies in potential members' minds relative to competing offerings. Once a position is selected, product, price, place, and promotion strategies and tactics are designed to reinforce the sought-after position. These marketing mix components represent a bundle of individual dimensions that are designed to work together to create a competitive advantage.

THE OFFICIAL HANDBOOK FOR HEALTH CLUB SALES

MOTIVATION AND GOAL SETTING

Fitness consultants often find that they have the needed knowledge and sales skills but have trouble getting around to using them, or else they work hard and long but find that what they accomplish fails to bring them lasting satisfaction. The missing ingredient is motivation.

Numerous definitions have been given for motivation. Perhaps the simplest is that motivation is the reason for taking action. This definition can be expanded slightly to say that motivation is the *impetus* to begin a task, the *incentive* to expend an amount of effort in accomplishing the task, and the *willingness* to sustain the effort until the task is completed.

The question most asked by club managers and owners, "How can we motivate our sales force?" The answer most given is, "You can't." The reason for this answer is that the question typically implies that somewhere there are strategies, techniques, or gimmicks that, once discovered and implemented, will double or triple sales motivation and productivity. Genuine and lasting motivation is not something management does, but rather a process that management fosters and allows to happen.

The primary responsibility for developing and sustaining motivation rests with you; the club's role is to provide a supportive climate in which the development and sustaining of motivation is encouraged. Bob Nelson, author of *1001 Ways to Reward Employees*, says, "What motivates people the most takes just a little time and thoughtfulness." Recognize them as individuals and you're giving them what they most crave. Read *The Lighthouse Story* for an inspirational idea that cost just a few dollars but paid enormous dividends.

The Lighthouse Story

Jonathan Berger, director of strategic accounts for Square D/Schneider Electric, had a salesperson on his team close a very important account that put a fairly large bonus in the sales rep's pocket. So Berger decided to take the extra step that made this sale a truly memorable triumph. He knew the sales rep's wife had a passion for photographing lighthouses, so he sent her a small crystal lighthouse with a note that recognized her husband's achievements and thanked her for her support and the time she had invested. The wife wrote Berger back and said, "Never has anyone in any company ever acknowledged my existence or the contribution I make to my husband's career." This story is good enough to pass on. So relate the story to a sales manager friend of yours!

Practical Motivation for Fitness Consultants

All motivation theories agree that motivation arises as a response to either an external or internal stimulus. Recognizing those stimuli that operate in your own experience can help you discover ways to control either the stimuli or your responses to them in a way that produces

Chapter 6 — Preparation for Success in Fitness Sales

a positive, sustained motivational power and the success you desire. Motivation may arise in *fear*—the fear of punishment or withholding of acceptance if behavior does not conform to expectations. It may come from *incentive*—the promise of reward for desired behavior. But the most effective type of motivation is that arising in *attitude*—behavior chosen because it fits your internal values and standards.

Fear Motivation. Fear as a motivating force has some value. Fear is a natural emotion designed as protection from danger. Fear motivation has some advantages.

1. It protects the individual from self-destruction or harm.
2. It protects society from undesirable behavior.
3. It is sometimes the quickest way to accomplish a desired reaction.

In spite of these advantages, fear motivation has serious disadvantages that more than offset its benefits.

1. **Fear is external.** It is effective only as long as the enforcing power is stable. When the sales manager is out of sight, fear motivation is materially weakened.
2. **Fear is temporary**. Threats or punishment may control behavior for a time, but people tune out warnings if they discover that threats are not always carried out.
3. **Fear is negative.** It is directed largely toward not doing something or toward doing something unpleasant merely because it is an imposed duty rather than a chosen activity. A warning not to do something creates a void that may be filled by another equally undesirable behavior.

Incentive Motivation. The use of incentives for motivation is generally considered more enlightened than the use of fear. An *incentive* is the promise of a benefit or reward to be earned in return for certain behaviors. The attempt to produce motivated activity by offering incentives is common in health clubs. Some common incentives used include the appeal to work harder for memberships to earn increased commissions; contests, certificates, and plaques for quotas reached, and bonuses. You have to understand what motivates each individual on your team and use that information. Like fear motivation, incentive motivation has advantages.

1. Incentive motivation calls for extra effort. When a promised reward is highly desirable, fitness consultants put forth almost superhuman effort to win it.

2. Incentive motivation is positive and promises something desirable. Sales reps are not frozen into inaction by fear of being punished or deprived.

Like fear motivation, however, incentive motivation carries built-in disadvantages.

1. **Incentive motivation is external.** Behavior depends upon the initiative of the person who offers the reward rather than upon the fitness consultant who will earn it.

2. **Incentive motivation is temporary.** You may put forth a great deal of effort to win a sales contest or to earn some desired reward but not continue that level of activity or effort once the contest is over.

3. A promised reward that is **not perceived as desirable** provides no motivation for action.

4. Incentives once earned often come to be regarded as **rights** instead of a special privilege for outstanding performance. For example, fitness consultants who qualify for a bonus by high productivity and enjoy this reward for several months feel incensed if the requirements for getting a bonus are raised and they fail to meet the new quota, even though they improve their membership sales.

Attitude Motivation. Attitude motivation operates on the concept that the only lasting and uniformly effective motivation is the personal motivation that comes from the internal structure of the individual. It is based on a strong self-image and a belief in the possibility of success. Attitude motivation is self-motivation. All great salespeople inherently possess this powerful, internal drive. Self-motivation can be shaped and molded, but it cannot be taught.

Self-motivation is the result of the choices made by individuals in response to conditioning influences. Fear and self-doubt are the habitual attitudes of some people, but others choose, instead, to respond to life positively. For example, some salespeople who are told they're too inexperienced decide that they are and always will be. Then they wait for someone to tell them what to do. However, others respond to the statement by choosing to believe that their condition is temporary. As a result, they are willing and eager to try new activities, stretch their imaginations, and attempt new goals. They do not wait for someone else to motivate them; they are always reaching out for new experiences. These fitness consultants are self-motivated. What you are, then, is not entirely a result of what happens to you. *What you are is a result of how you react to what happens to you, and your reactions are a matter of choice.*

The advantages of attitude motivation are the opposites of the disadvantages of fear and incentive motivation:

Chapter 6 — Preparation for Success in Fitness Sales

1. **Attitude motivation is internal.** Because attitudes come from within, you do not need to wait for an outside stimulus to make appropriate choices and take action.

2. **Attitude motivation is permanent.** An attitude, once thoroughly established, continues to operate on an automatic basis until you do something to alter it. Self-motivation is the only kind of motivation that can be sustained over a long period of time.

Attitude Motivation Through Goal Setting

The single most important tool for developing self-motivation is a program of personal goals. A personal goals program creates desire—one of the most powerful emotions operating in human experience. If you want to be able to choose where you will go with your sales effort, and how you will get there, you need clear goals and strategies. Only then will you have the power to direct your efforts.

Daily Activity Sheet. A daily activity sheet is a useful time management and goal-setting device that should be used by every consultant everyday. Table 6.2 is an example of a daily activity sheet you can use to keep track of your goals and your progress for your benefit as well as for your manager. It is also important to keep a table or list of your daily appointments and referrals, including the time of appointments and the outcome. Good managers will review these sheets to see where they can be of assistance in helping you reach your production goals.

Table 6.2

Daily Activity Sheet

Date/ Time	Member/Guest Name	Walk-In or Appt.	New Program?	Worked out with Client?	Current Diet	Current Aerobic Level	Other Comments

THE OFFICIAL HANDBOOK FOR HEALTH CLUB SALES

It's All a Matter of Perspective

Two salesmen fell on hard times and ended up broke in a small town in Montana. They needed money to move on and learned that the town paid $20 each for wolf pelts. They sensed the opportunity. That night they set out with a couple of clubs and some borrowed supplies and made camp in the distant hills. They were no sooner asleep than one was startled by an eerie howl. He crawled outside the tent to find himself surrounded by hundreds of snarling wolves. Back into the tent he crawled and shook his buddy. "Wake up!" he cried. "Wake up! We're rich!"

It's all a matter of perspective.

A written plan of action keeps you on track and headed toward the achievement of your goals. You know exactly what to do next. A written plan also reveals conflicts between various goals so that you can plan ahead and make a reasonable schedule for the time and resources needed to reach all your goals. Deadlines provide you with the needed time frame for achieving your goals. They give you something to aim for.

Crystallized Thinking. Daily club goals are essential for every fitness consultant. Effective club managers hold one-on-one meetings with every employee and discuss goals with them. You and your manager should agree on a goal that you both feel is achievable. You must write down and date your goals. Monitoring your status keeps you focused. If your goals are hazy and poorly defined, you cannot plan concrete action steps for their achievement. Without specific action plans, much of your time and effort is wasted. You must know what you want to achieve.

Sincere Desire. A burning desire to achieve the goals you want often makes the difference between a *wish* and a *goal*. A *wish* is something you would like to have but are not willing to invest enough time or effort in order to achieve it; a *goal* is something you want so intensely that you will exert whatever effort is needed to reach it. The more goals you achieve, the more desire you develop. The greater your desire, the more you can achieve. Desire is an ascending spiral of success.

Supreme Confidence. Success demands supreme confidence in yourself and your ability. Self-confidence enables you to undertake challenging goals and believe you can succeed. Self-confidence lets you see problems as opportunities and obsta-

Chapter 6 — Preparation for Success in Fitness Sales

cles as stepping-stones to success. Self-confidence builds your credibility so that the prospective member is open to considering the solutions suggested. Self-confidence makes it easy to ask for the membership—not once, but again and again until the sale is closed successfully.

The secret to developing this kind of confidence is a growing list of goals accomplished. Each time you succeed in reaching a goal you have set and worked toward, you gain added belief in your own capability to achieve. Confidence in your own personal ability is the greatest source of security you can possess.

Dogged Determination. Determination to stick to your plan of action until your goal is achieved is an outgrowth of desire and confidence. When you have a burning desire to achieve your goals, you are not easily swayed by others' thoughtless comments, by the disapproval of someone who does not understand your goals, or the active opposition of those who fear to be compared with you in either effort or results. Determination gives you the creative freedom to discover new tactics for achieving your goal when your first effort fails and to think up more ideas until you discover a way that works.

SUCCESS AND THE TOTAL PERSON

Health clubs emphasize that their sales forces are essential to success. However, clubs may not always pay attention to what constitutes success for an individual. Too often success for fitness consultants is measured only in terms of the amount of memberships generated. This narrow view of success has been responsible for destroying the self-confidence of untold numbers of fitness consultants. An understanding of what success really means frees you to become all that your potential allows.

One of the most comprehensive definitions of success is this: *"Success is the progressive realization of worthwhile, predetermined, personal goals."* This definition is especially applicable to fitness consultants, who can begin their careers with relatively little training compared to that required of other professionals. Because success is *progressive*, you can be successful immediately just by choosing to pursue goals that are personally fulfilling and then beginning to work toward them. Obviously, such a beginning is not made at the level expected of a master salesperson with long experience but at a level consistent with present reality. When you learn this truth, you have the patience to study, learn the art of selling, and practice your skills.

Those "worthwhile, predetermined goals" must involve more than money and position or the success that is achieved is likely to be hollow. Those who concentrate only on career success and neglect other areas of life find their lives less than happy. Money and position are fairly low on the hierarchy of needs that all people experience. For this reason, *goals must be set in every area of life*: physical and health, mental and educational, family and home, spiritual and ethical, social and cultural, financial and career.

Total personal growth in these areas is effectively pictured in Exhibit 6.5 as spokes on a wheel. If some spokes are uneven, the wheel that represents total life achievement is not round. The ride is bumpy, and you feel dissatisfaction and a vague sense of uneasiness or unhappiness. Unmet needs prevent the enjoyment of achievements in other areas. Monetary success means little to the salesperson whose family life is shattered, health ruined, or the respect of friends lost. All areas of life must be included in your plan for becoming a "total person."

Exhibit 6.5

The Wheel of Life

Preparation for Success in Fitness Sales

REFOCUS

- Preparing for success in fitness sales includes these areas of special importance: fitness knowledge, product knowledge, motivation, and goal setting.

- Fitness knowledge includes knowledge of muscular strength and endurance, cardiovascular health, body composition, and flexibility.

- Product knowledge includes knowledge of the entire health and fitness industry and specific knowledge about nutrition, exercise, your club, and the competition.

- Positioning refers to the place your club occupies in customers' minds relative to others. Once you select a position, design product, price, and promotion strategies to reinforce the desired position.

- Motivation comes primarily from one of three sources: fear, incentive, and attitude. Fear and incentives used as motivating forces are limited in effectiveness because they depend on someone else as the source. Attitude motivation is internal and permanent.

- Use a daily activity sheet to record your goals and track your accomplishments for you and your sales manager.

- Successful goal setting begins with crystallized thinking about what is important to you, then developing a plan of action with deadlines for its achievement.

THE OFFICIAL HANDBOOK FOR HEALTH CLUB SALES

What Causes Low Sales

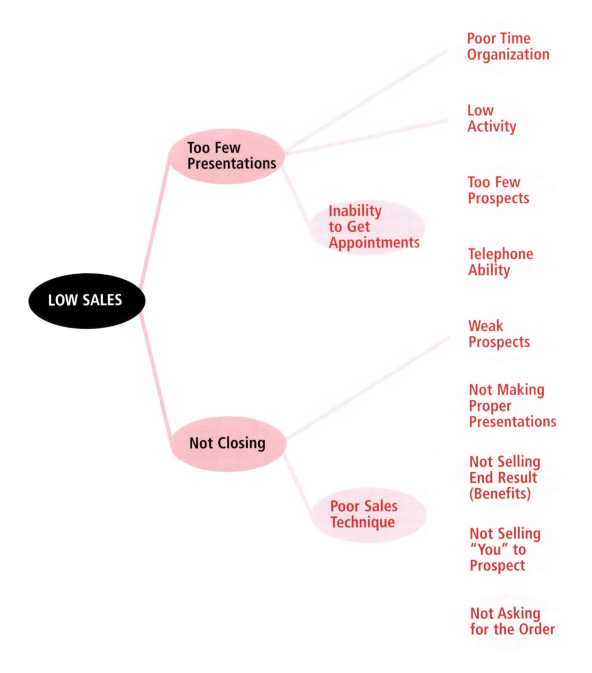

Brains & Muscle

Skilled, Seasoned, Sharp

Skilled
in her knowledge of the retail market

Seasoned
in her negotiation skills

Sharp
in her sense of responsibility to her tenant

Peggy Sells specializes in fitness clubs and is the exclusive representative to World Gym Express.

Peggy Sells
Sales & Leasing

Colliers Turley Martin Tucker is the largest full-service commercial real estate firm in the Central United States with over $2.2 billion in annual transactions, managing over 110 million square feet of office, retail and industrial space for both corporate and institutional clients. The Partner Program, CTMT's corporate services division transacts leases or administrates the portfolios of more than 20,000 locations totaling 90 million square feet throughout the U.S., U.K. and Canada.

There is only one leader.

We know the **State of Real Estate**™

Commercial Real Estate Services

5250 Virginia Way
Suite 100
Brentwood, TN 37027
ph 615.301.2800

www.ctmt.com

Chapter 7

Becoming a Master Prospector

FOCAL POINTS

- The nature and importance of prospecting.
- Who is a prospect.
- Qualify prospects using the MADDEN test.
- Internal and external prospecting methods.
- Technology in the management of prospect information.

THE CONCEPT OF PROSPECTING

Becoming a master salesperson begins with becoming a master prospector. A salesperson without prospects is as out of business as a surgeon is without patients. Great salespeople ask the right questions, know how to close, and have excellent follow-through. But the one trait they demonstrate more consistently than any other is constant prospecting enhanced by creative approaches that build value and relationships.

Opportunities are everywhere but know that it's not just the numbers – but it is a "numbers game". The more people you talk to, the better chance you have of getting one of them to a closing situation. Mastering the basics of prospecting makes you an expert in the art of searching and finding potential members. Competent prospecting saves time, and time is money.

If your closing ratio is lower than you like, your major problem may be that you don't have enough good prospects and not that you are a poor closer. If you see enough people, sooner or later you sell to someone.

Chapter 7 — Becoming a Master Prospector 106

It's a business of percentages. For example, if you have a list of twenty names, 10 of those leads may set up appointments, 5 of your appointments will actually show, and 2 or 3 of those will likely close. That is why it is so important to focus serious time and energy on prospecting to make the numbers work in your favor.

> "I'd rather be a master prospector than be a wizard of speech and have no one to tell my story to."
>
> — Paul J. Meyer

Confucius taught, "Dig the well before you thirst." This means you need to locate qualified prospects in advance—before you need them. You should have at least 5-7 appointments every day, so develop multiple sources from which names of prospects flow constantly.

QUALIFYING THE PROSPECT

Establish a pattern for prospecting. When all you have is a name, you have only a possibility of developing a prospect. Figure 7.1 illustrates the process of moving a name from the status of lead to that of qualified prospect. Truly qualified prospects are those who are exactly right for you because they possess the necessary characteristics that make them logical buyers for membership. A good definition of the best prospect is this:

A *Class 'A' qualified prospect* is one to whom you have been referred by a person the prospect respects or may already be a member, one who has the ability to make

Figure 7.1

Action of the Fitness Consultant in Turning Leads into Qualified Prospects

Sales Lead → Prospect → Qualified Prospect

Research needs, history, ability to pay, decision making ability, etc.

Evaluate information gained, add personal information

the decision to pay for membership, and one about whom you have all the personal information you need to make a good presentation.

To determine if you have a truly qualified *Class 'A'* prospect, use the **MADDEN** test described below to ensure that they: Have money, are approachable, have desire, have decision-making ability, are eligible, and have a need you can help satisfy.

M **Money.** You will save yourself many headaches by determining a prospect's ability to pay before spending your time and energy gaining a client who may quickly become more of a liability than an asset. Don't spend your valuable time giving a tour to someone who does not have any intention of paying or does not have a bank account.

A **Approachable.** Everybody is approachable when it comes to fitness. Few of us have our ideal body or fitness level. The key to approaching prospects and gaining an appointment to tour the facilities is to get them talking about their fitness goals, and you can then focus on what will best satisfy their needs.

D **Desire.** The prospect may be quite satisfied with their present health club and have no interest in changing. You can sell such a prospect only if you *create or discover a desire* that will motivate the prospect to move from the present health club to yours. The prospect may desire to save money, enjoy more convenience, have access to a wider variety of services, receive quicker results, and be in a more enjoyable atmosphere—all of which may have been the basis for selecting their present health club in the first place.

D **Decision Maker.** Before a tour is conducted the decision maker must be established. If the person you are speaking to is not the decision maker, make an appointment to have the prospect return with the individual who can make the final decision.

E **Eligible.** Determine whether the prospect is eligible and of age to purchase a membership. Some prospects may be committed to a competitor's contract and cannot afford a second membership. You must also establish that they have the necessary financing to join your club.

N **Need.** Determine the need for your club's services. To accomplish this you must ask questions and listen carefully before the tour to determine what the prospect's buying motives and goals are in order to uncover their specific needs, and then decide if your health club has the facilities that can effectively satisfy those needs.

Chapter 7 — Becoming a Master Prospector

> **Develop a prospecting consciousness — a prospecting awareness; it is the ultimate key to your success in professional selling. Prospecting is to successful selling what breathing is to living. There are prospects by the millions if you open your eyes and see them.**

METHODS OF PROSPECTING

Practice in prospecting invariably develops skill, provided the methods of practice are correct. Incorrect practice on a musical instrument produces only a greater ability to make errors. So it is with prospecting; aimless, hit-or-miss prospecting, no matter how much of it is done, generally leads only to failure. To streamline the job of prospecting and produce better results, master a number of different methods and use the ones that work best for your particular situation.

There are two general areas of prospecting for fitness consultants – internal and external. The following is a list of fifteen useful external and internal prospecting techniques. All of them work. What's important is that you pick the ones that work best for you!

Internal Prospecting

1. *Referrals*—Names given to you by members at the point of sale or on the workout floor, or from someone else who feels good about you and your health club.

2. *Upgrades and Renewals*—Sell a member a personal training package or other programs by calling new and current members to see how their workout program is going. Try to upsell.

3. *Centers of Influence*—Individuals who believe in what you are selling, influence others, and are willing to give you names and help to get them into your health club.

4. *Past Guest Register*—Follow up on unsold guests with a thank you card or a telephone call.

THE OFFICIAL HANDBOOK FOR HEALTH CLUB SALES

5. *Fitness Parties and Drives*—Provide missed guests with an additional opportunity to enroll at discounted prices.

External Prospecting

1. *Group Prospecting*—Bringing a number of people together at the same time and place and capturing their names and other information about them. Some examples are trade shows, speaking engagements, meetings, and luncheons.

2. *Planned Cold Calling*—Calling on a lead without making an appointment and knowing very little or perhaps nothing about the person.

3. *Direct Mail*—Choosing a mailing list of individuals, businesses, or professional people who appear to be qualified and sending them guest passes or promotional information that requests a reply or a visit.

4. *Lead Boxes and Fish Bowls*—Placing drop boxes in local businesses with an information card for prospects to fill out.

5. *Guest Passes, Flyers, and Door Hangers*—Handing out day or week passes, promotional flyers, and door hangers to local businesses and large apartment complexes.

6. *Civic Groups*—Joining various civic groups such as the Chamber of Commerce gives you opportunities to meet people who can become prospects for membership.

7. *Networking*—Sharing customers and information with salespeople from non-competing businesses.

8. *Company-initiated Prospecting*—Your club may provide initial prospecting for its fitness consultants, which frees you to have more face-to-face appointments with qualified prospects.

9. *Web Sites*—A health club can market its services and find customers utilizing the power of the Internet.

10. *Observation*—Prospects are everywhere, so keep your eyes and ears open. Scan local newspapers and trade publications.

INTERNAL PROSPECTING

Referrals

The use of referrals is one of the most powerful prospecting techniques. A *referral* is a name given to you as a lead by a current member, a friend, or even a prospect who did not join but felt good about you and your club. The factor that makes this prospecting method so valuable is its *leverage*. Until the proper time to use that leverage arrives, a referral is just a lead like any other.

Referrals work because people are naturally fearful or skeptical of strangers, especially those who try to persuade them to make some kind of decision. People accept you and your product more readily if someone they know and respect has sent you to see them.

Gain More Referred Leads. Salespeople do not have more referrals because they don't ask or because they don't know how to ask. There are two reasons why people do not immediately give you referrals. The first is that they find it difficult to think of names to give you. Basically, they just do not want to exert the mental effort to decide who might be interested. The second reason is they consider themselves to be "conscientious objectors" – they say they just do not give referrals.

Exhibit 7.3 illustrates a step-by-step approach to use when asking for referrals. Practice and rehearse it with members who think you are great or have given you referrals in the past. Customers think of themselves as professionals and they like to buy from professionals. Asking for referrals needs to become an automatic, habitual part of every presentation you make.

P.O.S Referrals. The first method of soliciting referrals is at the point of sale (P.O.S.). After the paperwork is complete and signed, present the benefits of referrals to the customer. Here is an example of how this may sound:

> *"By the way, Ms. Grimmett, you will have guest privileges at the club. Here is how the guest program works. Of course, we want you to invite as many guests as possible, but there is a $10 fee. However, if you have a pass or appointment for that guest, I can waive that fee. What I would like to do now is fill out passes for you with the names of the people who you think might be interested. What is the name of your first guest?"*

THE OFFICIAL HANDBOOK FOR HEALTH CLUB SALES

Many clubs offer incentives for new members to provide referrals. For example, your club may offer new members a free membership if five of their referrals enroll within a 30-day period. Or you can give away free t-shirts, gift certificates, or anything that may entice the new member to provide you with high quality leads.

Exhibit 7.3

A Six-Step Approach for Gaining More Referred Leads

1. Ask for referrals with respect

Open the dialogue something like this, "I have an important question I want to ask you." This will capture your client's attention and indicate to them just how significant this is to you.

2. Ask for their help

Soften them up by saying, "I'm trying to build our membership, and I would value and appreciate your help."

3. Explain in detail the course of action you are proposing.

Tell them what will happen if they give you a referral, and let them know that you will remain professional.

4. Gain their permission to explore

You might give them another softening statement: "I can understand how you feel." Then go on to say, "I was wondering if we could agree on who you know that might also benefit from membership. Are you comfortable with this?"

5. Narrow their focus by describing the prospect profile you are looking for

Once you have been given names, make a first step toward qualifying them. Ask your client, "if you were in my place, who would you see first?" Ask why. Then find out which one to contact next.

6. Be sure to thank the individuals for giving you referrals regardless of whether they did or did not join

Chapter 7 — Becoming a Master Prospector 112

Servicing Members. Another successful method to gain referrals is from current members on the workout floor. Building rapport with an existing member establishes an obligation on their part to help you with your business. Referrals solicited from this method are easy to approach, they show for appointments more often than leads from other prospecting methods, and they are generally easier to close.

When to Ask for a Referral. Make asking for referrals a part of the selling cycle. A logical time to ask for referrals is right after the close. A customer who buys is sold on you and likely to feel good about giving you names. Sometimes, however, a customer wants to use the facilities before giving any referrals. Salespeople are taught to go after referrals at the wrong time. They start asking for referrals before the ink on the contract is even dry. You can't ask for referrals; you must earn them. The best referrals come from satisfaction, not a signature on a contract.

Upgrades and Renewals

Not only can your current members provide you with top quality leads, they themselves are an area of internal prospecting. Never miss out on an opportunity that is right before your eyes. Notice which members seem to be struggling or which members have not come in for several weeks and contact them. They may be in need of personal training or a nutrition plan and just didn't know who to ask. By showing care and concern for your members, you not only develop friendships, you gain opportunties for upsells and may even get more quality referrals.

It is easier and less expensive to upsell existing members and fully flesh out their potential than to prospect for new clients. It is estimated that it costs 5 to 10 times more to go out and get a new customer than to keep the customer base you currently have. Some clubs furnish you with the names of past members who, for one reason or another, are no longer active. If yours does not, you can certainly ask for this information.

Centers of Influence

One of the best sales sources you can have is a person who believes in your health club, is influential with a number of people who are potential customers for you, is willing to give you the names of these people, and will help you get them in for an appointment. Such a person is called a *center of influence*. When you have several centers of influence, you will always have plenty of prospects.

THE OFFICIAL HANDBOOK FOR HEALTH CLUB SALES

People respect the center of influence to the extent that an introduction from this source virtually assures you of a sympathetic hearing.

You can find centers of influence among community leaders—social, political, business, cultural, or religious leaders. Cultivate their friendship, sell yourself to them, and ask them to help you. Centers of influence *may or may not* be actual members, but they must be sold on you and the value of the service you represent.

Centers of influence are one of the most valuable assets you can have as a salesperson. Follow up every lead they provide; then report your results to them and thank them for their help. Find a way you can show your gratitude by being of service to your centers of influence. A two-way relationship is rewarding to both parties.

Past Guest Register

Always follow up on guests who have recently tried the gym. Just because prospects use the facilities and do not join does not mean that they won't at some point in the future. Shaun Schimmelman, general mananger of World Gym Express in Brentwood, TN, reminds his salespeople that an individual's situation may change to where they find the motivation to join. Shaun uses one example of a man who toured the facilities, liked what he saw, but for some reason did not become a member. Shaun called the man back a few weeks later just to follow up, and the gentleman came in that very day and joined. Why the abrupt change? He had a mild heart attack the previous week and realized the neccessity of a personal health and fitness program. This example illustrates that people's situations and needs constantly change, and if you are persistent with a prospect, it may pay off in the future.

Fitness Parties and Drives

Fitness parties with free gifts and food is a great way to bring in new prospcets and entice members to bring in guests. For example, you can throw a party the last three days of the month for all members and businesses that are nearby. Holidays provide excellent opportunities to create excitement, have fun, and sell memberships. You may also sponsor a blood drive or a canned food drive at your club.

Chapter 7 — Becoming a Master Prospector   **114**

EXTERNAL PROSPECTING

Group Prospecting

Some clubs use group prospecting with great success. The idea is to bring together a number of people, from eight to twenty or even more. The group may meet in a business, office, a conference room, or at your club. The purpose is to inform prospects about your health club's benefits.

One effective version of this method is the corporate luncheon. This is a useful technique that gets you "belly-to-belly" with a larger number prospects. Contact the manager of a nearby business and set up a day and time to bring them lunch at their office. Offer the manager a free membership and then present the benefits of your gym to the employees as they enjoy the lunch you bought. Talk about fitness in general, discover their needs, and show them solutions to those needs that your gym can provide. The result: you sell memberships.

A variation of this method is to look for groups of potential prospects and offer to be a *guest speaker*. Members of civic clubs like the Toastmasters, Kiwanis, Lions, and Optimists may be ideal prospects for you, and they are always looking for speakers who have helpful information for their members. If you establish your credibility and sincerity, you may be able to close your speech with a brief presentation of your health club. Be sure to meet as many members of the audience as possible before and after the meeting, ask for their business cards, and then give them guest passes. Because these people have heard you speak, they already feel they know you. If they were impressed enough to want you to call, you know you have a qualified prospect.

Planned Cold Calling

One prospecting method that is available to any salesperson is cold calling. Cold calling can become an enjoyable part of your day if you accept the reality of the situation. Cold calling serves as an excellent supplement to other prospecting efforts if it is carefully planned for maximum effectiveness. Here are some guidelines for cold calling:

Supplement Your Prospect List. Be careful that cold calls never take so much of your time that you neglect calling on qualified prospects and existing members. Set aside a specific amount of time each week for cold calling but never at the expense of more profitable sales activity.

Preplan Cold Calls. Develop several effective door openers and experiment until you find which ones work best for you. Give the prospect something related to your club, such as a newsletter, brochure, or share a fitness idea. Your door opener should be something that causes the prospect to remember you when you later call for an appointment to tour the club.

Remain Enthusiastic. Set a goal to turn every cold call into a *warm call*. When you make cold calls, the person you should talk to is almost certainly not in or too busy to receive you. If you remain enthusiastic in spite of such responses, you make a positive impression on the receptionist or administrative assistant.

Direct Mail

The success of direct-mail prospecting depends upon the management of mailing lists. Some lists are better than others, and the best investment of your time and budget demands careful planning and analysis. Exhibit 7.4 has some suggestions for sources of direct-mail lists.

Exhibit 7.4

Suggested Sources for Building Direct-Mail Lists

Membership rosters

- Professional societies and trade associations (medical, accountancy, manufacturers, air conditioning, electricians)
- Country clubs
- Civic clubs (Kiwanis, Lions, Civitan, Optimist)
- Religious Groups
- Women's organizations (Altrusa, AAUW, Junior League)
- Special-interest groups (Audubon Society, garden clubs, environmental protection groups)
- Community business groups (Chamber of Commerce, Jaycees, Business and Professional Women)

City directories and telephone books

- White or yellow pages, depending upon need

People you have done business with in the past

- Such as home repair or building, banking, auto service and repair

Chapter 7 — Becoming a Master Prospector   **116**

If you are using a computer to store lists, develop a coding system to show which types of lists produce the highest percentage of responses. Code the names of people with whom you get in touch. Even if you do not sell to them immediately, they have some interest and might become active prospects at some later date.

Lead Boxes

Lead Boxes are an inexpensive way to get leads from high traffic businesses in your area and can be a very effective means of increasing sales by attracting new people to the club. It is a very simple program but requires attention, professionalism, and a systematic approach to be completely successful. If you use this technique correctly, here is an example of the results you may get:

5 boxes = 50 Leads = 25 Appointments = 5 Actual Shows = 2 Sales

Below are ten steps to follow with your lead boxes that will increase your sales production and enhance the image of the club:

1. *Effort* – Time and effort are necessary in order to maintain this program. You must be willing to expend the extra effort.

2. *Magnetism* – Design an attractive and eye-catching backdrop. The box needs to have magnetic appeal.

3. *Marketing* – You must have the right offer to entice people to fill out the entry blank form. For example, offer a free one or two-week membership.

4. *Volume* – Get out as many boxes as possible. Each consultant should have at least five boxes in the target market.

5. *Location* – Make sure boxes are in a 5 to 10-mile radius of the club. If they are not producing leads, pull the boxes. Use high traffic areas where people have a tendency to wait such as ice cream shops, dry cleaners, etc.

6. *Affirmation* – Getting permission to put out these boxes requires some experience. Look professional and ask for the decision maker. Give a brief description of the box and if necessary, offer managers an incentive such as a trial membership for themselves or their employees or set up an "employee of the month" program where they can award their best employees with free passes.

THE OFFICIAL HANDBOOK FOR HEALTH CLUB SALES

7. *Service* – It is crucial to the success of your boxes that you service them twice a week. On Monday during non-prime hours, gather the accumulated leads and replenish entry blank forms and pencils. Do the same on Thursday. Then begin calling the leads to set up appointments for the weekend.

8. *Organization* – Keep the leads separated so that you can remember which box the leads came from. When you return to the club, report to your manager so he can track your progress.

> One innovative way to gain information is an organization entitled LeTip International, which has over 400 chapters across the U.S. and Canada. Most of the members are salespeople who exchange tips and leads. Each chapter meets precisely for 75 minutes once a week between 7:16 and 8:31 a.m. You must attend 90 percent of the meetings and pass on at least two qualified leads a month — or else be terminated from the club. One particular member made six sales which he credits to receiving information directly from his chapter of LeTip.

9. *Telemarketing* – Before you start calling, sort through and discard any obscene or illegible forms. Call the younger leads as well because they can give their passes to parents or family members.

10. *Goals* – Set and meet goals. Establish quotas for yourself based on the amount of boxes you put out, the number of leads you expect to generate, how many leads will convert into appointments, and finally how many sales will be produced.

Guest Passes and Flyers

Handing out guest passes and flyers promoting specials for your club is one of the easiest and fastest ways to spark interest in the facilities and get prospects in for tours. Just remember that wherever you go you may have the opportunity to hand out passes, so be sure to have plenty with you at all times. Never miss an opportunity to prospect!

Joining Civic Groups

Membership in civic groups can give you opportunities to meet people who are prospects for your health club. Their meetings provide you with regular times to meet more people and to build relationships. Exhibit 7.6 lists some tips for using membership in civic clubs as prospecting opportunities.

Chapter 7 — Becoming a Master Prospector

Exhibit 7.6

Tips for Using Membership in Civic Clubs for Prospecting

1. Carefully select the groups you join.
2. Assume leadership responsibilities to work for positive visibility.
3. Set contact goals for each organization meeting.
4. Follow up with contacts.
5. Maintain an information file on the contacts made in each organization.
6. Use "remeet" goals to help you develop closer relationships with people.
7. Reach out to new members.

In selecting groups to join, consider the kinds of prospects you need to meet. Join a group whose purposes you can support and one that will stimulate your own thinking and creativity. Look for ways you can assume a place of leadership in the organization, preferably in a position with high visibility so that you become known to most of the members as soon as possible. Perform your role in the group competently so that your name is automatically associated with excellence in the minds of its members, and give unselfishly of yourself to the group. If you are interested only in what you can get from the group, they will soon see through your insincerity.

Networking

Networking is the active cooperation between people in businesses to share information about the business climate, specific happenings in the business community, and prospects. Networking incorporates the three C's—connecting, communicating, and cooperating.

THE OFFICIAL HANDBOOK FOR HEALTH CLUB SALES

One powerful networking technique you can use is called the "Business of the Week" Program. In this program, you partner with a local business for one week, allowing them to advertise in your gym with brochures, flyers, coupons, etc. During that week, all employees of that company can workout for free and at the end of the week, they have the opportunity to enroll at discount rates. This partnership is mutually beneficial because the company gets free advertising, and you and your club get new memberships.

Company-Initiated Prospecting

The purpose of company-initiated prospecting is to free up time for fitness consultants to concentrate on their top priority—face-to-face appointments with interested prospects. This is where results are generated.

Trade Shows. Trade shows in the United States attract over 100 million visitors each year. And, globally, trade shows are a more significant part of the marketing process than in the United States. Health and fitness companies use trade shows to demonstrate new and existing training machines and techniques, enhance their corporate image, provide information to those who visit the booth, and also use the opportunity to examine competing companies. The decision to exhibit at a trade show is a complex one that must be based on consideration of a number of variables:

1. Which trade shows will produce the most interest and the largest number of prospects?

2. Is the goal on-the-spot membership sales or discovery of leads for future sales?

3. What kind of display should be planned?

4. How many salespeople will be needed to staff the booth, and should there be personal trainers there for demonstrations?

5. How can we ensure high visibility for our exhibit and our name?

6. How will we preserve the information gathered?

A company has just 20 seconds to send out a powerful message to get people to visit their booth. For that reason, set up creative and memorable exhibits designed to catch visitors' eyes.

Chapter 7 — Becoming a Master Prospector

Harnessing the Power of the Web

You or your health club can set up a home page with a nominal initial expense and use these home pages to advertise gym services and offer special deals. Fitness consultants can market their businesses very inexpensively because of the online relationships they form.

Make Use of Affiliate Program Marketing. The Internet is also a great prospecting tool, especially as a way to partner with others. Are there Web sites that sell to the same types of customers that also buy what you sell? If so, your products might complement what they're doing in a way that would allow for an affiliate-type of arrangement. For example, you could advertise on a site that sells low-carb or low-fat foods.

An innovative e-marketing tactic to drive traffic to your Web site is to target your marketing at specific groups of prospects that are likely to have an interest in your facility. This is done by compensating the referring site for any sales that are made to customers that link from its site to yours. Unlike banner advertising, where you are essentially paying for impressions, this approach allows you to only pay for results.

Power of Observation

No matter what other methods of prospecting you elect to use, your own keen powers of observation provide many of your best prospects. Keep your eyes and ears open because prospects are everywhere. The daily newspaper, for example, is an excellent source of prospects.

Wedding announcements, business promotions, reports of civic activities, winners of contests, lists of graduates, notices of new business openings, new partnerships or planned mergers—all these and many others focus your attention on people who may be prospects. For example, call the people in the new job annouacements section. They may have just moved to town and have not yet joined a gym. You could even call the new mothers highlighted in the paper who will doubtless be looking to get back into shape after pregnancy.

MANAGING PROSPECT INFORMATION

All your good work in prospecting goes down the drain if you do not have a system for managing and using the information you find about prospects. The type of system you use is not the primary consideration; what is important is

THE OFFICIAL HANDBOOK FOR HEALTH CLUB SALES

accuracy, completeness, and ease of use. You can use a file box and individual cards. However, if you use a computer, you can easily achieve the same results with the added advantages of handy printouts and provisions for additional listings of names. Whether you use manual or computer records, the purpose and result are the same.

Initial Recording of Leads

Be sure to keep an organized list or spreadsheet of all leads, no matter what method of prospecting they came from. For leads gained from referrals, be sure to include who they were referred by. If you gain a lead from a corporate luncheon or other group prospecting technique, include the company or business they are affiliated with. For leads obtained through lead boxes, be sure that you indicate where the box was located when you record their names and information. The point is, you want to have the most accurate information possible on prospects before calling on them or making an appointment. Remembering details sets you and your club apart from the rest.

Classification of Prospects

When you first find the name of an individual, assign a classification indicator to the name. One handy classification system uses the letters **A, B,** and **C.**

- ***Class A*** prospects are those about whom you have adequate information to make a good presentation and most likely came from a referral from someone they respect. You know they have the money to buy and the authority to make a decision.

- ***Class B*** prospects are those about whom you may not know whether they have the authority to make a decision or whether they can afford to buy. You may not have a referral to help open the door. When one or more of these items is missing, take extra time to discover their fitness goals and needs that your club can meet.

- ***Class C*** prospects are people whose names you have found in some way, but about whom you have little or no information other than a name. They are leads, not prospects.

Prospecting activity involves not only finding new leads but also qualifying existing leads by adding information that allows you to move them up to ***Class A*** status.

Chapter 7 — Becoming a Master Prospector

Scheduling Contacts

When you have classified a prospect as *Class A*, determine when you will initiate contact, either by telephone, personal visit, or direct mail, according to the method of approach you choose. Use a *tickler* file arrangement of your prospect cards or computer records to see that you take the proper action on the date assigned. The same tickler file will help you schedule later contacts if your first attempt to schedule an appointment is not successful. Once a prospect's name enters your file, it stays there permanently until you close a sale or determine that the person is not a prospect. If you make a presentation and do not close, choose a time for a new attempt and schedule an appropriate time for contacting the prospect again.

When you discover that a person is not a viable prospect for you and will probably not become one in the foreseeable future, that person can still be an important contact. The impression you have given of your company by your professionalism may cause that person to recommend you to someone who will prove to be an excellent prospect.

Automating Prospect Information

As your client base grows, you will find that the need to interact with them requires the use of computer technology. This is why the most widely used software programs in selling, outside of word processing, are contact management programs. These powerful programs were developed to help you collect, organize, classify and keep track of prospect information. It's like having a super *Rolodex* for your desktop or laptop computer.

Applications for database technology are limited only by the creativity of the fitness consultant. For example, you might begin your day by calling up a list of follow-ups who visited the club the week before. Check the best way to organize the day based on where you'll be, and what names you have in that area. Then send thank you cards to all the prospects who visited the gym the day before. In addition, you can generate call schedules and short-range forecasts, provide scheduled contact lists in chronological order, and prepare graphs showing likely trends in sales based on your current closing percentages.

Becoming a Master Prospector
REFOCUS

- Prospecting is the skill that keeps you in business. Once you have leads, determine whether they are true prospects that have a need for your gym's services and are in a position to make a buying decision.

- Make sure they pass the *MADDEN* test.

- Two of the most effective prospecting methods are referrals and centers of influence. When someone they respect makes the introduction, you have a built-in sales assistant — the influence of the person who provided the lead and the initial contact.

- Group prospecting is securing names of possible prospects at trade shows, through corporate luncheons, or in any situation where you have the opportunity to meet a number of people. Cold calling also provides a supplemental source of new prospects.

- Networking is a valuable source of new prospects for fitness consultants who are willing to share information about their customers or clients. It's all about connecting, communicating, and cooperating.

- Efficient management of information means that needed data is always at your fingertips. Utilize filing systems to keep track of prospects as you record initial information, upgrade prospects, and schedule the time you want to contact each one.

Chapter 7 — Becoming a Master Prospector

— CARDIOVASCULAR —

— LIFE FITNESS STRENGTH —

— HAMMER STRENGTH® —

Built to Lead »

Nobody wants to be second best.
Not us. Not you. Not your members.

To be a leader, partner with one. To make it happen call **800.634.8637**

Life Fitness

AD CODE: AD-FSS-FL

lifefitness.com

Chapter 8

Preapproach and Telephone Techniques

FOCAL POINTS

- Importance of the preapproach.
- How the preapproach fits into the sales cycle.
- Methods for making telephone calls.
- The six-step telephone track.

PREPARATION AND PREAPPROACH

The path to success in fitness sales is often described by this formula: seeing enough of the right people at the right time. That sounds logical enough! The most exacting part of the formula however, is the "right people." The answer to that is simple: Everyone needs to stay in shape or get healthier, so you have a continual source of prospects. The real key lies in your diligence in collecting information about the leads you record in your prospecting system.

When someone gives you a referral, ask questions to learn what you need to know about that prospect. Is the referral a relative, friend, or business associate of the member. Are they currently involved in a program? Is the member getting good results? How many days a week does he/she workout? What type of activities do they participate in? Once you start making your calls you will be able to refer back to this information often to help build some common ground and set the appointment. The various activities that provide this necessary

Chapter 8 — Preapproach and Telephone Techniques　126

information are called the preapproach. The preapproach is the planning and preparation done prior to actual contact with the prospect.

The sales cycle is a continuous process with no clear break between one phase and the next. In practice, you cannot separate the prospecting, preapproach, approach, and need discovery elements into different segments. They seem to blend together and become one. They are discussed separately for convenience, but the exact point where one phase ends and the next begins is never clear. Figure 8.1 illustrates the absence of clear dividing lines between these steps in the relationship selling process. Qualifying prospects must therefore be accomplished during the approach and need discovery phases by asking questions and through observing, listening, and interpreting verbal and nonverbal signals.

Prepare for the Club Presentation

There is much more to preparation than simply gathering and reviewing information. *Rehearsal* eliminates the stammering, nervous speech habits, and repetition that sometimes result from lack of preparation. Allow time in your daily schedule to prepare your sales approach and presentation. Decide how you can make the best possible use of the club's facilities in each presentation. Plan how

Figure 8.1

to incorporate visual aids such as the cardio equipment or free weights into your presentation for maximum effectiveness.

Visualize Successful Selling

Fitness consultants can learn a great deal from the training habits of world-class athletes. Many track stars use visualization techniques to help them focus on a specific event. An integral part of their training consists of what is called "mental toughening sessions." They run the race over and over in their minds. Edwin Moses, over a 10-year period, won 122 consecutive races in the 400-meter hurdles. His power of visualization became so acute that when he mentally visualized hitting a hurdle, he actually felt the pain in his leg.

You can practice this same type of mental exercise. You can positively affirm the feeling you want to create and visualize the outcomes you want to obtain. Think about what you will say and anticipate the prospect's responses. Create a mental hologram and live it over and over in your mind. Practice out loud; your mind believes the sound of your own voice. *Remember that your mind cannot separate a real experience from an imagined one.*

Building Your Self-Confidence

One of the benefits of preapproach planning is to build your self-confidence. Knowing that you are prepared gives you an added measure of confidence that is transmitted to the prospect. The opposite of self-confidence is fear, and fear comes primarily from the unknown. A definite plan for each prospect means you are more likely to be accepted. By giving off an air of self-confidence and getting down to business immediately without wasting the prospect's time with unnecessary questions, you increase the likelihood of a successful close.

Conquering Fear

Many fitness consultants develop anxiety before getting on the phone or making a presentation, causing them to do poorly or scrap the correct procedure entirely. This is why conquering fear is an important part of preapproach planning. What is truly important in becoming successful is to overcome your fears by first identifying them and then taking positive action. When contacting people who you have never spoken to, there is no need to be intimidated. What you are about to offer them is something that could change their lives. Health and fitness is beneficial to everyone. Be confident in yourself and the product and services you are offering.

Fear can also result if you do not feel prepared to answer questions prospects may ask you. Be sure you know your club and its services well and have information nearby when you make your calls. Sometimes a prospect may question you and will make you feel inadequate if you cannot answer the question. Never provide incorrect information just to answer a question. This can hurt you and the club's credibility.

Know your product, keep abreast of changes in the industry, and always provide correct and accurate information. If you are stumped on a question, let the prospect know that you are unsure but that there is someone on the staff who is qualified to answer the question.

TELEPHONE TECHNIQUES

The phone is a critical tool for the fitness consultant. There is no other way to conveniently contact so many people in so short a period of time. Good telephone techniques enhance your image and preconditions the prospect to receive you favorably. Phoning for an appointment implies that you are courteous and considerate of the prospect's time. The phone call helps to create a selling situation because, just by agreeing to see you, the prospect tacitly indicates interest in joining your club.

Every telephone inquiry the club makes costs money, so you can benefit yourself and your club by improving your telephone techniques. When you are skilled and trained to conduct yourself professionally on the phone, you increase the likelihood of each call becoming a membership sale.

Make an appointment quota that will give you a goal to achieve, such as *5 new appointments* per day. You should spend at least 90 minutes each day on the telephone, and take excellent notes for each appointment in a telephone inquiry log, commonly known as a T/I, which can then be used as a guest register for those appointments you have made.

Getting the Appointment - A Mini Sale

You must regard the use of the telephone to set up appointments as a true sales activity and not just a necessary evil. You must also remember what you are selling. The *mini sale* is selling the prospect on the idea of giving you an appointment; your purpose is not to sell a membership on the telephone, but to meet face-to-face with the potential member.

Making First Impressions

Do you come across as being sincere, honest, confident, knowledgeable and likable? The quality of your voice, the hesitation in your voice, the volume, the strength of your speaking style all convey an image to another person. If you sound weak and tentative or use words like *well, sort-of, kind-of, maybe, perhaps,* that says to the prospect, "I'm not one bit sure that this is going to be a good investment of time for you." Lots of people also include phrases like, *"Well, to be honest with you,"* which says to the prospect that you aren't always honest.

Remember you're projecting your personality over the phone. How you say something can be as important as what you say. Try to put a smile in your voice. The most successful salespeople project positive voice qualities such as sincerity, courtesy, and confidence. A survey conducted for Jacobi Voice Development revealed the type of voice characteristics prospects are most annoyed by. Table 8.1 illustrates the most negative or annoying qualities.

Table 8.1

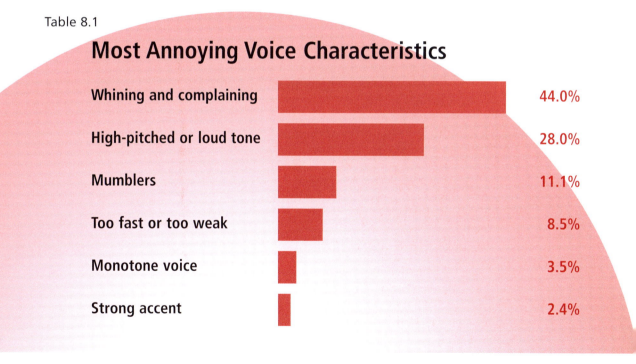

Most Annoying Voice Characteristics

Whining and complaining	44.0%
High-pitched or loud tone	28.0%
Mumblers	11.1%
Too fast or too weak	8.5%
Monotone voice	3.5%
Strong accent	2.4%

Organizing the Call

Inadequate preparation reduces the effectiveness of your delivery. Here are some hints to help you get organized for phone calls and then stay on track:

1. **Sell the appointment not the membership** – Remember you are selling the prospect on coming in to see the club, not to join over the phone.

2. **Organization** – Keep a lead book to track and follow-up with ALL LEADS including T/I's, referrals, lead boxes, upgrades, tanning packages, corporate, etc.

3. **Telephone scripts** – Have telephone scripts at every phone station.

4. **Always speak clearly and professionally** – Speak deliberately, talking at a constant pace conveys a message of confidence.

5. **Answer questions with questions** – This technique will help you maintain control of the conversation.

6. **Pen and note pad** – Always make calls or answer the phone with a pen and something to write on.

7. **Never apologize for calling anyone** – You will reveal insecurity and weakness by doing this.

8. **Courtesy** – Regardless of the prospect's response, show respect and leave a good impression.

9. **Enthusiasm**- Make the prospect want to come in. This must happen in the first 10 seconds. Statistics show that you have 10 seconds to capture a prospect's attention.

10. **Smile, sit up straight, and do not eat** –These traits shine through when you are on the phone.

11. **Alternate of choice questioning** – Be sure to use such questioning as, "What day would be better for you, today or tomorrow?"

12. **Never give out prices over the phone** – You put yourself at a disadvantage by giving out prices over the phone before the prospect sees the club.

Before you ever pick up the telephone, go through a mental checklist to ensure that you are fully prepared. Exhibit 8.1 gives some additional strategic checkpoints to consider when you are preparing to use the telephone to set up appointments. You must know what you are going to say before you dial a single number.

Exhibit 8.1

Key Points to Consider When Preparing to Use the Telephone

1. Arrange a definite time each day to telephone. Determine a specific number of calls to make during that time period.

2. Arrange for privacy to avoid interruptions. Make as many calls as you can in the allotted time. Your attitude is critical; without a positive attitude, using the telephone is mentally exhausting.

3. Develop a well-written, structured script. Know exactly what to say before you call. However, never make your call sound like a canned spiel.

4. Verify that you are actually talking to the person you intended to call. Be sure you have the correct pronunciation of the name. Use the name several times during the call.

5. Tell the prospect just enough to get the appointment. You know a lot more than you need to tell at this time.

6. Show excitement and enthusiasm in your voice. Give your voice the emotional feel of shaking hands over the telephone. Put a smile in your voice. Place a mirror by the phone and watch your expression.

7. Never argue; be sure to ask for the appointment. Always offer a choice of times so prospects can choose a time that is convenient.

8. Sell your own name. Ask the prospect to write it down to be sure you are remembered when you arrive for the appointment.

9. Be courteous. Say thank you and begin sentences with phrases like, "May I ask . . ." and "If I may . . ."

10. Watch your language. Choose words carefully for impact. Repetition of nonfunctional expressions like, "I see," "uh huh," "you know," and "fantastic" are irritating and unprofessional.

Chapter 8 — Preapproach and Telephone Techniques

THE SIX-STEP TELEPHONE TRACK

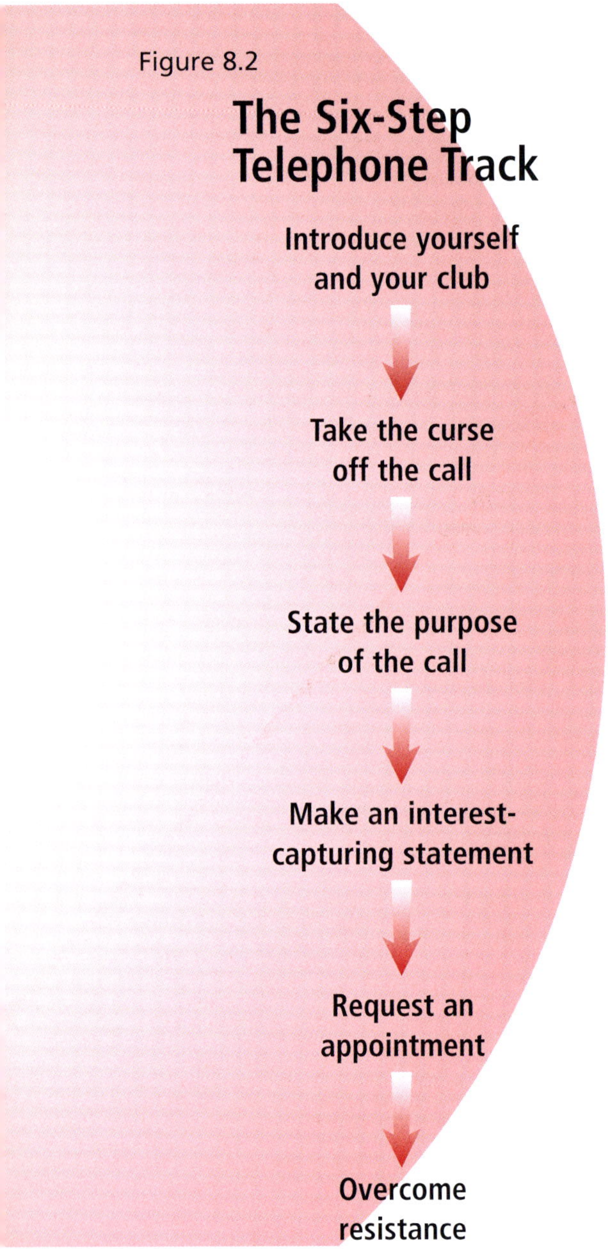

Figure 8.2

The Six-Step Telephone Track

Introduce yourself and your club

Take the curse off the call

State the purpose of the call

Make an interest-capturing statement

Request an appointment

Overcome resistance

The key to using the telephone effectively is to engineer conversations that sound like talk. They have to be two-sided, but cleverly get people to sell themselves on seeing you and your club. When you try to set an appointment by phone, you don't have the advantage of being able to show your prospect what a great product you offer. Instead, you need a careful strategy that allows the prospect to take an interest in what you're saying and agree to meet with you face-to-face. Use the six-step outline in Figure 8.2 to plan your appointment-setting calls so that the next time you talk to prospects, you're sitting face-to-face with them.

Step 1: Introduce Yourself and Your Club

Most sales relationships depend heavily on the initial impression. When you call on the telephone, the prospect will have made a judgment about you before your first fifteen words are said. How you introduce yourself, therefore, and what you say immediately thereafter are vitally important. A weak or tentative opening puts you at a severe disadvantage throughout the rest of the call. Your opening words should tell who you are, indicate the club you represent, and confirm that you are speaking to the correct person:

Good morning ... I am Mark Wainscott, a fitness consultant for Total Fitness Gym. Am I speaking to Mr. Ed Clay? ... Good. Mr. Clay, ...

Smile as you speak so that you transmit the impression of a warm, friendly personality. Watch the rate at which you speak. Prospects instinctively pay more attention to someone who speaks

133   *THE OFFICIAL HANDBOOK FOR HEALTH CLUB SALES*

at a moderate rate. A too rapid rate of speech seems nervous or sounds as though you are reading a canned pitch. If you are too slow, you come across as lazy or unconcerned, or the prospect feels that talking to you will be a long, time-consuming process.

Step II: Take the Curse Off the Call

The telephone call is an interruption of your prospect's day. To sell people on the idea of granting you an appointment, you must detach their attention from what they were doing or thinking when the phone rang and attract it to what you propose. It helps if you think and talk about your call as a service you are offering rather than as an interruption for which you must apologize. You can take the curse off the call with a statement and a question to soften the impact of the interruption. For example,

1. *It will take just about a minute to explain why I'm calling. Is it convenient for you to talk now?*

2. *Mr. Clay, do you have a minute to speak with me now, or did I catch you at a bad time? ... (If the prospect indicates the time is inconvenient...) ... When would be a better time?*

A prospect who is totally preoccupied with other matters may refuse to speak with you. In this case, calling back at a time the prospect suggests is better. When you do call back at the suggested time, the odds will be greatly improved that your message will receive a favorable hearing.

Step III: State the Purpose of the Call

Follow Step II with a brief, hard-hitting, lead-in statement about why you are calling—just enough to capture the prospect's attention but short of describing the benefits you will present in Step IV. If the lead was from one of your members, be sure to use that person's name. You need to present the member's name up front so that there is a common denominator between you and the prospective guest. The prospect automatically assumes that you are reputable and reliable and that you deserve a hearing. In the majority of instances, a referral alone is enough to get the prospect to hear you out during this first telephone call. For example:

Chapter 8 — Preapproach and Telephone Techniques   **134**

"I'm a friend of Dustin Smith, and he recently enrolled with us. Have you spoken to Dustin about our club? As a new member, he can invite guests to enjoy the benefits of Total Fitness Gym for one week. We would like to personally invite you to come and experience what is going on at Total Fitness Gym.

If the lead was from a lead box, be sure to mention this and the location of the box so the prospect remembers where he filled out the information card. You may also want to refer to a letter, free pass, flyer or any other direct mail piece sent to a prospect that gives you the opportunity to call and inquire if he received it. This tactic gives you a purpose for calling and provides an acceptable type of lead-in statement. Here is a sample:

Mr. Clay, thank you for taking a minute of your valuable time to speak with me. My purpose in calling is to find out if you received the guest pass I sent you last week to come in and try out our club free for a week.

Then ask some simple questions that will uncover some of their fitness needs. For example:

In order to best serve you when you come in to see the club, What are you interested in? (Pause).... Free weights, aerobics, nutritional guidance, etc., or what are you doing for exercise right now?

Another variation of this would be:

What I would like to do now is find out a little bit about what you're interested in accomplishing so we can help you when you come for your free week. So, to begin with, what specifically would you like to change about your body? (Lose fat, tighten muscle, etc.)

After you have established a legitimate purpose for the call and discovered some basic needs, you are ready to move to the next step.

Step IV: Make an Interest-Capturing Statement

Once you have the prospect's attention, your task is to convert attention into interest so that you can expect a favorable hearing. Interest is established by promising a health benefit or offering a service. Use product benefits and club services to answer the prospect's unspoken question: "What's in it for me?" Offer the prospect a benefit from listening to you, offer a service, or offer to do something *for*—not *to*—the prospect. Be sure to say how long the actual personal visit will take, and assure the prospect that everything you have to say can be covered in that length of time unless the prospect wants to explore certain areas in greater detail. Here are two examples:

1. *Mr. Clay, we've found that most people are just waiting for an invitation to come into a health club, and we'd like to extend that invitation to you right now to come see how Total Fitness Gym is changing the way our members look and feel about themselves.*

2. *The feedback from our members show that they have been pleased with the services and atmosphere of the club. Members like your friend Dustin say that the environment and facilities really make it easy to reach their fitness goals and get in shape. In fact, you may be aware that Dustin has lost ten pounds and reports that in his last check-up, his cholesterol was lower. Isn't that amazing?*

Rather than making a statement, you may ask a question to capture the prospect's interest:

Total Fitness Gym has a personal training team and nutritional specialists who guarantee results. You are intersted in getting in better shape aren't you?

People always want to be in better shape and would answer this question in the affirmative. You could then suggest that you have a specific plan and request a personal visit to discuss it with the prospect.

Step V: Request an Appointment

Remember that your goal at this point is to secure an appointment with the prospect so that you can make a complete presentation. Avoid giving interview information over the phone; the more information you give, the more problems the prospect may see. The prospect can easily say, "I'm not interested" into a telephone. Then you have nowhere to go. The conclusion could be much different when you give an excellent presentation in person. Next time, try the "KISS" approach to setting the appointment: *Keep It Simple, Salesperson!* The telephone itself encourages brevity, so just ask for the appointment confidently and directly.

Chapter 8 — Preapproach and Telephone Techniques

1. I'm sure you agree that we should get together to discuss how we can accomplish this for you. Would this Thursday at nine be good for you? . . . or perhaps Friday morning would be better?

2. The best time for me would be tomorrow afternoon at 2:00 or Thursday morning at 11:00. Which would be more convenient for you, Mr. Clay?

Notice that in each example the prospect was given a choice of times rather than asked, "When would it be convenient to see you?" which makes saying no too easy. You simply want to create enough initial interest to set up an appointment. Resist every temptation to get into specifics on the telephone. You are *selling an appointment*, not the membership. After you have set up the appointment, be sure to say "thank you" and then allow the prospect to end the call. It is important for you to *hang up* last, because the prospect may think of something at the end and should hear your voice instead of a click.

Step VI: Overcome Resistance

Using the telephone to set up appointments gives rise to two types of objections: an objection to receiving a telephone call and an objection to granting an appointment. A prospect who was engaged in an activity of interest or importance may feel irritated by an interruption and prefer to resume that activity. This prospect's goal is to get you off the phone by refusing to become interested in what you have to say.

Prospects who do not want to grant an interview often fear that they cannot successfully defend their own ideas or decisions when faced by an experienced salesperson. They are afraid that they will join. This type of objection can be overcome in three steps:

1. Agree sympathetically with the objection. This builds the prospect's ego.

2. Switch from the prospect's objection to your idea or purpose for the interview.

3. Ask for the appointment.

Design the telephone approach in the six-step format presented above and then practice it until it feels comfortable and natural. *Internalize it rather than just memorize it.* When you combine the six-step telephone approach with confidence and friendliness, you are likely to find yourself dealing with more responsive and receptive prospects.

SAMPLE TELEPHONE SCRIPT

The following is an example of a telephone script that you can follow and personalize once you begin to feel more comfortable with the six-step telephone track.

STEP 1: Introduce Yourself

Good morning, I am Ben Webster with Total Fitness Gym. Am I speaking with Ms. Erin Scensny? Good!

STEP 2: Get Approval to Continue

Ms. Scensny, it will only take a minute to explain why I am calling you today. Is it convenient for you to talk now? Thank You!

STEP 3: State Your Purpose for Calling

Ms. Scensny, as I mentioned I am with Total Fitness Gym. Our mutual friend Mrs. Lisa Elkins is a new member here and mentioned that you may be interested in our program. We have reserved a free workout session for you. I'll be responsible for helping you with your workout. Please share with me what is most important to you for fitness and health. Are you interested in weights, personal training, nutritional guidance, etc?

STEP 4: Capture Interest

Ms. Scensny, I would like the opportunity to share with you how Total Fitness Gym is helping people just like you reach their fitness goals and feel great about the way they look. It will take me about fifteen minutes to show you around the club, and if you feel like our club would improve or enhance your workouts and fitness level, I would consider it a privilege to help you get started with us.

STEP 5: Request Appointment

Ms. Scensny, I am sure that you are interested in staying healthy and keeping yourself in shape aren't you? Then I think we should get together and explore how our services may help you accomplish that.

Which will be best, tomorrow or the next day? What time of day is good for you; morning, afternoon, evening? Do you know where we are located? We'll see you at 3 o'clock. Remember, wear something comfortable to work out in, and please bring a friend with you if you like.

STEP 6: Overcome Resistance

Prospect: *I am not interested at this time.*

Fitness Consultant: *What are you not interested in, the free guest pass or getting in better shape? It just takes a few minutes to tour the club. Shouldn't everyone take a few minutes to find out how to get fit, stay fit, and be healthier? When is it best for you, today or tomorrow?*

Prospect: *Can't you just give me the rates over the phone?*

Fitness Consultant: *Ms. Scensny, our programs and membership rates are structured to meet everyone's needs. We would prefer for you to come in as my guest and then we can give you all the information you'll need. Will today be good for you?*

Prospect: *I already have a membership at another club.*

Fitness Consultant: *Are you satisfied with the services and the facilties there? Are you interested in having a guest pass to try something new? Or maybe you would like a club that is closer to your home or work. I would be happy to give you a free trial membership here at Total Fitness Gym. It will only take a few minutes to get you started. Would this afternoon or tomorrow be better for you?*

Going the Extra Mile

You may want to send a letter along with a guest pass to referrals. A truly professional fitness consultant will go that extra step and mail a letter to referrals prior to the phone call to let them know you will be calling. Again, this will help build credibility for you and your club and will unquestionably increase your appointment ratio. Here is how a letter may read:

Dear Mary,

Linda Smith is a mutual friend. She is a member at Total Fitness Gym. Linda would like to invite you to come in as her special guest. Enclosed is a guest pass especially for you. I will be calling you soon.

Thank You,
Your name

This extra note should be short and to the point. It is up to you to make the most of your telephone time!

THE OFFICIAL HANDBOOK FOR HEALTH CLUB SALES

Preapproach and Telephone Techniques
REFOCUS

- Planning and preparation are essential to securing an appointment for a personal sales interview.

- The attempt to set up a sales interview is a mini sale in which the product is a live sales interview, and the purpose of the call is to sell the prospect on the idea of granting that interview.

- Save the detailed description of your product and its benefits for the actual face-to-face meeting. Keep the telephone discussion focused solely on getting the appointment.

- It is vital that you hang up last. The prospect may be thinking of something and should hear your voice instead of a click.

- The six-step telephone track for making appointments includes:
  - Step 1: Introduce yourself and your club
  - Step 2: Take the curse off the call
  - Step 3: State the purpose of the call
  - Step 4: Make an interest-capturing statement
  - Step 5: Request an appointment
  - Step 6: Overcome resistance

Part IV

The Face-to-Face Relationship Model of Selling

» Pro Recumbent Bike
» Pro Upright Bike

» Treadmills
» Natural Runners™
» Stairclimbers
» Spinner® Bikes

Best known for its leading cardiovascular equipment, Star Trac offers a complete line of high-quality fitness equipment that will create a distinctive look for any fitness facility. From health clubs and YMCA's, to rehab centers and hotels, Star Trac equipment has been designed to be the user-focused choice for fitness equipment around the globe.

For information on the full line of Star Trac equipment and services, please call **1-800-228-6635**, or visit **www.startrac.com**.

Copyright © 2004 Star Trac. All rights Reserved. Spin, Spinner and Spinning are registered trademarks of Mad Dogg Athletics Inc.
Natural Runner is a trademark of Star Trac

going the extra mile

Chapter 9

Approaching the Prospect

FOCAL POINTS

- The purpose of the approach.

- First impressions and ways to control them.

- Surface language inhibits the ability to establish rapport.

- Controlling elements of the greeting.

- Ways to get attention and capture interest.

- Different types of approaches.

PURPOSE OF THE APPROACH

Your prospecting and preapproach efforts have uncovered potential members, and you have successfully arranged a personal meeting at the club with a prospect. What happens during the opening of the face-to-face encounter profoundly impacts the success of the whole presentation and your ability to close the sale. The approach, also known as the meet-and-greet, is important because it determines the character of your future relationship with a prospect, including how receptive the prospect will be to your presentation and whether the close will be difficult or easy.

Although the overall success of the meeting depends on more than the approach, an effective approach can create a favorable buyer-seller environment. The approach is often overlooked or taken for granted. Although it is usually considered in the context of the first meeting with a prospect, every meeting with a potential member or current member begins with an approach.

Chapter 9 — Approaching the Prospect　**144**

You never get a second chance to make a good . . .

FOLLOW the river and you will find the sea. Determination is the key.

INDIVIDUALS cannot consistently perform in a manner which is inconsistent with the way they see themselves.

REMEMBER . . . If you fail to plan, you plan to fail.

SOME people dream of worthy accomplishments, while others stay awake and do them.

THE single most important ingredient in the formula for success is knowing how to deal with people.

IF you don't take care of the customer . . . somebody else will.

MANAGE your time and your choices — and you'll manage your life.

PREPARE yourself for leadership. Be a living example of the excellence you expect from others.

RUNNING a business is no trouble at all as long as it's not yours.

EVERYTHING you say and do is a reflection of the inner you.

SINGIN' in the rain of life is better than letting it dampen your spirits.

SELF-ESTEEM, commitment and action determine your outcome.

IF we could kick the person responsible for most of our problems, we wouldn't be able to sit for a week.

ONE way to avoid criticism is to do nothing and be a nobody. The world will then not bother you.

NO one is useless in this world who lightens the burden of another.

Choose a job you love and you will never have to work a day in your life.

145   *THE OFFICIAL HANDBOOK FOR HEALTH CLUB SALES*

Fitness consultants tend to use the same approach over and over, but prospects and circumstances are not the same; instead, you ought to make a practice of using various types of approaches that fit the needs of a specific situation, whether talking to new prospects or members. Use should have multiple approaches memorized and ready to use depending on each selling situation. An effective approach achieves four key objectives:

l. To make a favorable or *positive impression* on the prospect

2. To gain the prospect's *undivided attention*

3. To develop *positive interest* in your proposition

4. To lead *smoothly* into the need discovery phase of the interview

FIRST IMPRESSIONS

Impress the prospect with a show of good manners, clear enunciation, good grooming, and appropriate dress; when you look and act like a professional, the prospect, consciously or subconsciously, begins to trust you. People make quick decisions based on feelings, emotions, or hunches. The more positive their feelings, the more they hear and accept what you say. The opening moments of the approach must be designed to create an atmosphere of trust.

Remember the importance of the "3 10s" when approaching a guest for the first time. The 3 10s are: 1) the **1st 10 seconds** of the initial meeting with a prospect 2) the **1st 10 words** that you say and 3) the **1st 10 feet** you walk with the potential member upon greeting them and shaking their hand. These three elements are critical for your initial contact and tell volumes about you.

When guests walk into the club it is important that their first impression is a positive one. Do guests see a clean club full of energetic people? Does the receptionist greet them immediately and properly? When the salesperson approaches prospects are they greeted professionally? Paying attention to what may seem like minor details can make or break a sale.

Your objective here is to personalize the sale as quickly as possible. We know that more than 85 percent of sales are based on emotion and only 15 percent based on facts. This stage will begin the relationship building process with your prospect and must begin very favorably. This is why you should always be calm and exude a sense of pride in yourself and your club.

Chapter 9 — Approaching the Prospect

Every personal characteristic is watched and evaluated; your approach must be impeccable. Exhibit 9.1 presents some guidelines for making the first impression favorable. *After all, you never get a second chance to make a good first impression.*

Exhibit 9.1

There's No Second Chance to Make a Good First Impression

When meeting a prospect for the first time, pay attention to:

Visual factors

- Correct any detail that could become a visible distraction: a cluttered office, a messy or untidy gym, or inappropriate grooming.
- Nonverbal communication is powerful. Pay attention to what the prospect sees in your body language as well as in what you wear.
- Don't wear jewelry such as lapel pins, tie pins, or rings that advertise your membership in a specific organization that may not be recognized or admired by some people.

Organization and Professional habits

- If you are out prospecting and not in the gym, be prompt, even early getting back to the gym. Set you watch five minutes ahead if necessary.
- Present a clear agenda. Prospects know they are meeting with you to consider joining your health club. Make it clear that you are there to help them, not waste their time
- Be prepared with as much information as possible about the prospect (individual and company).

Building rapport

- Be sure to pronounce the prospect's name correctly. A person's name is a personal identifier; mispronouncing it takes away some of the owner's status.
- If you pay the prospect a compliment, make it specific and of personal interest.
- Recall the importance of proxemics. Respect the prospect's personal space.
- Look for common ground like mutual friends, membership in the same religious or civic group, or similar hobbies.

Your Actions

- Shake hands, maintain eye contact, and greet the prospect warmly, but never say, "How are you?"
- Refrain from personal habits like smoking or chewing gum or careless language that might be offensive to some people.

Your Attitude

- Be enthusiastic. Enthusiasm is infectious if it is sincere.

THE OFFICIAL HANDBOOK FOR HEALTH CLUB SALES

Although first impressions may be dependable signposts, first impressions do have some weaknesses:

- They are likely to be based on feelings and emotions.

- All behavior traits do not show up simultaneously, and an initial short meeting may not provide enough time for all traits (either favorable or unfavorable) to surface.

- The prospect may deliberately control behavior and allow you to see only certain chosen personality traits.

- Some event immediately preceding the meeting may strongly influence the prospect's current behavior.

Be willing to wait before you conclude that you and a prospect have a personality conflict that cannot be overcome. Your job is to establish rapport, build confidence, and make the prospect feel comfortable while visiting your health club. Do everything in your power to satisfy the needs of your prospects, and refuse to allow first impressions to prevent a mutually beneficial sales experience.

SURFACE LANGUAGE

Surface language–including grooming, clothing, accessories, posture, and all other aspects of appearance–vitally affects first impressions, even though surface language factors actually provide limited or shallow insight into the true person. Fitness consultants must be sure the statements they make with their surface language are favorable because the impressions formed during the first few minutes of an initial encounter between two people could be lasting. Successful consultants increase the odds in their favor by taking advantage of the power of first impressions. Visual impressions almost always come first. Fortunately, you can do a lot to shape the visual impact you make when a prospect first sees you.

Projecting an Image

As an effective salesperson you want your clothes to command respect, inspire credibility and create trust – you must come across as the authority on health and fitness. In keeping with the health and fitness image, an employee's personal hygiene and neatness are of primary importance. You are expected to wear and

Chapter 9 — Approaching the Prospect   **148**

maintain a neat clean uniform (or appropriate attire for your position if a uniform is not specified) as well as care for the rest of your personal appearance. Your clothes speak volumes about you, your club, your work, and how you relate to members.

When you know that you are dressed appropriately, you feel good about yourself. When you are confident and at ease, you emanate an air of competence that the prospect unconsciously accepts and interprets as credibility. Total appearance is important because the prospect's initial attention is focused on you and not on your club. If you want to be successful, you must look successful. A fitness consultant who wears tattered or worn clothing, for example, creates a negative impression and sets up this line of thinking in the mind of the prospect:

1. This consultant is dressed cheaply. He must not be making much money.

2. Because he's not making much money, he must be having difficulty selling memberships.

3. If gym memberships are not selling, something must be wrong with the facilities.

4. I don't want to be a member of an inferior fitness club.

Dress Conservatively. Your objective is to focus the prospect's attention on the benefits of joining your club. Anything that detracts from that focus works against you. Conservative dress gives the prospect the impression that talking with you is safe and that you are familiar and dependable. Although "conservative" varies from one region to another , that variation is not extremely wide. Dressing conservatively suggests stability and dependability; following extreme fads of color, cut, and pattern may suggest just the opposite.

Dress Appropriately. You should plan to dress as well as your prospect. People feel comfortable dealing with those who seem to fit into their own lifestyle. Joe Girard, who according to the *Guinness Book of World Records* is the world's greatest salesman, says, "I believe a salesman should look as much as possible like the people to whom he sells.... I never wear clothes that will antagonize my customers and make them feel uneasy."

Your gym may require a uniform or dress guidelines to follow. If not, keep in mind that customers buy you long before they buy a membership. If your clothes are too formal or carry too much of an aura of authority, you cause the prospect to feel overpowered. If you dress too casually or carelessly, prospects may unconsciously feel that you do not consider them or their business important.

THE PROPER GREETING

Choice of Greeting

In order to increase the odds of making a good impression during the meet-and-greet, use the business etiquette *Rule of Ten*. The first ten words you speak should include a form of thanks: "Good morning, Mrs. Eubank. Thank you for agreeing to see me," or "Good afternoon, Brian. It's a pleasure to meet you." Casual questions like "How are you?" or "How ya' doing?" have lost all semblance of meaning. How does the prospect respond? "Great" or "Just fine, thank you," but what if the prospect is not feeling great and what if business is not going great? If a prospect covers up real feelings with a conventional answer, a vague feeling of uneasiness results from the untruth. If the prospect responds to your question with a long list of ills or problems, no response you make can turn attention naturally toward your sales presentation. How would you answer the simple question "How are you?"

Another way to handle the first meeting with a walk-in prospect who may not have made an appointment is to have the front desk attendant do the introduction. The front desk attendant should smile and greet the prospect, then call you to the front. Here is an example of the front desk attendant greeting:

Attendant: *"Steve, this is Dave. He would like some information about the club today."*

Fitness Consultant: *"Hello, Dave, I'm Steve. Welcome to Total Fitness Gym! Dave, to best serve you I would like to take a few minutes of your time to better understand what you are trying to accomplish. Then we'll take a quick tour of our fantastic facility. Oh, by the way, don't let me forget to mention to you about our first time visitors incentive!" (Simply start walking towards the office)*

The Handshake

Your voice inflection and how you shake hands are as important as what you say. These three elements of the greeting taken together tell a prospect your mood. The handshake, particularly, is a revealing form of nonverbal communication. Exhibit 9.2 presents helpful guidelines for an effective handshake.

Chapter 9 — Approaching the Prospect 150

Exhibit 9.2

Guidelines for an Effective Handshake

1. Maintain eye contact for the duration of the handshake.

2. You may wait for the prospect to initiate the handshake (to avoid offending those people who "do not like to be touched").

3. If your palm tends to become moist from nervousness, carry a special handkerchief with powder and pat your hand several times just before greeting the prospect. Be careful not to leave a residue of powder on your hand that might be transferred to the prospect's hand or to your clothes.

4. Apply firm, consistent pressure on the hand. Avoid the limp-wristed, wet-fish or bone-crusher handshakes.

5. The hands should meet equidistant between you and the prospect in a vertical position. If you turn your wrist so your hand is over the prospect's, this nonverbal gesture implies the intention to be dominant. If you turn your wrist so that your hand is on the bottom, you are signaling a submissive nature.

Small Talk or Get Down to Business

In the initial meet-and-greet before the gym tour begins, both parties may have what might be called relationship tension. Prospects fear being sold something they do not want, and fitness consultants face the fear of being rejected. The opening few minutes of conversation are designed to find a comfort level for both parties so that rapport can be established. The purpose of small talk at the opening of the appointment is to gain an advantageous, positive beginning that breaks the ice and eases the tension. Small talk may be a discussion of topics entirely unrelated to fitness. This warm-up period may take five minutes or more. Consider this time "chit-chat with a purpose." Here are four basic questions that are nonthreatening, easy to answer, and objective:

1. Are you a native of this area?

2. Were you educated there? (Based on answer to Question 1)

3. Are you a family person?

4. What do you do for a living?

THE OFFICIAL HANDBOOK FOR HEALTH CLUB SALES

This type of socializing at the beginning eases tension and may give you some insight into your prospect's behavioral style. It warms up a cold environment and has the side benefit of providing additional information about the prospect. If the prospect seems withdrawn or even hostile, this warm-up conversation helps you determine whether that is the prospect's real personality or whether they are having an especially bad day.

People love to tell you what they do in their spare time, talk about their accomplishments, or tell you about their families. This non-selling conversation is important. An ideal topic for initial chit-chat is one that relaxes the prospect, is of interest, and relates–if possible–to your objective so that you can move easily into the attention getter and then into need discovery.

> ## PEOPLE HAVE NO CONFIDENCE
> ### in salespeople whose only interest is self-interest, who seek to use their clients instead of being of use to their clients.

Use of the Prospect's Name

People do not like to have their names forgotten, misspelled, or mispronounced. Typically, when we are introduced to someone, we hear our own name, then we might hear the other person's name. In *How to Win Friends and Influence People*, Dale Carnegie says, "A person's name is to them [sic] the sweetest and most important sound in any language." If we forget a name or mispronounce it, we send out this message: "I care more about me and my name than I do about you and your name." Imagine how a prospect feels when you say, "So you see, Mr ... ah ... uh ..., excuse me (shuffle for prospect card or appointment calendar) uh ..., Mr. Danner, I mean, Tanner." The prospect probably stiffens, the environment turns a bit frosty, and they may well walk out without a membership. Now recall how pleased you were when someone remembered your name after just a casual meeting several weeks previously. You would stand in line to do business with such a person.

Chapter 9 — Approaching the Prospect   152

Improving your memory for names is not as difficult as it may seem. Several books are available to help you devise a method to correct a careless memory for names. Table 9.1 gives some suggestions for remembering names.

Table 9.1

How to Remember Your Customers' Names

Five steps to remembering names:

Pay attention
Ask to have the name repeated (even spelled). It will impress the person.

Concentrate
Look for characteristics that distinguish this person from others.

Associate
Relate a characteristic with some gimmick to help you recall the name.

Observe
Study people regularly to strengthen your ability to see characteristics and practice your imagination.

Repeat it
Use the prospect's name several times during the interview.

Suit the Approach to the Person

Most people today have more work than they can hope to complete during regular working hours. Prospects may react with resentment toward anyone who appears intent upon "stealing" precious time to engage in "small talk." How much or how little time you give to small talk or chit-chat depends on the behavioral style of the prospect, the circumstances of the moment, and the nature of the visit. If you sense that the prospect wants to get on with the tour, then move on.

THE OFFICIAL HANDBOOK FOR HEALTH CLUB SALES

Gain Attention and Capture their Interest

As the cartoon says, first you've got to get their attention! Develop a carefully constructed, attention-getting statement that focuses the prospect's attention solely on you and your proposition. Remember that prospects are probably thinking about work, or where they are going, or a meeting they have – in other words, they may be focused on things other than you and your club. Unless prospects want to listen, they won't. Give them a reason. Just as the newspaper uses a headline to make you take notice, you must have an attention-getting opening statement that breaks through preoccupation and focuses attention on the selling situation.

The two basic methods of getting attention are: 1) through an appeal to the senses and 2) through the introduction of a benefit.

Appeal to the Senses. An appeal to the senses gets the prospect involved in the presentation. Use a little more dramatization. Show something the prospect can see; hand the prospect something to hold. For example, you can use the "dumbbell technique". If the prospect wants to lose a certain amount of weight, you ask the prospect to pick up the corresponding amount of weight with the dumbbells. After they hold it for a about a minute, tell them to put the weights down. Then say, "Now, Michelle, isn't it a good feeling to lose that weight?" This gets the prospect visualizing their weight loss.

"First you've got to get their attention!"

Introduction of a Benefit. Introduce a benefit by a statement that relates to the prospect's fitness needs or goals. Highlight the values of your gym. The prospect always wants to know, "What's in it for me?" Matt Kinear, a fitness consultant in Atlanta, certainly knows how to get a prospect's attention. He routinely uses a corny but effective prop: a simple bag of bread with a note that reads, "Our members say we're the greatest thing since…sliced bread."

An effective attention getting statement requires preparation. If you have done your homework in gathering preapproach information, you already have enough to have some idea about both the needs and the social style of the prospect. If you spend a few minutes in "small talk" you gain further clues to confirm or adjust what you already know.

TYPES OF APPROACHES

Because every prospect and every selling situation is different, you ought to have several approach methods available and use the one that best fits the particular circumstance. Learn the principles of each of the different types of approaches so that you can use whichever one is appropriate for a particular situation. How many approach techniques are enough? You cannot have too many. The personality style of prospects, the mood they're in during the meet-and-greet, and your own feelings and mood that particular day suggest the need to have an opening for every occasion and every situation. You may have to deviate 180 degrees from the opening and presentation you had planned.

Self-Introduction Approach

This approach is commonly used but is probably the weakest approach to use alone. A smile, a firm handshake, and a relaxed but professional manner should accompany the introduction. Address the prospect by name, pronouncing it correctly, state your name, and present your business card. Although the business card is optional, it is a useful reminder of your name, and the prospect is not embarrassed by finding it necessary to ask you to repeat your name. Here is an example of a typical self-introduction:

> Good morning, Blakele. Welcome to Dan's Aerobics and Fitness Center. My name is John Andrews. It's nice to meet you. I'm glad you could come in to see our facility today." (Accompany this with a firm handshake and a smile to begin to establish trust).

To increase the effectiveness of the self-introduction approach, follow it immediately with one of the other approaches. The consumer-benefit approach, for instance, is generally a good fit.

THE OFFICIAL HANDBOOK FOR HEALTH CLUB SALES

Consumer-Benefit Approach

Give the prospect a reason for listening and suggest a risk for failure to listen. The benefit statement should be unique and appeal to the prospect's dominant buying motives, such as lowering their cholesterol or losing weight. It should be sincere and must not sound like a gimmick. Something new and different about your facilities that paves the way for the rest of the presentation is a good choice.

Good morning, Mr. Carter. I am Kevin Davis with Lee's Gym and Fitness. I'm glad you stopped by to take fifteen minutes for me to introduce you to our facilities that will, first of all, give you 24-hour access – secondly, provide you with cardio, circuit, and free weights training, as well as give you access to professional certified personal training, and third—and probably the best part of all—is that it will help you reach and maintain your fitness goals.

Do you have fifteen minutes?

This example combines the self-introduction and the consumer-benefit approaches. As a fitness consultant, you want to offer value to your prospects and members, so presenting this benefit statement may cause the prospect to seek more information. Such a statement often sparks questions from the prospect that lead directly into the presentation.

Curiosity Approach

The curiosity approach works best when you know something about the prospect. Used sensibly, this approach is an effective opener. You might say something like this:

Erin, have you been wanting to join a gym, but aren't sure where to begin with a new fitness routine? Or maybe you haven't been able to find enough time away from the kids to get to the gym? Do you know that you can get started today and have free personal training sessions to get you going, plus free child care while you work out?

People with certain behavioral styles, particularly analyticals and drivers, may find this approach offensive, especially if it sounds gimmicky.

Chapter 9 — Approaching the Prospect   156

Question Approach

The question approach quickly establishes two-way communication. It enables you to investigate the prospect's needs and apply the benefits your facilities provide to those expressed needs. This type of approach indicates your interest in the prospect's problems and draws attention to the need to identify problems. You may frame a leading question designed to obtain mental commitment from the prospect and at the same time show a major benefit. Here are two examples of how this might be done:

1. *Mr. Fisher, you do want to lower that cholesterol and strengthen your heart as your doctor recommended, don't you?*

2. *Do you feel you would have more confidence in your daily life if you reached your weight loss goals? Wouldn't it be amazing to walk into the office looking great and knowing it?*

Qualifying Question Approach

A variation of the question approach seeks a commitment from the prospect. This *qualifying question approach* asks the prospect to consider membership; it can help determine whether you have a prospect who is cold, lukewarm, or red hot toward joining your gym. Here are two illustrations of how this technique could be used:

1. *Mr. Armstrong, if I can satisfactorily demonstrate to you that the weight training, group aerobics classes, and cardio equipment provided by our gym will help you reach your fitness goals within the next year, would you willing to join with us?*

2. *Mrs. Woods, we are looking for individuals who have the desire to reach and maintain a healthy fitness level. And I believe you are one of those people. If I can show you how you can reach and maintain your own goals, would you be willing to invest in your health with us?*

If the prospect says yes, you have a sale, provided you can back up your statement with valid proof.

Compliment Approach

Opening with a compliment is like walking on eggshells, but this opening is highly effective if used properly. Follow the same guidelines you would use in any situation: Offer compliments with empathy, warmth, and sincerity. The purpose is to signal your sincere interest in the prospect. Sources for information upon which the compliment is based vary. Information from a person who provided a referral or from something the prospect said in the initial meeting can tell you about accomplishments or traits that you genuinely admire. Here is an example:

> *I am impressed with your genuine desire to change your lifestyle and become happier and healthier. You must be proud of your decision to get in shape.*

This type of compliment not only builds rapport but also directs the prospect's train of thought toward health and fitness. Whenever a compliment is used as an opening, it must be *specific*, of *genuine interest* to the prospect, and *sincere*.

Referral Approach

The referral approach is especially useful because it helps you establish leverage by borrowing the influence of someone the prospect trusts and respects. If you use a referral card signed by the person who provided the prospect's name, you can give it to the prospect to introduce yourself and your gym. This approach enhances your credibility and increases the likelihood that the prospect will give you full attention. Here are two good examples:

1. *Miss Eubank, your neighbor Jaime Rader has recently become a member of our gym. She told me that you are also interested in getting healthier and staying fit, and she suggested that you would like to hear about what our gym has to offer. (Give the referral card to the prospect.)*

2. *Mr. Donovan, I am Chris Elkins with West Coast Gym. Melanie Jacobs, who just signed up with us, suggested that I contact you. She thought you would like to have an opportunity to consider whether our gym facilities, personal training, and free tanning could also be of benefit to you.*

Product Approach

This approach is a hands-on method to interact with the prospect to produce a positive reaction. The product approach provides a visible image that the prospect can hold or use that helps demonstrate the benefits of membership.

Using the product approach stirs interest, permits a demonstration, makes a multiple sense appeal, and usually creates in the prospect a feeling of commitment to listen and to participate actively in the presentation. For example, you may want the prospect to try out the new elliptical trainers by saying:

> *"Kathy, this is a new way of doing cardio that is very popular because of how it specifically targets the legs and glutes. Our members also like it because they say it is fun! And it is zero-impact so it won't hurt your joints. Hop on and give it a try!"*

To summarize, whatever approach device you decide to use, it should be directly related to your plan for beginning the need discovery phase of the presentation. The exchange of conversation in the approach phase allows you to move smoothly into the questions you plan to ask to discover the needs of the prospect. Because the actual presentation of benefits cannot begin until the prospect agrees to having a need for what you have to offer, whatever you can do to make need discovery seem a natural process will be helpful.

Approaching the Prospect
REFOCUS

- What you do and say in the initial moments of the meet-and-greet has a profound effect on the success of the close. Plan those initial moments carefully. The first 10 words out of your mouth are crucial.

- Be aware of the power of first impressions. You never get a second chance to make a good first impression.

- Proper dress and grooming give the prospect the feeling that you are competent. Appropriate choices in dress and grooming let the prospect focus on your sales message instead of on your physical appearance.

- The greeting is important to create a favorable first impression. Use the prospect's name often and begin with some "chit-chat with a purpose" to feel out the mood and behavioral style of the prospect.

- Have a firm handshake, maintain eye contact, and make use of voice properties that reflect confidence.

- Confirm or modify your impressions of the prospect's behavioral style and adapt your plans for the presentation accordingly.

- A number of different types of approaches are available: (1) the self-introduction, (2) consumer-benefit, (3) curiosity, (4) question, (5) qualifying question (6) compliment, (7) referral, and (8) product. A good approach forms a natural transition into the need discovery phase of the selling process.

Chapter 9 — Approaching the Prospect 160

Now That You Can Sell...
You Need Leads!
We Can Get Them!

Consumer **DIRECT** Target fitness minded people in your area.

Business **DIRECT** Increase your membership with corporate wellness programs.

New **CONNECTS** Catch consumers & businesses when they are most likely to buy – when they move in.

Referral **PLUS** Expand your sales force! Reward your members for referring a friend: it's like adding a sales rep to your staff.

Cross **MEDIA** Hit mailboxes AND newspapers (inserts or display ads) for a multi-media blitz.

$100 OFF Your First Order
Just mention this ad. Call for details. Some restrictions apply.

- ✓ Direct Mail
- ✓ Newsletters
- ✓ Guest Passes
- ✓ Door Hangers
- ✓ Inserts
- ✓ Lead Boxes

...And More!

Preferred Vendor of **Total Fitness Systems, LLC**

Call Now!
800-792-8812

LOREX INC.

www.lorexinc.com/Fitness

Chapter 10

Identifying Needs Through Questioning and Listening

FOCAL POINTS

- The purpose of asking questions.
- Selecting questioning tactics.
- Specific questioning techniques.
- Various types of questioning methods.
- The importance of listening.
- Improving listening skills.

THE PURPOSE OF ASKING QUESTIONS

Telling isn't selling; asking is! For many years, salespeople in the fitness industry learned that selling is talking. The message seemed to be to tell the prospect everything you know in hopes that something you say will touch the right spot and the prospect will join. The result of this kind of thinking was a salesperson who kept the prospect pinned down with constant chatter that resembled oral machine-gun fire.

The problem created by that theory of selling lies in its assumption that every prospect wants to get or stay in shape for identical purposes and in the same manner. But in actuality, each prospect has unique needs. Of the many benefits your facilities have to offer, only a few will be key motivators to a particular prospect. The challenge is to determine their buying criteria before beginning your presentation and then use only the specific benefits that address their particular situation.

Fitness consultants are diagnosticians. If you went to your family doctor complaining of severe back pain, and the doctor—without asking any questions—wrote a prescription for a medicine to be taken three times a day for the next month, would you take it? Of course not! You would not believe the doctor could make an accurate diagnosis and prescribe the appropriate medicine without making a thorough examination and asking a number of probing questions. You would expect the doctor to understand your problem—not the problem of back pain in general—before prescribing a solution for you. Your prospect has the right to expect the same professional attention from you.

Need Discovery and the Sales Cycle

The evolution of relationship selling has reached the point where the need discovery step in the sales cycle is more important than making the presentation, handling objections, or closing. Figure 10.1 shows the relationship between need discovery and the other basic steps in the face-to-face sales process. At this point of need discovery—not in the close—the sale is most often lost. The dotted line around need discovery in Figure 10.1 is a reminder that this step is often skipped or given inadequate attention by many fitness consultants. In reality, more time should be spent in the approach and in discovering needs than in any other steps of the process.

Need discovery is the foundation upon which a successful sale is built. Telling prospects what they need is a mistake. Asking questions that allow prospects to

Figure 10.1

discover their own needs and share them with you sets you up as a sounding board for the solutions they "discover" while considering your proposal. Prospects are more receptive when they feel that the solution is their own idea.

Need Discovery During the Pre-Tour

Although need discovery begins the moment you first contact a prospect, the pre-tour phase of the presentation is the point when you confirm the prospect's reasons for considering membership. The pre-tour presentation contains the most important portion of your entire presentation. Your initial approach and questioning of the prospect will determine the outcome of your presentation.

During this stage there are four characteristics about prospects you must work to discover. Remember to take prospects into your office or in a quiet lobby. There you will begin qualifying prospects to find their:

1. Needs

2. Wants or emotional stimuli

3. Ability to enroll

4. Decision making capabilities

You will use a sales interview or pre-tour sheet such as the one in Exhibit 10.1 to write down information as the prospect tells you. A pre-tour sheet is a list of questions that targets prospects' areas of concern and reveals the reasons why they are considering joining a health club.

The most essential element in this stage is to gather information so you will have plenty of opportunities to tell the prospect how they can reach their goals at your facility. Once you understand the prospect's needs, you can begin meeting those needs. This is called "need/satisfaction" selling. You can enjoy yourself and have more financial success if you stop trying to get just what you want and start helping others get what they want.

Specific Planning of Questions for the Pre-Tour

You must retain control of the questioning phase of the interview so that you obtain the required information and do not detour into irrelevant areas. The old standbys – *who, what, when, where, why,* and *how* – are a vital part of the sales interview. Decide in advance what questions you will be asking.

Chapter 10 — Identifying Needs Through Questioning and Listening

Exhibit 10.1

Sample Pre-Tour Sheet for Need Discovery

Fitness Goals

What are your primary fitness goals? (What specific areas are you most concerned with? Ex. Legs, arms, stomach, etc.)_____
_____ _____

Draw Stick Person

(Use the stick person to have prospects circle their problem areas)

1. Lose Weight _____ Lbs
2. Gain Weight _____ Lbs.
3. Tone up _____
4. Increase Muscle Mass_____
5. Improve appearance_____
6. Cardiovascular improvement_____
7. Firm Up_____
8. Increase strength_____
9. Have more energy_____
10. Increase Flexibility_____
11. Increase Stamina_____
12. Improve athletic performance___

1. Special event coming up _____

2. Why is this important to you? _____

3. How long have you been thinking about getting started on a fitness program?_____

4. By what date would you like to reach your specific fitness goals?_____

5. On a scale of 1 – 10 how committed are you?_____

6. What made you choose our gym?_____
_____

7. What made you come in today?_____

It is important to determine what guests want to accomplish and get them thinking about and visualizing reaching their fitness goals. They must believe they can change. The following is a set of eight useful pre-tour questions that will elicit information in the quickest and most efficient manner consistent with the prospect's social style and situation:

1. *"Have you ever been in the club before?"*

   Find out if they were a guest or a previous member. Find out when they used the club and what they liked or disliked.

2. *"Are you a guest of a current member?"*

   Find out if they already know someone else who is working out. Be sure to give the current member a reward, such as a month of free membership, when the guest does join.

3. *"Is this membership just for you?"*

   This will help you determine who the decision-makers are as well as if there is any family or business add-on possibilities?

4. *"Where is the club closet to? Home, work or both?"*

   Find out if the club is within a 5-mile radius or the crucial travel time.

5. *"What time of the day will you use the club? Morning, afternoon or evening?"*

   This is a powerful question that assumes the guest is going to become a member. When would they think about the time that they would use the club? Of course, when they join!

6. *"How much time are you able to invest to reach your fitness goals?"*

   The answer you are given to this question will be useful during the presentation to eliminate the time objection.

7. *"Are you happy with your current fitness level?"*

   Help prospects realize that you and the club are the ideal solution for them.

Chapter 10 — Identifying Needs Through Questioning and Listening   166

8. *"Do you have any physical or medical limitations that would prevent you from exercising?"*

This would be the only valid reason not to move forward and join the club. This question will also increase the credibility of you and the club.

Research shows that prospects are more likely to buy if you establish points of agreement early in the interview. To accomplish this…

- *Plan* your questions in sequence to gain information in a logical order.

- *Predict* beforehand all the possible answers to each question so that you are never left wondering what to do next.

- *Prepare* a smooth transition from every possible answer into the next logical question.

Some consultants hesitate to ask questions because they are afraid the prospect will refuse to answer. However, prospects that refuse to cooperate during the need discovery phase are unlikely to cooperate at the end of the sale either. Communication is a two-way street that demands participation by both you and the prospect. If you are to involve prospects in the sales process, you must be prepared to ask the questions that maximize participation. The right questions never materialize out of thin air. Your questions should attempt to achieve these specific objectives:

1. To discover the prospect's **"hot button"** or dominant buying motive.

2. To appeal to their **emotional** reasons for joining a health club.

3. To agree on a time frame to help eliminate **procrastination**.

4. To help them visualize their **goals**.

5. To get them thinking about their level of **commitment.**

6. To eliminate thoughts about checking out the **competition** before deciding.

7. To help the prospect develop a **sense of urgency**.

8. To ensure that the prospect is able to make the **decision** to join.

THE OFFICIAL HANDBOOK FOR HEALTH CLUB SALES

The following is a list of questions that are specifically targeted to achieve the objectives listed above:

1. **Hot Button:** *"What are your primary fitness goals?"*

   This is known as finding their "hot button". Draw a stick person and have then circle the areas of their bodies that they want to change. Follow this with questions like:

   - *"What specific areas of your health or appearance are you most concerned with?"*

   - *"What would you like to change about those areas?"*

2. **Emotional:** *"Why is this important to you?"*

   This question is key. This is the emotional reason why they are there. Remember that it is important to determine what the guest wants but it is essential to determine why.

3. **Procrastination:** *"How long have you been thinking about achieving these goals?"*

   This information will be helpful during the presentation when you eliminate procrastination.

4. **Goals:** *By what date would you like to accomplish your goals?"*

   Just like in business, things that have a time frame for completion get done. Look for special events or times of the year. This will help them from putting off joining.

5. **Commitment:** *"On a scale of 1 – 10, how committed are you?"* (10 being the greatest and 1 being the lowest)

   If their commitment level is lower then a 7 think of ways to make that number higher throughout the presentation.

Chapter 10 — Identifying Needs Through Questioning and Listening

6. **Competition:** *"Why did you choose our gym?"*

This question will help eliminate "shop around" or "think about it" objections. After they have told you all the reasons why they chose your club it will make it more difficult to tell you why they shouldn't get started.

7. **Sense of Urgency:** *"What made you come in today?"*

This question will establish the urgency of the situation. Whether it is a special we are promoting or their own personal fitness goals.

8. **Decision Maker:** *"Have you discussed this with your spouse / significant other or parent?"*

If they answer yes, follow this up with, "Are they supportive?" This will again establish the decision maker and possible family add-ons.

Because the sale is made in the mind of the buyer and not in the mind of the fitness consultant, using the questioning process to gain agreement on key issues is paramount. Then you must assist the prospect in prioritizing those health and fitness issues and agree that those are the key issues or concerns to address before they make a decision to join.

STRATEGIC RECOMMENDATIONS

As you select specific questioning techniques, keep these tactics in mind:

Avoid Technical Language That Might Confuse the Prospect. Many prospects considering membership have never set foot in a gym before and are likely to be nervous about using the equipment for the first time. You cannot assume that everyone knows how to use resistance machines or even the cardio equipment. Just remember that your goal is to promote understanding and not to demonstrate your own personal erudition.

Make a Smooth Transition from the Approach. Chapter nine presented four specific objectives of the approach: to make a favorable first impression, to gain attention, to create interest, and to serve as a logical transition into need discovery and the pre-tour. This transition requires that you tell the prospect exactly what you intend to accomplish during the pre-tour session. You are to provide a *clear agenda* for the sit-down discussion. Always let the prospect know what you want to accomplish. You can set up the desired atmosphere by <u>requesting permission</u> to ask questions. Here are two practical *permissive questions*:

1. *I believe our facilities can provide you with a number of ways to reach your fitness goals, but in order for me to be sure, I need to know a little more about your particular situation, would it be OK if I ask you a few questions?*

2. *"Sheila, in order to determine how our facilities and service best meet and serve your needs, I would like your permission to ask you a few personal questions. Will that be all right with you? Oh, and may I make some notes while we talk?"(say this as you are walking and lead them into the office or quiet spot)*

Phrase Each Question So That It Has One Clear Purpose An ambiguous question or one with multiple meanings creates misunderstanding between you and the prospect. Proceed logically, one topic at a time. Murphy's law operates here: Anything that can be misunderstood will be misunderstood. A corollary to this principle is equally important: Phrase each question to produce the maximum amount of information so that the number of questions needed to elicit the needed information is as small as possible.

COMMON QUESTIONING TECHNIQUES

General Types of Questions

The major types of questioning techniques are summarized in Exhibit 10.2. Questions are generally classified by the type of answers required and by the purpose they are intended to serve. Begin the questioning process with closed-end questions or fact-finding questions that are easy to answer and therefore not threatening to the prospect. If the first few questions are reasonable, the prospect begins to gain confidence and feel comfortable with the process. The next questions then, although progressively more challenging, seem easier to handle.

Closed-End Questions. These questions are designed to reveal background information about the prospect's business, general workout habits, and family. They ask an either-or type question or request a choice from a series of suggested responses. Closed-end questions are usually answered with a very brief response, often a single word. They ask for a yes or no response or a choice between two alternatives.

Chapter 10 — Identifying Needs Through Questioning and Listening **170**

Here are some examples:

- How long did it take you to get here today?
- Did you come from home or work?
- What do you do for a living?
- Where do you live/work?
- Do you exercise on a regular basis now?
- Does your spouse exercise?
- How would you rate your current fitness level on a scale from 1-10?
- Who will be watching the children while you exercise?

Exhibit 10.2

Types of Questions and Probing Techniques

General types of questions

Closed-end questions

Provide a series of responses from which the prospect selects one, are easy to answer, used to get feedback, and can be used to get prospect commitment.

Open-end questions

Identify a topic but do not provide structured alternatives for responses, usually begin with "how" or "what", cannot be answered "yes" or "no", and are designed to stimulate the prospect's thinking.

Classification of questioning techniques

Amplification questions

Ask prospect to expand on an answer. Do not direct thoughts but encourage prospect to continue talking. (Nonverbal gestures, silence, and continuation questions)

Getting agreement on the problem

Make a formal statement of the problem, get prospect to agree, and attempt to get commitment.

Internal summary questions

Assimilate information presented, put it in perspective, and ask if the interpretation is correct; may repeat all of prospect's last response in the form of a question.

171   *THE OFFICIAL HANDBOOK FOR HEALTH CLUB SALES*

You may also phrase closed-end questions to get feedback or to gain commitment.

1. Would you like to begin working out today or would you like to schedule your free personal training session for sometime later in the week?

2. Who will be involved in deciding whether to join our gym?

Use closed-end questions as a substitute for telling the prospect something. A question can sometimes make a point in a more telling manner than a statement because the prospect must think to answer it, and thinking makes a stronger impression than hearing. Consider these two ways to impart the same message:

1. Our facilities will satisfy all your health and fitness needs.

2. How much would you invest to be able to finally reach your health and fitness goals?

The first method tells the prospect something. You hope the prospect is impressed, but that may not happen. Unless the prospect reacts strongly enough to the statement to break in with a comment, any skepticism is buried until some later point, where it emerges as a vague objection or stall like, "Well, I don't have the time to reach all my goals right now." The second question, however, gains attention because the prospect has to think about an answer. Disbelief surfaces immediately where it can be dealt with instead of being postponed until later when you are trying to close. Exhibit 10.3 lists the various purposes served by asking closed-end questions.

Exhibit 10.3

Purposes of Closed-End Questions

- Uncover specific facts.

- Reduce prospect tension because they are easy to answer.

- Check understanding and receive feedback.

- Maintain control by directing the flow of conversation.

- Reinforce prospect commitment to a specific position.

Open-End Questions. These broadly phrased questions allow prospects plenty of room to answer. They require explanations. Open-end questions encourage prospects to express their needs by explaining their preferences, expectations, or judgments. Open-end questions tend to be *general* rather than *specific*. Use them when you want the prospect to talk freely during the pre-tour and tour. You can encourage the prospect to verbalize feelings by asking questions that begin with "What do you think?" or "How do you feel?" Talking out loud often helps people clarify and organize their thoughts.

The reason you ask open-ended questions is to get the prospect talking so that they will reveal information which enables you to create a presentation that meets their needs. It also keeps you from talking too much. You want to be a listener, not a talker. Open-end questions help you and the prospect sort out ideas and begin to make decisions. Here are some examples of questions that give prospects the freedom and responsibility to express their own thoughts:

- How did you find out about our club?

- Tell me about the last time you exercised on a regular basis?

- What was your level of fitness like then?

- In your opinion how do you feel about training partners?

- Tell me about your eating habits?

- Tell me how you feel when you wake up in the morning?

- What is your energy level like throughout the day?

- In what area's would you like to trim down or fill out?

- Describe the level of stress you deal with throughout the day?

Open-end questions reveal attitudes that you must be aware of if the sale is to be closed. You cannot easily ask a prospect, "Are you motivated by vanity?" but you can ask open-end questions designed to detect this emotion, and you then have the answer to the direct question you cannot ask. Exhibit 10.4 lists the properties of open-end questions.

THE OFFICIAL HANDBOOK FOR HEALTH CLUB SALES

Exhibit 10.4

The Properties of Open-End Questions

- Allow the prospect to move in any direction.

- Cannot be answered with "yes" or "no".

- Ordinarily begin with "how" or "what".

- Designed to stimulate the prospect's thinking and increase dialogue.

- Help determine dominant buying motives (rational or emotional).

- Uncover the social style of the prospect.

CLASSIFICATION OF QUESTIONING TECHNIQUES

The questions you ask can also be classified by the purpose they are intended to perform. Three basic classes of questions can be used: *amplification, internal summary* or *reflective*, and *questions to gain agreement on the problem*. Either open-end or closed-end questions may be asked for any of these purposes, depending upon the situation. If one type of question does not provide all the information needed, another type can be used to get a more specific response or to elicit a better sense of the prospect's point of view.

Be careful how you phrase the questions you ask. Place responsibility for not understanding on yourself rather than on the prospect. "Do you understand what I said?" or "Did you get that?" or "Are you with me?" seems to imply that the prospect may not be too bright. You must take responsibility for any possible misunderstanding by asking, "Have I explained this clearly enough? Is there some part I need to clarify or go over again?"

Amplification Questions

These questioning techniques encourage prospects to provide additional information and encourage them to explain the meaning of a statement made. Amplification questions help both fitness consultants and prospects. At times prospects may not make themselves clear; they may wander off the subject or may stop

Chapter 10 — Identifying Needs Through Questioning and Listening   **174**

talking before you can fully understand their position. In a subtle manner, these techniques ask the prospect to expand on or clarify the meaning of a statement and help identify the frame of reference used.

Nonverbal Gestures. *Visual cues* such as nodding the head or leaning forward show that you are listening, believe the prospect is on the right track, and understand what the prospect is saying. You may also *inject appropriate words* or phrases to encourage the prospect to continue: "You don't say?" "Is that right?" "That's interesting!" You may imply a question by the nonverbal choice of silence accompanied by a slightly raised eyebrow.

Silence. *Silence* is a powerful sales tool. When prospects avoid telling you the whole truth, the knowledge that they are being less than honest makes them uncomfortable. Your silence convinces them to go ahead and tell you the whole story. Silence allows you to slow down and relax the pace of asking questions. Some prospects want to think and contemplate longer than others before responding to your questions. Give people time to reply at their own pace. Silence also gives you valuable time to formulate your next question or comment.

Continuation Questions. *Continuation* questions encourage prospects to continue talking by making a positive request for more information. Such questions do not push for a particular response or for agreement; they just encourage more communication from the prospect. Here are two examples:

- What additional thoughts do you have regarding your current fitness level?

- That's just the kind of information we must have to help pinpoint your needs. Please go on.

Exhibit 10.5 outlines the advantages of using amplification questions.

Exhibit 10.5

Advantages of Using Amplification Questions

- Encourages the prospect to continue to provide revealing information.

- Allows you to rephrase what the prospect appears to have intended.

- Invites the prospect to expand or clarify any point of disagreement.

- Narrows down generalizations and clears ambiguities.

Internal Summary Questions

Probes designed to get prospects to think, see, and consider your interpretation of the situation may be called *internal summary or reflective* questions. Summarize what you understood the prospect to mean. You want to assimilate the information provided, place it in the perspective that suits your purpose, and ask if the interpretation is correct. You achieve this by repeating all or part of the prospect's last response in the form of a question or by rephrasing the entire idea expressed by the prospect, feeding it back in a slightly different form, and asking for confirmation.

These types of questions are useful throughout the interview. Successful fitness consultants know about summarizing the key benefits just before asking for the membership:

> *Now, as I see it, we've agreed that you would like a 3-year membership, at a monthly $29.99 investment, with free tanning and a free personal training session and that will get you started today. Am I right about that?*

The summary question may be used to underscore points on which you already agree. An occasional summary of the points to which the prospect has already agreed will fix them firmly in the mind of the prospect and demonstrate just how wide an area of agreement there is between the two of you. Such summary techniques are especially useful during the close.

Getting Agreement on the Problem

In *Open the Mind, Close the Sale*, John Wilson says that the salesperson's failure to confirm the problem is one of the biggest mistakes in selling. The whole purpose of asking questions is to determine whether the prospect has a problem or need that you are capable of solving. State the problem in your own words and get the prospect to agree, "Yes, that's it." Never begin the actual presentation phase of the sales process until the problem has been clearly established in the minds of both you and the prospect. Begin the *formal statement of the problem* by using such phrases as these:

- Let me attempt to summarize what we have been saying.

- As I understand it, here is (are) the problem(s) we must solve.

- Based on your answers to my questions, I see the problem as...

Chapter 10 — Identifying Needs Through Questioning and Listening

After you pinpoint the problem, you must seek confirmation. Get the prospect to agree by following your summary of the problem with questions like these:

- If I show you how easy it is to get started today with one of our certified personal trainers to help you reach your fitness goals, would you commit to our program?

- Is that a fair statement of the way things stand?

- If I can satisfactorily demonstrate a solution to these concerns of yours, would it be enough to earn your business?

If the prospect agrees with the problem statement, you are ready to present the specific benefits of membership that can solve the problem. Even if the prospect disagrees with your summary of the problem, you have both learned by sharing information.

LISTENING

About 80 percent of our waking hours is spent communicating, about half of that listening. Effective listening is not just hearing what the prospect is saying. Faulty listening results in misunderstanding and lost opportunities. Research indicates that 60 percent of misunderstandings in business are due to poor listening. Fortunately, improved listening skills can be learned.

To succeed as a fitness consultant, you must be able to offer a membership in a way that satisfies the buyer's needs. Presenting features and benefits is not always enough. How they are presented may be as important as what is presented. Listening is the key to finding ways to present benefits that enhance the possibility of a close.

Effective listening helps fitness consultants catch verbal and nonverbal signals indicating a prospect is interested in joining their gym. "Unfortunately, good listening skills usually require a change in our behavior," says Barry Elms, CEO of Strategic Negotiations International. Psychologists claim that listening uses only about 25 percent of our brain's capacity. The other 75 percent either thinks about what to say next or stops listening if the conversation is boring or of no interest.

Improving Listening Skills

To improve your listening skills, practice these five mental activities as you are listening:

1. **Be Patient.** Listen more and give "nonverbal nods" of encouragement. This allows speakers plenty of time to answer questions and encourages them to express their ideas. Speak at the same speed as the other person: Matching speed is a rapport builder. In addition, find the person's *mental rate of speed* and then adjust or modify your thinking to that rate. Even though the guest is saying something exciting, wait until the message is complete and you are sure that you understand it all before you contribute your own thoughts.

2. **Avoid Prejudgment.** Not only should you allow the prospect to complete a message before you comment or respond, but you should also wait until you have heard what they have to say before judging its meaning. Making value judgments colors your thinking and creates *emotional blind spots* that block your ability to make a buying recommendation. Jumping to conclusions is a common fault of poor listeners. As the cartoon indicates, assuming you know what is coming next can seriously damage your understanding of the actual meaning intended.

Chapter 10 — Identifying Needs Through Questioning and Listening   178

3. **Take Notes.** Remembering everything a person says is difficult. In the pre-tour, be sure to use the pencil-and-paper approach to selling memberships. Divide your notepad into two columns. On one side note what the prospect says. Then in the other column sketch out your proposal to meet those expressions of needs, requirements, or desires. Find the happy medium between trying to record everything you hear and recording nothing. The mere physical action of writing down a few key words reinforces your memory and understanding. You can go back to the prospect's own words to help show how your club satisfies the individual's needs and goals.

4. **Reinforce.** Anchor in your mind and in the prospect's the points made by the prospect. Use your own reinforcing responses to achieve this purpose. If the prospect says that personal training is important, respond, "Yes, that is very important." Later, bring up the fact that your gym offers a special package rate that includes sessions with certified personal trainers. If the prospect says, "I work such long hours that I can't find time to get to the gym," respond, "That has to be a problem." Then later emphasize how your gym is open 24 hours a day for just that reason.

5. **Capitalize on Speed of Thought.** We can process about 600 words a minute, but even a fast talker gets out only 100 to 150 words in that time. Thus you can think about four times as fast as the average prospect talks. All that spare time is valuable. The poor listener uses it to fidget impatiently, to think about what happened earlier in the day or what will happen later, or to plan what to say as soon as the prospect takes a breath. Successful salespeople have a plan to follow for using this time profitably:

- *Anticipate where the prospect is going.* If you guess right, your thinking is reinforced. If you are wrong, compare your thoughts with the prospect's; look for the main point the prospect is making.

- *Mentally summarize the message.* Pinpoint problems, misconceptions, objections, or misunderstandings. What you learn can be an excellent guide to the items that should be stressed in the presentation and at the close.

- *Formulate a response*, but not before you hear everything the prospect wants to say. Listen, understand, and then turn the prospect's words to your advantage.

- *Listen between the lines.* Nonverbal messages are as important as verbal ones. Watch facial expressions and body movement; listen to the tone of voice and for volume changes.

Identifying Needs Through Questioning and Listening
REFOCUS

- Asking questions is the primary tool for identifying problems. Need discovery during the pre-tour lays the groundwork for the presentation and close. When you ask the right questions, prospects clarify problems in their own minds as well as in yours.

- No standard set of questions is universally applicable. Your gym's amenities, your preapproach information, and the prospect's social style help determine the questions you ask.

- Questions may be either closed-end or open-end. A closed-end question asks for a yes-no response or a choice between alternatives. Open-end questions ask for opinions, explanations, or judgments.

- Ask questions according to their structure: amplification, internal summary, and questions designed to gain agreement.

- Listening is one of the most neglected skills in any type of training program. Taking notes focuses your attention on what the prospect is saying and avoids prejudgment of ideas. Reinforce what you hear by comparing the prospect's ideas with your own

- People can think at a rate much faster than they talk. Use this spare thinking time to anticipate where the prospect is going, mentally summarize what you hear, form a response, and refine the message as your listening continues.

Chapter 10 — Identifying Needs Through Questioning and Listening

Like They Say, The Apple Doesn't Fall Too Far From The Tree.

Strive is proud to announce the latest addition to our family. With the exact same quality of the adult line and new safety features, Strive's kidzSmart Strength line is sized perfectly for children ages 9 to 14. Strive also offers the Y.E.S.™ (Youth Exercising Safely) program which is an exciting, educational children's exercise program, designed to establish health and fitness habits that will last a lifetime.

Kidz Selectorized Chest Press

800-368-6448 • 724-873-5780 • FAX: 724-873-5770 • www.strivefit.com

Chapter 11

Making the Presentation

FOCAL POINTS

- Making an engaging presentation.

- Devising units of conviction.

- Tactics for making a presentation.

- Methods for getting the prospect involved.

- The significance of a demonstration.

- Transition from the club presentation to the price presentation.

DEVELOPING A PERSUASIVE PRESENTATION

Some experts are predicting that salespeople are soon to be relics on the road to extinction. Not true! Professional fitness consultants will prosper in the future if they understand this: There are big differences between data and information. You must have **knowledge** in order to believe in something. It is essential that you have knowledge about the fitness industry. You must be able to match your club's **product** and **services** to what the potential member is trying to accomplish. In the past, traditional club sales reps simply presented facts and data. How "data dense" are most sales presentations?

Here are some interesting and surprising facts about most sales presentations:

- The typical salesperson presents six to eight features or benefits during the sales presentation. Twenty-four hours later the average prospect remembers one benefit about the club.

Chapter 11 — Making the Presentation　　182

- In 39 percent of those cases they remember the one benefit incorrectly.

- In 49 percent of the cases they remember something that wasn't even mentioned at all.

Prospects want to join a gym that not only provides what they need to reach and maintain their goals, they also want it explained in a language they understand. The future of relationship selling is going to be based on real-time value and how well fitness sales professionals become trusted advisors in guiding guests and members to a solution to their fitness concerns and needs. Salespeople must become better knowledge managers and not just people who are trying to close a deal. If you believe in yourself and you are knowledgeable about all areas of the fitness business then you will be more confident. The more **confident** you are the more **successful** you will become.

Strive for Passion, not Perfection. More often than not, people join because of the rapport building you establish with guests and members. Selling is all about relationship building. There are thousands of clubs chomping at the bit. It all comes down to the way you present yourself and your club, and the value you create for the customer. People-reading skills help fitness consultants adapt to their prospect's social styles.

Mark McCormack in his book *What They Don't Teach You at the Harvard Business School* says there are three fundamental selling truths: (1) If you don't know your product, people will resent your efforts to sell it. (2) If you don't believe in your product, no amount of personality or technique will cover that fact. (3) If you can't sell your product with enthusiasm, the absence of it will be infectious.

Nobody buys from a dispassionate seller. If you don't believe in your club and its benefits, no one else will. The more options a fitness sales rep creates for the prospect, the greater the chance for a sale. Don't worry about making the perfect presentation. It probably will not happen! Besides, the prospects are looking to you for knowledge of what you're selling and how it can help them satisfy a lifestyle need or simply become healthier. You must truly believe in what you're selling and *show some passion* when doing it – that is far more important than perfection.

Begin with Planning

Does everything begin with planning? Yes, everything important begins with planning. Exhibit 11.1 is one man's account of the results he suffered from his failure to plan his immediate future. Random, haphazard action never leads to success in any worthwhile endeavor, and in this respect, selling is no different from any other undertaking. How well you plan what takes place during the club presentation plays a major role in the success you achieve when closing time arrives.

In reality, planning and preparing for the sales presentation begin when a name is first recorded in your prospect files. As information is gathered about the prospect, you are subconsciously planning how to approach this person, what features and benefits of your club are most appropriate, and what kind of close is likely to be

Exhibit 11.1

Failing to Plan My Immediate Future

I am writing in response to your request for additional information. In block #3 of the accident form I listed "not planning my immediate future" as the cause of my accident. I trust the following details will be sufficient.

I am a bricklayer. On the date of the accident I was working alone on the roof of a new six-story building. At the end of the day, I discovered about 500 pounds of bricks left over. Rather than carry them down by hand, I decided to lower them in a barrel by using a pulley that was fortunately attached to the building at the sixth floor..

Securing the rope at ground level, I went to the roof, swung the barrel out, and loaded the bricks. Then I went back to the ground and untied the rope, holding it tightly to ensure a slow descent of the 500 pounds of bricks. Block #11 of the accident report shows that I weigh 135 pounds. Due to my surprise of being jerked off the ground so suddenly, I forgot to let go of the rope. Needless to say, I proceeded at a rapid rate up the side of the building. In the vicinity of the third floor, I met the barrel coming down. This explains the fractured skull and broken collarbone.

Slowed only slightly, I continued my rapid ascent, not stopping until the fingers of my right hand were two knuckles deep into the pulley. Fortunately, I had regained my presence of mind enough to hold tightly to the rope in spite of my pain.

At approximately the same time, however, the barrel of bricks hit the ground and the bottom fell out of the barrel. Devoid of the weight of the bricks, the barrel now weighed approximately 50 pounds. I refer you again to block #11. As you can imagine, I began a rapid descent down the side of the building.

In the vicinity of the third floor I met the barrel coming up. This accounts for the two fractured ankles and the lacerations of my legs and lower body. The encounter with the barrel slowed my descent enough to lessen my injuries when I fell onto the pile of bricks. Fortunately only three vertebrae were cracked.

I am sorry to report, however, that as I lay there on the bricks, in pain, unable to stand and watching the empty barrel six stories above me, I again lost my presence of mind and let go of the rope. Now the empty barrel weighed more than the rope, so it came back down on me and broke both of my legs.

I hope these details explain sufficiently that my accident was caused by failure to plan my immediate future.

Chapter 11 — Making the Presentation   **184**

most effective. The final step of preparing is to crystallize all your plans and decide exactly how to proceed with making the presentation.

Call Objective

The most successful fitness consultants have specific objectives from the time a prospect enters the club. In most instances, the call objective is to present your club and secure a membership. In others, your objective is to discover the prospect's needs so that you may prepare them for later consideration or to persuade the prospect to set up a presentation with the decision maker who will make the choice to join. In these latter instances, you will probably plan another meeting that, taken together, will contain all the elements that may be considered parts of "the presentation." The difference is that you accomplish the various steps in *successive* interviews rather than in a *single* meeting with the prospect.

Just remember that in the health and fitness industry, people usually know after the tour whether they want to join, but may respond and react with objections in much the same manner others have before them. Learn how to respond to the common responses and this will make closing on the first meeting more likely, as long as you have done your homework and are prepared for the typical procrastination responses.

Sales Call Planning Sheet

It is a good idea to prepare a presentation plan in written form. The plan reveals the need for any additional information, makes it possible to check needs and goals against suggested solutions, and makes sure you have a clear picture of the entire situation before an individual arrives for the club tour. Exhibit 11.2 is an example of a sales call planning sheet that may be used for this purpose.

PRESENTATION STYLES

As long as people have been attempting to analyze the selling process, a running controversy has raged over the use of "canned" presentations. Opponents point to presentations that are obviously memorized, and delivered in a hypnotic manner likely to produce a mesmerized listener in the shortest possible time. Supporters of memorized presentations point to the many advantages of knowing exactly what to say and when.

THE OFFICIAL HANDBOOK FOR HEALTH CLUB SALES

The question is not likely to be settled once and for all because the difference lies more with the fitness consultant than with the method of delivery itself. In deciding how you will deliver the message you want the prospect to receive, consider the advantages and disadvantages of three basic choices: the memorized presentation, the outline presentation, and the extemporaneous presentation

Exhibit 11.2

Sales Call Planner

Call Plan What is the Objective of this call?	
Situation:	
Fitness Concerns: (What we can solve)	**Implications:** (that make the concerns urgent)
Explicit Needs: (that we hope to develop)	**Benefits:** (that we can offer)

Chapter 11 — Making the Presentation

Memorized Presentation

Some gyms supply their salespeople with a printed presentation and require them to memorize it. A few words of caution are in order when considering the use of a memorized presentation. Even though it is memorized, the presentation should never sound memorized. A memorized presentation should be practiced and its delivery polished until it becomes natural. It should be internalized to the point that it is a normal, personal message. The memorized presentation must be used as a framework or guide to lead you and your prospect through the sales process.

A well-prepared, memorized presentation offers a number of important advantages, especially to new fitness consultants.

Quick Productivity. If you are new to the club or to the selling profession, you can memorize a good presentation in much less time than one can be developed. Using a standardized presentation gets you into production quickly. Enough membership sales can be made during the initial learning period to supply basic income needs while you gain knowledge and experience.

Reliable and Proven Effectiveness. The memorized presentation makes sure you give the right information to the prospect. Nothing vital is omitted, and nothing erroneous is inserted. The presentation your sales managers may supply has usually been tested and refined over a period of years in actual selling situations.

Confidence Building. Using a memorized presentation can serve as a confidence builder. When you know the presentation has worked for others with no more experience than you have, you feel capable of using it successfully. When you succeed in closing a sale with the presentation, you gain even more confidence. Each success builds on the previous one, and you are *earning* and *learning* at the same time.

Outline Presentation

The outline presentation takes a great deal of thought and preparation. With this presentation technique, exact words are not planned in full detail. You know what content will be presented at each stage of the presentation but are confident enough of both knowledge and skill to believe that the right words will be available as needed. This is the same process that most experienced public speakers use.

THE OFFICIAL HANDBOOK FOR HEALTH CLUB SALES

The outline presentation is built by considering all the information available about the prospect. This is a commonly used presentation style for the health and fitness industry because it allows room to cater the presentation to the specific needs and wants of potential members. Most fitness consultants who use an outline method follow the same general outline for most presentations. They may, however, have several approaches or openings from which to choose, numerous features and benefits to present, and all sorts of evidence to present—all of which can be combined and recombined to meet the needs of the specific situation.

Extemporaneous Presentation

Some highly successful fitness sales reps, particularly those who have many years of experience, may be heard to say that they "don't prepare" for a presentation. Actually, their preparation time is distributed in a different way than that of the less experienced salesperson, but they do prepare.

The extemporaneous presentation follows the same principles that any other presentation incorporates, but experienced salespeople who use this approach are master people watchers. They understand people; they ask questions and listen. They are experts in discovering problems and identifying dominant buying motives. They know their product so thoroughly that they can seize almost magically upon the one benefit that will best appeal to the prospect. They possess such charisma that the air of trust and credibility they create makes objections nonexistent and painlessly places the prospect's name on the membership contract. People love to buy from them.

As a result, these master salespeople spend most of their "preparation time" in gathering additional information about the prospect rather than spending time in *consciously* matching features and benefits to prospect qualification information. This step is almost automatic and subconscious as a result of their long experience.

PRODUCT-ANALYSIS WORKSHEET

Prospects have neither the fitness knowledge you have nor an understanding of the type of service you and your club are prepared to render. You must not only know all the facts about your gym but also be able to relate your knowledge of health and fitness directly to the specific needs of the prospect. If you can recite all the muscle groups and know all about the latest dietary fads, but have no solid, convincing evidence of your club's value to offer upon which the prospect

Chapter 11 — Making the Presentation

can base a buying decision, you are afflicted with what has been called the *salesman's* curse: "You know your club better than you know how potential members can use it."

Before you can expect a signed membership form, you must figure out how to solve your customer's needs and then find a way to persuade the prospect that the solution your club offers is the best possible. You can do this by preparing *units of conviction*.

Units of Conviction

Units of conviction are concise, carefully prepared "mini-presentations" used as building blocks to construct the information you present. When the individual units of conviction are combined, they form what is referred to as a *product-analysis worksheet*.

Preparing a written product-analysis worksheet helps you evaluate the various characteristics of your club so that you are better able to present it to your prospects. When you prepare units of conviction and add them to your store of available options, they become a permanent part of your selling arsenal. A single unit of conviction consists of five elements:

1. A feature of your club

2. A transitional phrase

3. The benefits the feature provides

4. Evidence to support your claims

5. A tie-down question to gain the prospect's agreement

Features and Benefits. *Features* are the tangible and intangible qualities of your club and its services. Features are facts that are the same no matter who uses the facilities. The tangible features include observable factors such as the circuit and free weight equipment, cardio machines, locker rooms, and group exercise rooms—anything that can be detected through one of the five senses. Intangible features are also important: the service given by the fitness consultants, price of membership, availability of personal trainers, availability of help or assistance, and even the service and support that you personally promise.

Benefits, however, are the value or worth that the user derives from your club's services. Of the numerous benefits it has to offer, only four or five will be key motivators to a prospect, and these will be different for each person. Your task is to find out which ones are the key motivators.

Every feature of your product has numerous benefits. Remember, *one feature does not equal one benefit*. Examine the insert that follows and challenge your mind to perform some mental gymnastics to prove this point.

> **Features and Benefits**
>
> Every feature of your club has numerous benefits. Here's an exercise to give your mind a healthy benefit workout: What are the benefits of a 270-horsepower engine in a luxury car? They could include a smoother ride, power to spare when passing a slower car, quick acceleration away from a hazard, the feeling of being in charge, less wear and tear, higher resale value, etc.
>
> The point is, one feature does not equal one benefit. List your club's top 10 features, then come up with at least five different benefits for each feature. Remember, features only justify the price; benefits justify the purchase. This gives you 50 new ways to close more sales.

Transitional Phrase. The ability to translate features into benefits is one of the strengths of a professional fitness consultant. Even if you know which feature can fulfill the buying motive, you cannot expect the prospect to make the connection automatically. You must make the verbal transition. The prospect does not know your club as well as you know it and has to have features and benefits connected by transitional phrases. Some consultants call these *bridges*. While the actual words may vary, they are all designed to accomplish the same purpose: To connect, in the prospect's thinking, features and benefits. These phrases all serve the purpose of answering the prospect's question, "What's in it for me?" Some common transitional phrases are:

- "This is beneficial to you because…"
- "This lets you…"
- "This heads off all the problems of…"
- "What this means to you…"

Chapter 11 — Making the Presentation   190

Evidence to Support Claims. Just as you present benefits to head off the prospect's question "So what?" about the features of your club, you must present evidence to support the claims you make to head off the questions "Can you prove it?" and "Who says so?" Even if you have been unusually successful in establishing a high degree of credibility and trust with the prospect, you are unlikely to be looked upon as an all-knowing sage with all the answers whose statements are to be accepted without question. You must be prepared to back up what you say.

The Tie-Down. The "tie-down" is the final and essential step in building units of conviction during the presentation, although it usually consists of no more than a single question that asks for the prospect's agreement.

The tie-down is important throughout the presentation to check on understanding and agreement and to make sure the prospect is ready to proceed to the next point. One of the functions of the tie-down is to ask a series of questions, all of which the prospect can be expected to answer yes. Then when you attempt a close, the prospect more easily says yes again. Suppose, however, that you ask, "You agree with me about this, don't you?" and the prospect says, "No, I don't." Where are you now?

You are in a better position than you were before you asked the question because you now know you have a problem. Had you not asked the question and found out about the lack of agreement, you would have pushed on to the close and to failure. Now you are warned about the existence of a problem and can go back to find its source and correct it, ask another tie-down question, and move forward again when agreement is reached.

Relationships are like a two-way street, but you have to meet each other halfway.

THE OFFICIAL HANDBOOK FOR HEALTH CLUB SALES

FIVE STEPS TO A SUCCESSFUL PRESENTATION

Now that you have learned about units of conviction, and the difference between features and benefits, it is time to put it all together into an effective winning presentation. As a guideline, follow this five-step formula:

Step 1: Show

In this stage, show specific elements of the club. Your club is likely broken down into different areas from aerobic fitness to free-weights. Take guests through each area of your club and show them what they will find at each.

Step 2: Tell

Tell guests about the benefit of each area in relation to their interests and goals that were mutually identified during the pre-tour interview. This step includes the use of transitional phrases such as, "this lets you…" or "this allows you…" that helps translate those features into benefits. Be sure to have your pre-tour sheet with you so you can tailor your presentation to each guest's specific needs. Remember, it is up to you to determine which benefits are those key motivators for the prospect.

Step 3: Ask

Ask questions that are worded in such a way as to handle potential concerns that may have been revealed during the presentation. Each concern should be handled in the area of the club that pertains to the specific need addressed by the guest.

Here are three specific examples of how to combine the *show, tell, and ask* phases of your presentation for the different areas your club may have:

1. The Cardio-Respiratory Training Area

Show the Feature:

> *"We offer a large range of cardio equipment and a full schedule of aerobic classes."*

Chapter 11 — Making the Presentation 192

Tell a Benefit:

"These help you perform the types of exercises that are needed for the body to use fat for energy and to improve cardiovascular endurance."

Ask a Tie-Down Question:

"Wouldn't a wide selection of cardio equipment and classes help keep your exercise routine interesting?"

2. Free Weights Area

Show the Feature:

"We have two full sets of dumbbells ranging from 5 lbs. up to 100 lbs."

Tell a Benefit:

"This is beneficial to you because by having such a wide range of weights, you will not have to wait."

Ask a Tie-Down Question:

"Would you agree that by having such a wide variety of weights that range from 5 lbs. all the way up to 100 lbs, it should make it easy to get your work out completed in a shorter amount of time?"

3. Group Exercise Room

Show the Feature:

"We have built a state-of-the-art group exercise floor."

Tell a Benefit:

"What this means to you is that the floor will absorb the aerobic shock so there will be less impact on your knees and joints."

Ask a Tie-Down Question:

"Would you agree that this absorbent floor would alleviate stress on your knees and joints? "

Step 4: Demonstrate and Participate

Showmanship sells if it is more than mere carnival hoopla. There is a big difference between showmanship and *show-off-manship*. A demonstration is not your chance to exhibit your own strength or fitness knowledge, but rather a time to seize and hold the prospect's attention. The demonstration provides the evidence to support the claims you made when presenting the features and benefits. A good demonstration provides you with these benefits:

1. Captures the guest's interest

2. Strengthens your club's selling points

3. Helps the prospect understand the different aspects of your facilities

4. Stimulates your own interest

5. Cuts down on the number of objections

6. Helps you close the sale

The value of a demonstration is that it involves more than one of the physical senses. Demonstrate features that relate to the guest's interests. Allow them to participate in the presentation by trying several pieces of equipment themselves. Use the words **feel** and **benefit** during this stage! Remember these three points when determining how you will deliver your message to the prospect:

- If you rely solely on "telling" the prospect about your club, only the *auditory* sense is involved. If you add a demonstration, you include the *visual* sense.

- If you involve the prospect in the demonstration, you add the sense of *touch*. The more of the senses you can involve, the more quickly the prospect absorbs the information that leads to a sale.

- People remember 20 percent of what they *hear* and 20 percent of what they *see*. But they remember *50 percent* of what they *see* and *hear*.

Every presentation—no matter how it is organized—must get the prospect involved in the process. When prospects are shut out of the presentation or choose to remain aloof, say nothing, and contribute nothing, they do not join.

Chapter 11 — Making the Presentation   **194**

Here are specific principles to consider when using a demonstration as a part of your sales presentation:

Concentrate the Prospect's Attention on You. The CEO of a large corporation once called a meeting of his associates in his office. When they came in, he was juggling several tennis balls. Finally, he tossed aside all but one and said, "We all have many things on our minds—like these tennis balls. But we must put them aside and concentrate on one problem at a time or we'll waste time trying to juggle them all." This demonstration illustrates the situation when you give a presentation. You must focus the prospect's attention on one thing - what you are saying and showing them.

Get Your Prospect Into the Act. Invite prospects to operate one of the cardio machines or lift some free weights. As guests participate in the demonstration, be sure to include questions that will link each feature of the club to the benefits they will enjoy in relation to what they have told you they want to accomplish. As you demonstrate the elements of your club and encourage guests to get involved in the demonstration, ask questions such as:

- " Do you feel that working?"

- "Where do you feel it"?

- " Do you see how easy it is to use?"

- "Can you see the benefit you would get using this equipment"?

Paint a Mind Picture Using Metaphors. Metaphors imply comparisons between otherwise dissimilar things without using the words "like" or "as", often creating a dramatic visual image. Remember, "facts tell, stories sell." Painting a mind picture is a hook that grabs prospects and reels them in.

Steve Durk, a fitness consultant in Sacramento, California, uses this creative metaphor with prospects:

> *Picture yourself in a desert without a canteen. In the distance you see a water well. There's a bucket with a rope nearby. Now, would you jump into the well headfirst or would you use the bucket and rope? What our club can do for you is supply you with the bucket and rope—the tools you need to succeed.*

Metaphors, analogies, and similes can bring special life to your presentation. These are effective ways to reinforce concepts, while building rapport and winning people over to your way of thinking.

Use Testimonials. The gym floor presentation is also a great time to use testimonials and success stories from actual members. The best possible testimonial is for one of your satisfied members to tell the prospect what the club has done for them. This may actually help predispose the prospect to accept what you say.

Use these guidelines when planning this type of testimonial evidence:

1. The story must be *authentic*. It should be about someone the prospect knows or could contact for verification at the club.

2. Use *many details* to let the prospect know you are intimately familiar with the situation.

3. Relate it directly to the prospect's circumstances and fitness goals.

Use Statistics. Be sure to make use of statistics in your presentation. Call attention to shocking or interesting facts about the level of fitness – or lack thereof – in America, and other facts about the decrease in the risk of heart attack and stroke with regular exercise and a healthy diet.

Step 5: The Tie-Down

The final and essential step in building units of conviction is the "tie-down", which consists of a single question that seeks the prospect's agreement. The tie-down is used during the presentation to verify understanding and confirm that guests are ready to proceed and have accepted what you have told them. Here are some examples of tie-down questions:

1. *Considering these facts, you agree with me that we have a wide range of cardio equipment for every fitness level, don't you, Ms. Shores?*

2. *I believe you will agree with me, Mr. Lockridge, that this circuit training equipment is a better way to get started with resistance training, won't you?*

ADJUST THE PRESENTATION TO UNIQUE CIRCUMSTANCES

You have the option of approaching the task of presenting your club to the prospect using a variety of sales tactics. Which tactics you choose depend upon what you have learned about the prospect during preapproach qualification, what you observe in the opening minutes of the interview, what you personally want to do, and what kind of environment you find in the interview location. The only limit to the number of different presentation tactics is your own creative imagination.

Situational Selling

Master fitness consultants have a specific plan for every sales presentation, but they never feel slavishly bound by that plan. Relationship selling requires flexibility. No matter how much you learn about a prospect before they come for a tour, you can never be absolutely sure what kind of situation to expect when they arrive. Instead of finding a calm, receptive prospect ready to listen and evaluate your club, you may find one who is angry, resentful, or emotional. If planning has been adequate, you can shift gears and make a different kind of presentation, switch to another purpose, or even delay the presentation until a better time.

The ability to exercise this type of flexibility is called *situational selling*—fitting yourself to the situation and making each contact with the prospect beneficial to your ultimate purpose of closing a sale.

Interruptions

No matter how carefully you schedule a meeting, your best-laid plans may go astray. Telephone interruptions can be prevented by asking the front desk attendant to hold your calls until later. This tells the prospect that you believe the tour is more important than routine matters. When an interruption does occur, your sense of timing will tell you whether the discussion can be resumed or whether scheduling a later meeting would be better.

If you decide to continue, summarize what has been said up to the point of the interruption. If a problem or need has been identified, state it again and ask a question designed to gain the prospect's agreement. Review in detail the last major point made in your presentation, and again check for agreement or com-

THE OFFICIAL HANDBOOK FOR HEALTH CLUB SALES

mitment by asking a question. Be sure the prospect is back on track and is following your planned path of reasoning before proceeding.

PRICE PRESENTATION

After the club presentation and tour is complete, it is time to begin the price presentation. As you lead the guest back to your office, use this opportunity to transition into the price presentation by making the following statement:

"Let's go back to my office so that we can review together all of the important information about the club."

Once back in your office, you need to ask the guest permission to ask a few questions before the price presentation. For example, you may say, *"John, before I give you any more information may I ask a couple of questions?"* When the guest says, *"yes,"* he is also saying he will answer your questions. After gaining permission, you should use the following question to eliminate any minor issues that could surface as concerns when you confirm the membership:

"John, as your workout program begins, I am sure you will have additional questions, but before I explain the membership options, are there any concerns I can answer for you now?"

Once John asks any questions he may have or replies that he has no questions, add:

"John, I am glad we have gotten to this point. Let me show you how to become a member."

After the prospect's confirmation to continue, it is now time to explain the membership options your club offers. Remember the key is to stay positive and do not change the pace.

Most people will feel apprehensive if their first visit to your office is the part of your presentation when you discuss money. If, on the other hand, you have taken prospects to your office at the beginning of their visit and created a friendly and comfortable atmosphere, it will be a pleasurable experience. Prospects will eagerly return to the same seat with little resistance later.

Chapter 11 — Making the Presentation   198

The key is to keep the price presentation simple so you do not confuse the guest. If you present too many options or numbers you may likely hear, " *I need to think about it.*" When in doubt, follow this "anatomy of a price presentation" to keep it as straightforward as possible:

Anatomy of a Price Presentation

1. Start from the top of the membership form and work your way to the bottom so the guest can follow you logically.

2. Next, turn the form towards you and NEATLY note any discounts your club is currently offering.

3. Be sure to POINT out each element of the club as you recap and discuss.

4. Allow them to choose from more than one membership option. It takes away some of the pressure by giving them choices.

5. Look at the membership form during any silent moments to avoid intimidating the guest. Always look down, never look up during this crucial stage.

6. Make sure you always have a pen when you present prices. You cannot reduce or discount prices without a pen, and the pen will act as a magic wand which will allow you to direct your guest's attention to where you want it.

And remember, always congratulate them sincerely in their decision to join!

Making The Presentation
REFOCUS

- You can memorize a presentation or use an outline that allows you to present each of your selling points in an orderly and systematic way.

- Personalize each presentation to the needs of the prospect. One of the most important tactics available is prospect participation.

- One way to choose what you will present is to develop units of conviction. Each unit of conviction includes:

  1. A feature of your club

  2. A transitional phrase

  3. The benefits the feature provides

  4. Evidence to support your claims through demonstration and participation

  5. A tie-down to gain agreement

- Interruptions represent anything that distracts the prospect's attention from your message. You must learn to control these distractions and transform them into buying opportunities.

- The price presentation should be a natural and easy transition from the gym floor to the office. Be sure to gain agreement from the guest before proceeding into this phase of the presentation.

Chapter 11 — Making the Presentation   200

- 50 years of health club experience
- Group discount on equipment
- Expand and control profit centers
- P&L management
- Sales and marketing plan
- Recruit and hire general manager
- Forecast and trend statement
- Monthly club check to inspect the "systems"
- Budget creation and control
- Pre-sale set up
- Monthly sales quota
- 3 calls per day to your facility to monitor and push productivity
- Operation manual
- Business plans
- Sales manuals
- Continued education via monthly sales seminar
- Hire and fire staff

YOU HAVE THE VISION. *We have the plan.*

Total Fitness Systems is a full service, member driven management company that increases the value of your fitness club through professional, educated, and motivated fitness staff. The preferred management company of *World Gym International, Cybex International, Inc.* and *Cory Everson Fitness For Women*, TFS can help you open and operate a successful business or enhance your existing facilities by implementing its time-proven operating systems.

 Total Fitness Systems | 615-771-0228 | www.totalfitnesssystems.net

Chapter 12
Handling Objections

FOCAL POINTS

- Positive attitudes toward objections.
- Why prospects have sales resistance.
- Uncovering hidden concerns.
- A six-step plan for dealing with objections.
- Techniques to use to overcome objections.
- Tactics to employ in handling price concerns.

THE TRUTH ABOUT OBJECTIONS

The problem with the word "objection" is that it conjures up an adversarial relationship between the fitness consultant and prospect – where someone must win, and someone must lose. The relationship sales cycle is a mutually beneficial process that produces a jointly satisfying long-term connection.

So we must look at the word "objection" a bit differently. Professional salespeople look positively at the objections prospects offer. Objections move prospects nearer to the close and reveal their concerns. An objection often uncovers the key to a successful sale.

If the prospect has been properly qualified, objections are really *buying signals*. Offering an objection is another way for the prospect to say, "Here are my conditions for joining," or "I want to join as soon as you answer a few more questions or reassure me that joining your club is the smart thing to do." Welcome all objections! They are the verbal and nonverbal signs of

Chapter 12 — Handling Objections 202

sales resistance that give you the chance to discover what the prospect is thinking. These *objections or sales resistance* become leverage for closing the sale.

An *objection* is anything the prospect says or does that presents an *obstacle* to the smooth completion of the sale. Objections are a normal and natural part of almost every conversation, not just in sale-situations, but whenever people discuss any current topic. A purchasing decision usually involves some risk. To ease the fear of risk, people object, raise concerns, or ask questions in hopes of getting answers that will convince them that the buying decision is in their best interest.

Disagree Without Being Disagreeable

Getting into an argument with a prospect, particularly in response to objections, is one of the easiest and most disastrous mistakes you can make. Your purpose is to remove the objection without being objectionable. Remember that relationship selling is a win-win proposition. The negotiation process is not a battle that you win and the prospect loses; rather it is a situation of mutual cooperation and mutual benefit. You may well win the argument and prove you are right but lose the sale in the process. *People who are forced to agree seldom actually change their minds.* Never force a prospect into making a decision. Prospects are more likely to stay sold, brings their friends in, and renew their memberships if the decision to join was their idea.

Sales resistance contains elements of both logic and emotion. When people really want something, logic goes out the window and emotion takes control. The heart tends to rule the head, especially in the health and fitness industry where we can directly affect a person's self-esteem and confidence level. The first task in answering an objection is to calm the prospect's emotions by proving that you are open to reason. Pause before responding; then acknowledge that you respect the prospect's opinion and find the views expressed worthy of consideration. Show a measure of empathy. People are open to changing their opinions and attitudes when they are convinced that others value their opinions, understand how they can feel that way, and grant them the right to those opinions. *Thus, the key to maintaining a positive sales environment is to disagree without being disagreeable.*

TYPES OF OBJECTIONS

When the prospect objects, you must understand what type of sales resistance is being offered before you can handle it effectively. Sales resistance may be separated into four general types: the stopper, the searcher, the stall or put-off, and the hidden objection.

The Stopper

Prospects often have legitimate reasons why they feel unable to join. One type of valid objection is what might be called a *stopper*. Even Harry Houdini could not solve this one. The stopper is an objection to which no satisfactory solution can be found. For instance, if a prospect insists the only way they will join is if you can promise they will lose 30 pounds in one month, you cannot or at least you should not make that promise.

The Searcher

A second type is called a *searcher*, a request for additional information. Some prospects object simply to get more information, even though they have already mentally decided that they want to join. The customer just wants to be convinced that joining your club is the right thing to do.

Handle Valid Searcher Concerns with Finesse

How Negotiators Might Respond to Four Common Searcher Objections

I'm not interested.

- There is no reason why you should be interested until I show you how our club can help you feel better and reach your fitness goals. May I show you how we can help you do that?

- Do you mean you are not interested at this time, or at all? I'll call back in four weeks; hopefully, things will be less hectic for you.

I don't have any money for this.

- I can certainly respect that. If I could show you two ways the membership will pay for itself, would you be interested?

I am satisfied with the club I currently use.

- What do you like most about the club you are using now? [Then demonstrate how your facilities are better.]

I really like the competitor's gym.

- I am not surprised to hear you say that. Their club does have some interesting features. I know some of my happiest members are people who used to work out at that other gym.

Chapter 12 — Handling Objections   **204**

The Stall or Put-Off

When the prospect offers a *stall* or *put-off* objection, look for the true meaning. Frequently, the prospect is simply avoiding a decision. You should never experience a stall if you have properly qualified a prospect at the beginning. The stall could mean that you have not presented a compelling enough reason to buy. A stall is a classic sales killer unless you can create a sense of urgency to buy *NOW*. The stall is actually the prospect's way of saying, "I really don't want to think about your proposition right now because I would then be forced to make a decision." Here are some examples of how *stalls* are phrased:

1. "I have to leave in fifteen minutes; I have an important meeting."

2. "Just let me take your brochure home and read it. I will get back to you."

3. "I must talk this over with my husband."

Handling a stall is a test of your *attitude*. If you believe you have a qualified prospect whose needs will be satisfied by your club, then you do not allow a "*put-off*" to put *you* off. Here are some suggestions for responding to the stalls given above:

1. "We are both busy people. Can I have fifteen minutes to show you something that would increase your health and fitness level and help you finally reach those weight loss goals you told me about?"

2. "Mr. Ray, I thought that I had adequately covered the highlights and aspects of our gym. Obviously, I have not made myself clear at some point. Would you tell me what I have not explained to your satisfaction?"

3. "I certainly understand wanting to involve your husband in a decision like this. Can we ask him to join us now, or can he drop by this afternoon with you to get you both started today?"

The Hidden Objection

A fourth type of sales resistance is the *hidden objection*. This kind of resistance is more difficult to overcome. Chris Mitchell, a fitness consultant in Birmingham, AL, defines hidden problems as "unspoken hesitations which, if not addressed, can delay or prevent a sale." The prospect refuses to let you know the real concern. Many times the reason is quite personal, and the prospect prefers not to reveal it or has a vague feeling that cannot be easily articulated. You know the prospect has a hidden objection when the answers fail to make sense. The reasons for not buying are not logical based on the meeting up to that point. For example, a prospect may dislike revealing these real concerns:

1. "Circumstances have changed since you first contacted me. Recent family problems have caused severe financial hardships, and I do not have the ability to pay for a membership."

2. "I find this whole situation distasteful, and I don't want to deal with you. I don't like you, but social convention prevents my being blunt enough to tell you so."

3. "I really don't know what my objection is. It just doesn't feel right. Quite frankly, the club looks a little run-down to me."

GETTING TO THE HEART OF SALES RESISTANCE

The fitness consultant must get to the heart of the prospect's objection before it can be negotiated successfully. Before you can marshal the appropriate facts, logic, and evidence to resolve a vaguely stated objection, you must know the basis for the prospect's point of view. To make the correct response to customer concerns, you must know the underlying circumstances.

Most objections that an experienced salesperson hears are not original. If you have been selling for any length of time, your chance of encountering an objection you have not heard before is remote. Eighty percent of buyers will give you the same five or six objections. You should therefore be ready to handle each one in advance, and have practiced them in a training course or sales meeting first.

To deal effectively with the objections you hear, develop a worksheet to categorize them and the responses you use to answer them effectively. Write out your responses word-for-word, commit them to memory, and practice delivering each one so that it becomes a reflex action. Polish and refine your responses; keep a record of how they are received. You will soon be able to choose the best possible response from your prepared list for each situation you encounter. Exhibit 12.1 lists five basic categories of buyer resistance with examples of what the prospect might say or, in the case of hidden objections, might think.

Chapter 12 — Handling Objections

Exhibit 12.1

The Basic Categories of Buyer Objections

Club Objection
- The machines and equipment are not up-to-date.
- The club is too-crowded.
- Your club is not very well known; I prefer to deal with a large, established gym.
- Wasn't your club charged with some unethical price practices?

Objection to Salesperson (Hidden)
- You are poorly prepared.
- I don't like you.
- You have tried to dominate me from the moment I arrived.

Don't Want to Make a Decision
- I will come back at another time.
- I want to think it over.
- I don't have time to use a gym.

Service Objection
- Your staff may not be able to help me. I don't know the first thing about working out.
- I need someone helping me stay motivated at all times.
- Your personal trainers are too pricey when all I really need is some general guidance.

Price Objection (Possibly Hiding Real Objection)
- I can't afford it.
- Your membership pricing structure is out of line.
- I'm going to wait until your next membership special.

WHEN TO ANSWER OBJECTIONS

A lot more has been said about *how* to overcome objections than about *when* to answer them, but choosing the proper time to answer them is just as crucial as the answer itself. In determining when to answer an objection, you must consider the type, why it has been raised, the mood of the prospect, and in what phase of the presentation it is raised. Timing is important in any negotiation. Prospects introduce an objection at a time that favors their position. Why shouldn't you choose to handle it when the timing favors your position? Normally, there are four logical times for responding to the buyer's concerns:

1. Answer them *before* they arise.

2. Postpone the answer until *later* in the presentation.

3. Answer it *immediately* when it is raised.

4. Do not *answer an excuse*.

Anticipate and Forestall

Every club has both strengths and weaknesses. Because no gym is perfect, a prospect may well identify a negative feature or shortcoming in your facilities or services. Hoping that the prospect will fail to notice a negative feature is dangerous. Instead of waiting for the prospect to raise a specific objection, *anticipate* the objection and *forestall* or *answer* it in the presentation before the prospect can ask. You are thus able to make a more orderly presentation of benefits and maintain better control of the entire interview.

Weave into your presentation factual answers to anticipated objections so they are answered before the prospect verbalizes them. Anticipating objections requires a well-thought out, planned presentation delivered from the prospect's point of view and focusing on value. As an example of how you might *forestall* objections that come up over and over again, consider the two objections Rico Ochoa, a fitness consultant in Atlanta, was constantly hearing from prospects: "I don't have the money" and "I have to talk this over with my husband/wife." After the opening, get-acquainted chit-chat, Rico gets down to business by saying:

Mr. Mayer, I am working with people who can invest about $500 a year in something that will improve their health and well being, and who can also make their own decisions without consulting someone else first. Do you fit into these conditions?

This opener is admittedly forceful, but Rico prefers not to spend thirty minutes going through the entire presentation and then hear one of these familiar objections. Of course, dealing with an objection early in the presentation does not guarantee that it will not be raised again. However, you are at an advantage in such a situation for two reasons:

1. The objection has much less impact the second time.

2. You may recall the original answer, expand upon it, and then move into a close or back into the presentation.

Postpone the Answer

Some objections are better *postponed*. This tactic is logical when you are planning to cover that very point further along and the prospect has simply jumped ahead. To answer early might disrupt the flow of the presentation and make the answer less effective. For example, the prospect may ask about price–"How much is this going to cost me to join?"—before you have established the value of your club. If you answer immediately, the price may seem too high because the prospect has not yet learned enough about the facilities to make a value judgment. The price may depend upon which membership option is selected; in that case, you cannot quote an accurate price. You may need to build a better foundation before risking a confrontation with the prospect. You can postpone answering an objection by saying something like this:

That's an excellent question, and I can certainly understand why you want to ask it. Let me write it down so I won't forget to answer it. And if you don't mind, let's postpone the answer until later. I have some information we need to consider first. Is that all right?

Salespeople often get price questions early in the interview. Here are two ways to postpone the premature price question:

1. I can appreciate that you would be interested in the price, and I assure you we will discuss it completely, but before we consider the price, I want to be sure that my service can satisfy your needs. Will that be all right?

2. Mr. Osmond, your concern for price is quite understandable. The actual amount for membership, however, will depend upon the options you ultimately select. Let's consider the price after we establish how our facilities can help you with your goals. Is that fair enough?

The price question should be answered near the end of the meeting after need, value, and benefits have been discussed. Should the prospect *absolutely insist* that you answer immediately, then by all means do so. You do not want to risk the question remaining in his mind to block out everything else that follows.

Answer Immediately

Most valid objections should be answered when they are raised unless you have a logical reason to postpone them. If you feel the objection is valid and postponing an answer could cause problems, by all means handle it immediately. Answering an objection right away prevents it from festering in your prospect's mind and blocking out the more important information you are presenting.

"Never answer until you are sure of the real concern, and once it is discovered, answer in 30 seconds or less." A sincere and immediate response conveys professionalism, respect for the prospect's point of view, empathy, and listening skills. The right answer removes the resistance and promotes the sale.

Do Not Answer an Excuse

A final alternative is to simply not answer an excuse. Some issues don't have a worthwhile answer. On some sales calls, prospects raise concerns that have nothing to do with your discussion. They say things that have no relevance to the point you are trying to make. In reality, they are offering excuses for not joining rather than valid resistance.

Never try to answer an excuse. By acknowledging excuses, you may actually turn them into real objections in the prospect's mind. If you must reply to excuses, suggest to the prospect that you will answer them at the end of the presentation. If the question is a serious objection, the prospect will repeat it later.

Exhibit 12.2 summarizes the factors to consider in choosing the best time to deal with objections.

Chapter 12 — Handling Objections   210

Exhibit 12.2

Timing Answers to Objections: Points to Consider

Anticipate the Objection and Answer It Before It Arises

- This option should be considered only when you are fairly certain that the prospect will bring up the objection.
- Anticipating the objection prevents a future confrontation and shows your objectivity.

Postpone an Answer Until Later

- Postponing an answer allows you to present many more benefits that have the effect of reducing the significance of the objection.
- Postponing an answer allows you to maintain control of the interview by keeping to your own agenda.
- Postponing an answer gives you time to think about how you will answer the question. Better a good answer later than a poor one now.

Answer the Objection Immediately

- Answer immediately so the prospect can concentrate on the rest of the sales story.
- Answering immediately demonstrates that you are sincere
- An immediate answer prevents prospects from inferring that you are unable to answer.

Do Not Answer an Excuse

- Not acknowledging an objection is one way to separate it from an excuse. The serious prospect will repeat the objection.
- By not answering, you suggest that the excuse is not relevant and imply that bringing it up again is not necessary.

A SIX-STEP PLAN FOR DEALING WITH BUYERS' CONCERNS

Professional salespeople handle prospects' objections successfully by placing them in the proper perspective. They realize that well-handled objections become powerful aids. To handle them skillfully, you need a definite negotiation strategy so that you react naturally to buyers' concerns. Knowing that you have a strategy gives you confidence. Then you can welcome objections instead of shuddering at the very thought that the prospect may not go along with what you are saying. The six-step plan presented in Exhibit 12.3 should be internalized so that you use it instinctively and automatically.

Listen Carefully, Hear the Prospect Out

The relationship fitness consultant is happy when the prospect raises an objection because it provides the information needed to complete the sale. Never interrupt a prospect who is expressing an opinion. Listen carefully to what the prospect says. Observe the prospect's verbal and nonverbal behavior, and listen to what is *not* being said. Recognize the prospect's right to express opinions and concerns. The prospect is telling you what to do: "Give me more information," "Go over that membership agreement again; it wasn't clear," or simply "Reassure me one more time that this is a good decision for my health and well-being."

Exhibit 12.3

A Strategic Negotiating Plan for Overcoming Buyers' Concerns

1. Listen carefully and hear the prospect out.

Learning to listen is not difficult, just unusual. We were born with two ears and one tongue. Listen twice as much as you talk. The buyer will tell you what you need to know. Just listen!

2. Confirm your understanding of the objection.

The key is to clarify and classify the objection. What type of objection is it and into what category does it fall?

3. Acknowledge the prospect's point of view.

Prepare the prospect for your answer. Don't just tear into your answer. After all, the buyer has a reason for stating the objection. Show concern for his or her feelings. Practice empathy.

4. Select a specific technique.

No one technique works best for all prospects. It must fit your behavioral style as well as that of the prospect.

5. Answer the objection.

The answer must satisfy the buyer if a sale is to result, and it must be complete and prompt. Get a commitment from the prospect.

6. Attempt to close; if the close is not completed, continue the presentation.

After answering a major objection, ask for the membership. The worst that can happen is that the buyer will say no. If that happens, continue with the presentation.

Chapter 12 — Handling Objections

Confirm Your Understanding of the Objection

Restate the prospect's objection to make sure you understand just what it is. This is a critical negotiation tactic. Use your own words and repeat what the prospect was saying to *clarify* and *classify* the real objection, and to indicate to the prospect that you understood what was said. In addition, you give yourself time to formulate an answer. Restating the objection in a sympathetic manner dissolves the prospect's defensiveness and helps you avoid the temptation to argue. Say, "Now as I understand it, your position is … ," and then explain the prospect's position in your own words. When you prove you understand, the prospect is ready to listen to you.

Your purpose here is to *evaluate* and *isolate* the stated concern. Determine whether the reason given for not buying is the *real* reason, simply an *excuse*, or a statement *hiding* the actual objection. You may decide to answer immediately, not answer an excuse, or seek more information. If you need more information before you can answer, ask questions until you have the information you need. There are a number of questions you might ask the prospect that can help you isolate the real issue and confirm your understanding. They include:

1. Other than that, is there any other reason that would prevent you from joining?

2. I am glad you brought that out into the open. Is this your only concern?

3. If we can work together to find a solution to this important concern, would that help you make a decision to join with us today?

Acknowledge the Prospect's Point of View

All successful negotiators find points of agreement with their prospects before beginning to answer an objection. Agree as far as possible before answering, and take responsibility for any misunderstanding. If the prospect indicates a bad experience with your club, believe it. Find a way to cushion your response so that it has a chance of convincing the prospect. After all, prospects believe they have good reasons for not joining and give you those reasons. Instead of arguing directly, soften your answer and say something like this:

- *I can certainly understand how you feel, Mr. Maloney. Others have had much the same feeling when I first presented the concept to them. (Then provide a plausible explanation.)*

- *I appreciate your concern, Mr. Maloney, and you do have a relevant point. Thank you for bringing it to my attention. (And you really should appreciate it.)*

Select a Specific Technique

In the next two sections of this chapter, eight techniques are detailed for use in formulating answers to the types of sales resistance you may encounter. Not all of them work all the time. In deciding which of the techniques to use, take these factors into consideration:

1. The prospect's *behavioral* style

2. The *stage* of the negotiation process in which the objection is raised

3. The *mood* (argumentative or receptive) of the prospect

4. How *many times* the objection has come up

5. The *type* of objection (searcher, excuse, stall, or service)

You must decide quickly on the technique you will use and avoid showing that an objection has upset you. Keep in mind that far too many variables operate in a given selling situation to guarantee that every objection can be answered satisfactorily.

Answer the Objection

Negotiation is persuasion, not manipulation. Avoid explanations that merely cloud the issue and cause prospects to feel that you are trying to pressure them. The answer, however, must be conclusive; don't close off your answer with the question still up in the air. Present only as much information as required to gain the prospect's cooperation and commitment. Minimize the objection by not dwelling on it. Say just enough to dispose of it to the prospect's satisfaction. Be honest and factual, and do not promise anything that you, your club, or its services cannot deliver.

People have their own needs, viewpoints, and ways of looking at things. Be sure to consider the prospect's ego and help the prospect to win. Your answer should include a benefit and should be shaped to fit the behavioral style of that person. Finally, confirm that your answer satisfied the prospect. Gain agreement by suggesting something such as, "Am I correct in assuming that I have completely satisfied you regarding the variety of resistance training equipment we provide?"

Attempt to Close

Closing opportunities exist at various times throughout the entire negotiation process. Recognizing those times and capitalizing upon them is up to you. When you have successfully answered a major objection, you have created an opportunity to close, especially if you are near the end of the presentation. Attempt a trial close before continuing with the presentation.

The trial close gets a prospect's reaction without exerting any pressure for making a definite decision. It may be used at any point in the sales presentation to test the water to see whether you have presented enough information for the prospect to make a decision. Typical trial closes start with "If you were to join," "In your opinion," or "How do you feel about..."

If you receive positive buying signals from the prospect at this point, you can attempt to close. If the close proves unsuccessful, get back on track and continue the presentation until another opportunity presents itself.

FIVE SPECIFIC TECHNIQUES FOR NEGOTIATING OBJECTIONS

Keep in mind that with any technique you must produce evidence to prove the validity of what you say. Techniques do not establish belief and credibility; that is your job. Techniques are merely vehicles for organizing your answer and your support for it.

After an objection has been clarified and classified, you are in an excellent position to respond by using one or more of the following techniques.

THE OFFICIAL HANDBOOK FOR HEALTH CLUB SALES

1. Feel, Felt, Found

This practical technique overcomes a stall or a very personal concern. It can counter prospect hostility, pacify an unhappy customer, or inform someone who does not yet clearly understand the value of your club and its services. Answer the prospect with this language:

> I can understand how you *feel*.... I have had other members who *felt* the same way until they *found* out....

This approach serves several purposes. It shows prospects that you understand their concerns, and it reassures the prospect that having this kind of objection is normal. Now the stage is set to introduce information that can change the prospect's way of thinking. This technique says that other people who are now members had similar misgivings but changed their minds after they found out some new information. These new facts allow the prospect to reevaluate your proposition. This approach can also stress the facts without creating an argument or conflict. For example:

> **Female Prospect:** *"I don't want to workout with weights because I'll get big muscles and look ugly!"*

> **Fitness Consultant:** *"I understand how you FEEL, Mrs. Heggem. Many of our female members initially FELT the same way, however they have FOUND just the opposite to be true. You see, women do not have significant amounts of the male hormone testosterone in their system, which is largely responsible for building big muscles. They have FOUND that exercising with weights has added shapes and curves they've never had before, and improved strength, flexibility, and tone! Now, do you think you might add some weight exercising to your fitness program?"*

The Feel, Felt, Found idea is a very powerful technique that works very well. Practice using it along with the other techniques discussed here and your sales productivity will multiply!

2. Compensation or Counterbalance Method

At times, a prospect may join in spite of certain valid objections. The prospect may be partly right or may have misunderstood a portion of what you said. Accept and admit any truth in the objection. Admit that your club or one of its services does have the disadvantage that the individual has noticed and then immediately point out how the objection is overshadowed by other specific benefits of the facilities. Your job is to convince the prospect that the compensating benefits provide enough value that the disadvantage should not prevent them from joining. By admitting the objection, you impress the prospect with your sincerity and sense of fair dealing. Then you can select the real strengths of your offering to offset any negative feelings. A good way to deal with this situation is to provide documentation such as *statistical evidence*, *a third-party endorsement,* or the *case history* of a current member who faced a similar situation that relates to the potential member's fitness concerns.

3. Ask "Why?" or Ask a Specific Question

This method is helpful not only for separating excuses from real objections but also for overcoming objections. You can use questions to narrow a major, generalized objection to specific points that are easier to handle. If the prospect says, "I don't like to associate with your gym," ask, "What is it that you don't like about our club?" The answer may show a past misunderstanding that can be cleared up. If the prospect complains, "I don't like the look of your group classes," ask, "What do you object to concerning our aerobics classes?" The objection may be based on a relatively minor aspect that can be changed or is not true of all classes.

Another value of this method is that some objections sound flimsy once they are put into words. The prospect may conclude that the objection is of little consequence and write it off without your needing to do anything.

4. Deny the Objection

One way to answer buyer resistance is simply to assert that the prospect is wrong. This technique must be used with caution or it will antagonize prospects. You can sometimes tell prospects they are wrong but you have to be careful how you do it. You could *win the argument but lose the sale.*

The denial technique is useful when the person clearly has the wrong information. Either a portion of the presentation was misunderstood or someone else has supplied incorrect information. Point out that the information is wrong, but not by means of a direct, frontal assault. Present the denial sympathetically, thoughtfully, and with sincerity.

After listening attentively to the buyer's concern, begin by saying:

> "I don't believe I quite understand what you are saying." (This response allows the buyer time to cool down emotionally and perhaps to soften the statement. It also gives you the opportunity to regain your composure).

After the prospect repeats the incorrect information, respond in this manner: "I don't know how you could have gotten that impression. I really must have stated my position poorly; please let me correct it for you." A bit more forceful statement would be, "Fortunately for me, that is not the real situation. I have some other information that does not support what you just told me."

5. Boomerang Method

The boomerang method allows you to agree with prospects yet show them that their objections need not prevent them from joining. This method is often used in a situation where the point to which the prospect is objecting is actually a sales point in favor of joining. The boomerang method involves agreeing with the objection and then making another statement *that translates the objection into a reason for joining.* For example, here is a typical objection and your response if you are attempting to presell memberships of a brand new club in the area:

> **Prospect**:*"Your club is too new to this area. I do not want to join a club I have never heard of before. You may be closed in six months."*

> **Fitness Consultant** (**Turn the objection into a sales point**): *"There is no question that our club is new to your area; that's why we are eager to build awareness for our facilities. We intend to spend thousands of dollars to tell potential members about our gym. And because we are brand new, we have state-of-the-art-equipment and new techniques not yet available in any other club in the area. Plus, we have amazing specials and incentives that really benefit those who sign up early. We are even giving away free memberships at our open house!"*

The *boomerang method* works well when the prospect lacks complete information or perceives a drawback that actually may not exist. Be careful of the image you project when using this technique. If prospects feel that you are directly challenging them or perhaps patronizing them, then you could be in for a real battle. In that case, you might as well pull out your boxing gloves because you will have more use for them than you will for your membership forms.

Chapter 12 — Handling Objections **218**

A MINDSET FOR NEGOTIATING PRICE RESISTANCE

One type of objection surfaces so frequently that it requires additional examination. Your prospects and members want as much for their money as they can get. While that's not unexpected, you can't provide value-added service at reasonable prices if you give up too much at the negotiating table. How many times each week do you suppose a fitness consultant hears, "I just think your price is too high." To succeed in selling, you must see this type of sales resistance for what it is and overcome it.

Your club priced their memberships so they would sell. Never be afraid to ask the full value for your offering, but be prepared with *solid evidence* to support the price you are asking. Do not be defensive or *apologetic*. You must believe that the price you are quoting is actually much less than the value your club will give the prospect.

The following table is a list of related words that mean the same thing but create two very different images in the prospect's mind. Take a look at the words in the negative column, examine whether you use any of those words in your presentation when discussing price, and replace them with the positive words in the corresponding column to soften your price presentation and avoid potential objections due simply to your choice of vocabulary.

Creating Positive Pictures With Words

Negative Words	Positive Words
Contract	Agreement
Down Payment	Initial Investment
Monthly Payment	Monthly Investment
Objection	Concern
Deal	Opportunity
Sell or Sold	Get them Started
Cheaper	More Economical
Pitch	Presentation
Problem	Challenges

The price objection is more difficult to pin down because it can mean so many different things. The final price paid for membership depends upon the length of membership, the type of discounts available, whether any tanning packages are included, whether the member chose to purchase a personal training package, free trial periods, any money-back guarantees, and myriad other price-related variables. Then, too, the prospect may not really be objecting to the price but may just be hiding the real reason for not buying. When prospects say, "I can't afford it" or "Your prices are just too high," they may just be saying, "You have not convinced me that the value I will receive here is worth the price I have to pay to get it." Often the buyer's concerns or questions about price represent an incomplete sales job!

If your gym has exclusive features that are not readily apparent, convert them to benefits and sell those benefits as this classic example of Ma McGuire in Exhibit 12.4 illustrates.

Exhibit 12.4

Sell Benefits to Overcome the Question of Price

Two farm wagons stood in a public market. Both were loaded with potatoes in bags. A customer stopped before the first wagon.

"How much are potatoes today?" she asked the farmer's wife, who was selling them.

"A dollar and a quarter a bag," replied the farmer's wife.

"Oh, my," protested the woman, "that is pretty high, isn't it? I gave one dollar for the last bag I bought."

"Taters has gone up," was the only information the farmer's wife gave. The housewife went to the next wagon and asked the same question. But Ma McGuire "knew her potatoes," as the saying goes. Instead of treating her customer with indifference, she replied:

"These are specially fine white potatoes, madam. They are the best potatoes grown. In the first place, you see, we only raise the kind with small eyes so that there will be no waste in peeling. Then we sort them to grade out culls so you get only full-sized, good potatoes. Then we wash all our potatoes clean before sacking them, as you see. You can put one of these bags in your parlor without soiling your carpet — you don't pay for a lot of dirt. I'm getting $1.50 a bag for them — shall I have them put in your car or will you take them now?"

Ma McGuire sold two bags, at a higher price than her competitor asked, in spite of the fact that the customer had refused to buy because she thought the price was too high!

THREE METHODS FOR OVERCOMING THE QUESTION OF PRICE

Face the fact that you will not always have the lowest-priced memberships to sell in the area. Be prepared to justify your asking price and show that it is fair. Understand and be able to apply the differential competitive advantages you have in location, equipment, personal training, or member service superiority. There are a number of negotiation tactics that can help you overcome the price obstacle. You may respond to the question of price by using one or a combination of the following methods.

1. Break the Price Down

The price that sounds huge in its entirety often sounds much smaller when you break it down into weekly or even daily increments and compare it to how the customer normally spends extra money. If the prospect is really objecting to the absolute magnitude of the price, then a logical response is to *break the total cost down* over a period of time. Here is an example of how you might use this technique:

> *I am glad you mentioned price, and I can certainly appreciate your concern. $720 for a two-year agreement may seem like a lot. But just imagine, that's really less than $1 per day! So for less than the price of your daily cup of coffee and a newspaper, you can enjoy these state-of-the-art facilities with an experienced and helpful staff. What a small price to pay for better health! Like you said, don't you want to make your husband proud because you finally shed those last few pounds? You may just decide to take that beach vacation this summer because you will be feeling so good about yourself!*

Compare the one-time price of membership to the amount of money the prospect will save after years of using your club. The clearer you make the distinction between what your prospects pay and what they get, the easier for them to recognize your club's great value. Talk about the initial and ultimate costs. Look at the *price-cost-value* comparison from two perspectives: *Price* represents the initial amount paid; *cost* is the amount the buyer pays over time.

2. Use the Presumption of Exclusivity

What can you do when the price for your club's membership is higher than that being asked by a competitor? Stress those features that are *exclusively* yours. What does your gym have that the competition cannot offer? No two fitness clubs are exactly alike. You will find strengths and weaknesses in any offering. Analyze the competition to see why they have a lower price. If your analysis indicates that you are offering more, then your task is to drive home those exclusive features. You may have to show more interest in the prospect than a competitor who concentrates only on price. Go out of your way to isolate other needs of the prospect for which you can provide assistance.

If your club has a higher price, then it must be because you offer more to your members. Identify your superior advantages and convince the prospect that the extras can be obtained only from your club. In other words, justify the price with facts. Determine what the prospect wants more than anything else from your club and then identify the features that satisfy those fitness goals and wants. This is what Mack Hannan calls the *presumption of exclusivity*. Concentrate on those features until the prospect feels that only with you can his or her needs be completely satisfied.

If a prospect gives you a hard time about price, stop selling price. Show what the money buys. Make the price seem unimportant in comparison to the value received. You may proceed something like this:

> *Mrs. Myers, allow me to share some information with you. The lower prices of our competitor may not necessarily be the best for you. Let's look at the quality of our club and why we are more expensive. We hire only experienced staff and pay them a wage they deserve for their expertise, purchase superior-grade machines and equipment, and have a state-of-the-art group fitness and spinning room. Our price includes options for personal training; our staff is skilled at helping you at any time on the gym floor. You will have 24-hour access to the facilities with unlimited tanning, and we also provide child care during peak hours. We don't fight your complaints; we settle them promptly and equitably. The price paid for solutions to your fitness needs should be based on what gives you the best solution. Don't you agree?*

Draw the picture clearly and convincingly. Sell quality and exclusivity when the prospect argues price. If you sell the exclusive features properly, the prospect is not even thinking about price by the end of the presentation. Most buyers are fair-minded if you show why your club must get the price it does.

Chapter 12 — Handling Objections

3. Use Comparison

Be prepared to present logical reasons for the price you are asking. One way you can do this is to compare the quality of your memberships to something in the prospect's own daily life, such as where they work. If you asked the prospect about their job during the pre-tour, you could use the following example to stress that you both are selling superior services/products:

> *Mr. Becker, your own company makes a high-grade product that commands an exceptionally high price, and deservedly so. Your products warrant their outstanding reputation because of the top-quality materials used to make them, right?*
>
> *Well, our club provides only the top-of-the-line, state-of-the-art equipment along with sales professionals whose only goal is to help you reach your health and fitness potential. Oh, you can join less expensive clubs than ours, but you would not be satisfied with their limited services.*

Acknowledging the superior nature of your prospect's products and suggesting that their company and your club are two of a kind makes considerable sense. This approach elevates your club to the same level of pride prospects may have in their jobs.

If you choose to make comparisons, be sure you have facts to substantiate your claims. Case histories and testimonials are useful for this purpose. For example, Jake Shores, a veteran personal trainer in Charleston, SC, focuses on his current clients' achievements and performance and uses referrals to build trust. "My members are more concerned about what happens after they sign a membership agreement than the actual price," says Shores.

He provides prospects with a current members' referral list, encouraging them to contact any or all of them. Shores uses his club's reputation to build trust and justify the higher price of his personal training packages. Visual evidence and verifiable case histories produce powerful comparisons for justifying membership package prices.

THE OFFICIAL HANDBOOK FOR HEALTH CLUB SALES

Handling The Crunch Technique

There are seven words that drive fitness consultants crazy: **"You've got to do better than that."** Here are six responses from fitness consultants who handle the crunch technique with success. They use answers like:

1. *"I understand that you want a lower price, and we will be more than happy to lower it to the level closer to what you have in mind. Let's review the options that you'd like to remove from your membership package, so we can meet your needs."*

2. *"We are building our club up to a quality, not down to a price. A lower price would prevent us from staying in business and serving your fitness needs later on."*

3. *"It is my understanding that we were discussing the sale of a membership and not the sale of our club."*

4. *"How much better can you get than rock bottom? You see, our policy is to quote the best price first. We have built our reputation on high quality and integrity— and it's the best policy."*

5. *"I'd be glad to give you the names of two members so you can find out how much they paid for their membership. And you'll see it's exactly the same as we are asking you to pay. We could not develop our reputation without being fair to everyone."*

6. *"I appreciate the opportunity to do a better selling job. Obviously, you must have a reason for looking exclusively on the dollar side of the membership. Let's review the value that you'll be receiving…"*

Always remember when dealing with price objections that your prospects know it is unwise to pay too much, but it is actually worse to pay too little. Your customers may pay too much and lose a little money, but when they pay too little, they feel that they could lose everything because the club could not provide what they needed or wanted.

The common law of business balance prohibits paying a little and getting a lot—it can't be done. So be patient with your prospects and focus on the benefits if they still seem fixated on price.

Chapter 12 — Handling Objections

If the prospect has been properly qualified, objections are really *buying signals.*

Handling Objections
REFOCUS

- Success in handling objections depends upon your attitude. If you assume that the sale is over when you hear an objection, it will be. If you regard an objection as an invitation to continue negotiating, you are likely to enjoy a successful close.

- Objections enable prospects to avoid the risk of making a decision that has potentially unpleasant consequences.

- Some objections are valid and indicate either a logical reason for not buying or a need to present additional information before your prospect makes a buying decision.

- Classify and clarify the objections according to their type and apply the appropriate plan to overcome them.

- The six-step strategic negotiating plan for dealing with buyers' concerns gives you the opportunity to handle whatever objections you may encounter.

- Experts in overcoming objections record the objections, study them to determine which ones they hear most often, and develop logical answers to use in the future

- You will not always have the lowest-priced memberships. Apply the competitive advantages you have in equipment, facilities, staff, or service superiority and respond to the question of price with one of the following methods: break the price down, the presumption of exclusivity, or use comparison.

Chapter 12 — Handling Objections 226

Success in the End is What Counts — Not Failure in the Beginning

His failures far exceeded his successes:

- 1832 lost his job
- 1832 defeated in the race for the legislature
- 1833 failed in business
- **1834 elected to legislature**
- 1835 sweetheart died
- 1836 suffered a nervous breakdown
- 1838 defeated for speaker in the legislature
- 1843 defeated for nomination for Congress
- **1846 elected to Congress**
- 1848 lost renomination
- 1849 rejected for job as land officer
- 1854 defeated for Senate
- 1856 defeated for nomination for vice-president
- 1858 defeated for Senate
- **1860 elected sixteenth president of the United States**

Abraham Lincoln

Chapter 13

Closing the Sale

FOCAL POINTS

- Attitudes towards closing.
- Functions of the close.
- The value of persistence.
- How to deal with rejection.
- Knowing when to close.
- Different types of closes.

A CLOSING FRAME OF MIND

A *close* can be defined as a question asked or an action taken by a fitness consultant designed to elicit a favorable decision from the prospect to join. It is always related to the specific objective you identified for the club presentation.

Closing the sale is not really difficult for the salesperson who is conducting a professional presentation held under favorable conditions, including the presence of a qualified prospect. Although closing a sale is actually quite natural, far too many consultants have adopted such a distorted view of the close that they dread trying, even though the close is their only reason for being there. In fact, according to Chris Hegarty, in sixty-three percent of all presentations, salespeople fail to ask for the prospect's business. The usual scenario goes like this:

Well, Mr. Webster, that's about all I have to tell you. Is there anything else you would

Chapter 13 — Closing the Sale 228

like to ask me? No? Okay, I guess you can give me a call or stop back in if you would like to join. Have a good day. I enjoyed talking with you.

When you are watching the potential member walking away wondering, "What happened? I thought sure I had that membership. What did I do wrong?" The usual answer is that you did not do anything *wrong*. You probably just did not do *anything*.

The sale has actually been made or lost long before the time arrives to sign the agreement. The final step should be just a formality – a necessary step, but not one that requires making weighty decisions. Unless you complete the selling process by asking for the membership, the only title you deserve is *conversationalist*.

> When each step in the sales process is handled correctly, the close is the natural conclusion to a successful sales interview.

Closing is not a separate event tacked onto the end of a club presentation. It is something that happens all along during the course of the meeting. Closing would probably be easier to understand if someone had devised a better name for it. Because the word *close* suggests something that occurs at the end of a process, fitness consultants seem to feel that it is an isolated segment of the selling process that must be approached in some exact manner to produce success, but the opportunity to close may occur at any time during the meeting. The wise professional watches for and takes advantage of every closing opportunity. Close a membership as soon as you can get it! Closing begins the moment you speak the first word to the prospect and continues throughout the whole process until the contract is signed.

Failure at the close is the result of inadequate completion of the prior steps in the sales process: inadequate prospecting, incomplete qualifying of the prospect, or too little probing to determine the prospect's real fitness needs and concerns. As a result, the presentation has focused on the wrong features and benefits, or the wrong evidence has been supplied to support claims for your club.

A prospect's failure to join does not automatically brand you as a poor closer. Studying your entire performance to find the weak link in the chain is necessary. Focusing only on closing as an indicator of sales skill is like expecting to hear Tiger Woods say that putting is all that matters in golf. Of course, the final putt that wins the championship is the most obvious success moment, but secure agreement throughout the sales process and the final step is the easiest one.

FUNCTIONS OF THE CLOSE

The Need for a Close

Even when all the steps leading to the close have gone well, the prospect may still hesitate. Logically, the prospect would gladly sign the agreement when a professional fitness consultant has a quality gym and membership plan to offer, has presented meaningful benefits, has a carefully planned strategy for servicing member needs, makes an impressive sales presentation, and successfully answers all of the buyer's concerns. However, the *moment of decision* is difficult for most people. Buyers take many risks: They must live with the membership and pay for it, and they may be forced to justify the decision to someone else. Risks are threatening to most people. Of course, you may also feel some strain at the moment of decision. You may be asking yourself, "Have I told the prospect enough? Did I find the real need? Did I read the verbal and nonverbal clues correctly? Is this the best moment to close? What if the answer is no?"

> **The art of closing sales is not the process of persuading people to make decisions, but the art of making decisions with which people will agree.**

Reassure and Close. Consider how the prospective buyer is probably feeling and thinking. Do you remember the first time you jumped off a diving board? You thought, "the board is too high; I can't swim that far; I'll choke on some water; I think I see sharks." You thought about all the possible bad consequences. Perhaps a friend in the water encouraged you to try. When you finally jumped, you discovered that the water was fine, just as your friend had said. In the sales situation, you are the friend in the water, you know how the prospect feels and you offer the needed reassurance: "Come on in; you'll be glad you took that first dive; I'm here to help if you need me." Your attitude must be that you respect prospects and their decisions, whether or not they decide to jump in. You continue to reassure them until they finally make a decision. The next time you advise them to add on personal training or renew their membership, they will trust your recommendation more readily.

WIFE asks: Dear, do you have difficulty making decisions?

HUSBAND responds: Well, yes and no.

Once prospects agree that they can benefit from your club, your responsibility is to guide them to a close. You must never be discouraged by no. If you honestly believe that a sale is an exchange of mutual benefits, then a no should set up this train of reasoning: Prospects are asking me to explain once more that this decision will help them reach their fitness goals, so I will continue to reassure and close. Do not be discouraged when the buyer hesitates. People do not like to make decisions; without assistance and reassurance, some simply cannot make decisions at all. *There is no agony like that of indecision.*

A CLOSING CONSCIOUSNESS

A Closing Attitude

The most important factor in successfully closing a sale is not having the lowest priced membership or the biggest club. *Your attitude* is the crucial factor. You must have an absolute belief in what you are selling, and you must *expect* to be successful. If you assume that you will successfully close the sale, the prospect interprets your confidence as reassurance that the gym will provide the needed benefits. Your positive attitude makes the difficult decision, "Yes, I'll join" much easier. All they have to do is say, "Yes, you're right" when you recommend that they join. Confidence is contagious; it infects people and draws them to your side.

> *Mr. Evert, we have agreed on the large variety of cardio equipment we provide, the skill of our staff in assisting you to get started, the convenience of our club to your office, and the benefits you will receive from your personal training sessions. We could significantly speed up the process if we could settle now when you would like your first training session with Billy. Is Friday okay with you?*

When you maintain a positive mental attitude, a high level of self-confidence, and belief in your club, you create an atmosphere within which you can handle the day-to-day rejections that are inevitable in the world of selling. Steve Simms,

231 *THE OFFICIAL HANDBOOK FOR HEALTH CLUB SALES*

noted author and speaker, reveals how to *shake off the shackles of rejection*. When prospects don't join, you know that the rejection is seldom directed toward you personally. It is a reflection of their own differing opinion about what will best fill their needs or a result of their hesitancy to make a decision that they perceive as a risk. In other words, you have lost nothing except a little of your time, but the individuals who say no have lost the opportunity to benefit from using your club and of being your personal customer. The bigger loss is theirs.

Persistence

Kirk Bingham, a fitness consultant in Norman, OK, says, "You should push, but never be pushy." Bingham regularly calls on local businesses to convince them to come and try out his club. He suggests that "making repeat, *meaningful* calls demonstrates to prospects that you are not going to give up. The idea is to be graciously tenacious—without being obnoxious." Focused persistence involves asking whether doing *this* today will get you *that* tomorrow. Successful salespeople like Kirk Bingham never take no for an answer unless it is in everyone's interest to do so. If the business is worth having, it is worth going after repeatedly—with repeated calls or repeated attempts to close during a single call. The extra effort often makes the difference between success and failure.

How often do you ask prospects for their business? The answer often given is "one more time." Realistically, you should be prepared to ask *at least* four or five times. A study of several thousand salespeople demonstrates how important persistence really is:

1. 48 percent of those interviewed quit after the first contact with a prospect.

2. 73 percent give up after the second contact.

3. 85 percent quit after the third contact.

4. 90 percent give up after the fourth contact.

Shake the Shackles of Rejection

First of all, you can disassociate yourself from the rejection by pretending you're watching the disappointing encounter from a distance. In your imagination, pretend to step out and away from your body, then turn around and watch yourself and the prospect. From that view, the pain and discouragement of rejection are significantly diminished. You can also add humor by pretending you're watching your sales manager get rejected instead of yourself.

Second, try delaying judgment. When you finish a sales call that ends in rejection, refuse to evaluate your situation in a negative way. Disagree with any feelings that tell you things are awful, and instead say to yourself, "It's too soon to tell. Maybe this is awful, maybe it isn't. I'll decide later." Then, like Scarlett O'Hara, say to yourself, "I'll think about that tomorrow."

Steve Simms is president of Attitude-Lifter Enterprises and author of *Mindrobotics: How To Be Happy For The Rest Of Your Life.*

Chapter 13 — Closing the Sale

The most dramatic statistic from the study shows that the *ten percent* of salespeople who continue past the fourth contact, end up with *eighty percent* of the business.

People will not ask questions about your membership or facility if they weren't interested. Have you ever made a purchase without asking questions? People want to buy but they detest being sold. To close a prospect you must ask the right questions and work to maintain the rapport you have already established with them. Always agree with the prospect, never argue, and this can be done by never saying, "BUT." The word, "BUT" indicates a conflict, instead use, "AND".

> *"I understand how you feel, and here is another way of looking at it..."*

Selling must be a side-by-side, step-by-step process, involving both prospect and fitness consultant, in which you *earn the right to close*. When you understand the problems faced by prospects, stay with them through the problem-solving process, watch for buying signals, and time the close to fit the prospect's behavioral style, your chances of a successful close skyrocket. Opportunities to close occur a number of times during the sales process; recognize them, persist, and ask for the order. Exhibit 13.1 describes the kind of persistence needed for success in sales.

Dealing With Rejection

Exhibit 13.1

Persistence

One of the best examples of persistence is a story you probably loved as a child: *Green Eggs and Ham*. This Dr. Seuss classic describes the attempt of the "salesman," Sam I Am, to induce a wary "prospect" to try a meal of green eggs and ham. When his first straightforward offer is rejected, Sam I Am tries one assumptive close after another: "Do you want them here or there? Would you like them in a box or with a fox? Do you want them in a house or with a mouse?" Finally, the prospect tries green eggs and ham and is surprised to find them quite delicious. His no's seemingly never registered with the persistent Sam I Am. If you have not read *Green Eggs and Ham* lately, visit the children's section of the library and learn the story's important lesson about persistence.

Dr. Seuss, *Green Eggs and Ham* (New York: Random House, 1960)

So many fitness consultants leave the profession because of their inability to cope with the day-to-day sense of rejection they experience. They interpret a prospect's refusal to join as a message that says, "You are personally worthless." Sales professionals must learn to deal with rejection by keeping a positive attitude about themselves and how they make their living. True, they feel disappointment if they fail to close, but successful consultants focus in on the sense of accomplishment they feel when they do close a sale. To keep from being overwhelmed, accept the fact that rejection exists, see it for what it really is, and never make the mistake of allowing it to serve as an absolute measure of your own self-worth.

What is a good batting average in selling? Professional baseball players who average .300 (three hits for every ten times at bat) or more for a full season are a small minority of players in the major leagues. Imagine failing to get a base hit 70 percent of the time. Consider some of the great names in baseball history:

- Babe Ruth hit 714 career home runs, but struck out 1,330 times.

- Cy Young won 515 games, but lost 313.

- Ty Cobb stole 96 bases one year but was caught stealing 38 times.

Baseball fans ignore the failures and concentrate on the successes of their favorite players. The attitude of all professionals is, "I may have *failed,* but that does not mean *I am a failure.*"

A fitness consultant who never hears a 'no' is no salesperson, only an *order taker.* Rejection is as much a part of sales as getting dressed in the morning, and salespeople who can't or won't deal with it had better find another career. The first thing to remember when handling rejection is that you just can't take it personally. Refuse to permit anyone else to *make you* feel bad about yourself. Exhibit 13.2 describes six specific strategies for coping with rejection.

Exhibit 13.2

Six Tactics for Dealing with Rejection

- Remind yourself of exceptional salespeople and how many hundreds or thousands of rejections they had to face on their journey to success. You see, you are not alone!

- When you make mistakes, forgive yourself. Mistakes are great learning experiences, but to benefit from them you have to keep moving forward. Continue to generate, gather and harvest prospects. The more prospects you have, the better you feel.

- Give yourself a pep talk. Replace negative thoughts with positive ones such as, "I'm a great salesperson, and after they hear what I have to say, they'll want to buy from me."

- Remind yourself of the difference between self-worth and performance. Never equate your worth as a human being with your success or failure as a salesperson.

- Engage in positive self-talk. Separate your ego from the sale. The prospect is not attacking you personally. Say to yourself, "This prospect doesn't even know me; the refusal to buy cannot have anything to do with me as a person."

- Positively anticipate rejection and it will not overwhelm you. Expect it, but don't create it. Think in advance what your response to rejection will be.

Chapter 13 — Closing the Sale

WHEN TO CLOSE

Most of the sales you make will not close themselves. The closing curve shown in Figure 13.1 illustrates how the closing process works. The will-buy line (WBL) shows that some sales will be closed almost at once, others are easy sales, and that most can be closed with an interest-building club presentation. A few can never be closed. The key is recognizing the spots at which a close can be made—when the buyer gives a buying signal. The appearance of a buying signal is the critical moment during the presentation when a successful close is more likely.

When you sense the psychological moment to close do so immediately. A delay of even a few seconds may give prospects a chance to change their mind. If you fail to recognize these critical moments at which the prospect is most nearly ready to make a decision to join and continue to talk past them, the close becomes steadily more difficult. After a critical point is passed, you must buy back the prospect's readiness to decide. In other words, you must once again convince the prospect that joining is the proper decision. Talking too much and overselling is a much greater danger than underselling. Your attempts to close early and often eliminate the possibility of going past the point at which the prospect is ready to join.

The professional fitness consultant guides and directs the prospect's behavior. As you reach the point where the final decision is to be made, it's just as important for you to know *when to ask* for the membership as it is for you to know *how*

Figure 13.1

The Closing Curve

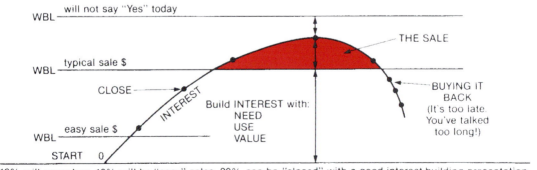

10% will never buy, 10% will be "easy" sales, 80% can be "closed" with a good interest-building presentation.

235 THE OFFICIAL HANDBOOK FOR HEALTH CLUB SALES

to ask. Instead of just watching passively for signs of interest, you must create situations in which interest can be generated and revealed.

The best psychological moment for closing may occur at any time during the presentation. When it comes, prospects *signal* in some way that you have convinced them and they are ready to join. You never have only one possible moment to close. You may be in the early stages of the presentation, you may have completely exhausted all the selling points you planned to present, or you may be somewhere in between.

RECOGNIZING BUYING SIGNALS

A *buying signal* is anything the prospect does or says that indicates readiness to join. Buying signals are all around us if we learn to recognize them. Unfortunately, it's all too easy to become so focused on your presentation that you overlook these signals even if they are obvious. Buying signals occur quickly and may be verbal, nonverbal, or both. Genuine buying signals show that the prospect has moved from evaluating the club to an appraisal of it. A buying signal may come in the form of a question. A prospect may ask you to repeat some point or benefit previously discussed or stop you right in the middle of the presentation to ask how soon they can begin with a personal trainer. However a buying signal comes, take advantage of it and close immediately. Always remember that when the prospect is ready to join, you will receive a signal.

The CHEF Technique

Just as the experienced chef in a fine restaurant knows precisely the right ingredients to blend to produce exquisite cuisine, similarly professional salespeople can exhibit chef like characteristics as they try to translate the combination of gestures fed to them by their prospects. Use the **CHEF** method to identify prospects' verbal and nonverbal buying signals.

Cheek Or Chin. When people touch or stroke their chin or cheek they are signaling satisfaction and gratification. Leaning forward and nodding the head in agreement says, I'm almost persuaded. In this instance, ask if you've answered all their questions, move quickly and ask for their business. Prospects that tighten their jaw muscles or cover their mouths suggest that they are not receptive to what you have to say. This is a critical time to ask questions to open them up.

Hands. Open and relaxed hands, especially with palms facing upward, are a sign that prospects may be ready to join. Rubbing their palms together signals that they are already assuming possession of a membership. Those individuals who steeple (like a church steeple) their hands together are indicating confidence or superiority. When the prospect's hands are fidgeting or forming a fist, they're more than likely skeptical, or worse yet, irritated. You must stop talking and find out what is wrong!

Eye contact. Maintaining consistent eye contact with you indicates the prospect is probably paying attention to what is being said, and the use and examination of the equipment shows the intensity of that commitment. This is a good time to request a buying decision. When the pupils of the prospect's eyes are dilated this signals relaxation, and you are on the right track. However, rolling or squinting of the eyes often means irritation or confusion. In addition, the rate at which a prospect blinks can indicate anger or excitement. A raised eyebrow can mean the prospect doesn't believe what you are saying. Something is wrong and you had better find out what that something is. If you sense this you might say, "You seem a bit uneasy with this. Please tell me what concerns or questions you have."

> Eye contact, or the lack of it, can signal to the salesperson a prospect's level of interest.

Friendly prospects. Prospects who are smiling, relaxed, or engaging you in conversation are telling you that you've earned their trust. A prospect indicates readiness to join by saying, "It sounds good, but I ought not to join." Give this prospect another reason to join. Reassure and ask for a decision. When prospects turn unfriendly, be sensitive and empathetic. After all, the basic reason for becoming experts at relationship selling is to create an atmosphere within which an act of trust can take place! People like to buy a membership from people who are like them.

The Trial Close

A *trial close* asks for an *opinion*; a *closing question* asks for a *decision*. A trial close, by asking for an opinion, serves as a thermometer that tells you whether the prospect is warm, hot, or cold to joining. It is designed to help you read the prospect's feelings and predict probable reactions. In Chapter 11, the tie-down question was discussed as one element in a *unit of conviction*. The tie-down and the trial close are used for basically the same purpose. When you get prospects agreeing with you throughout the presentation they are much more likely to agree with you when you ask the closing question, that is, when you make the formal request for their membership. You want to be careful not to talk past the sale. Close when the prospect wants to join.

Many fitness consultants think of closing as the last phase of a sales call. If they do, they may not get all the sales that they should. During every sales call there will be a number of opportunities to close the sale. How do you know the proper time? When in doubt, test the prospect with trial closes such as:

- "Is this what you're looking for in a gym?"

- "In your opinion, do you feel that the program I have outlined for you will meet your needs?"

- "Is there anything preventing you from taking the next step and enrolling with us today?"

- "What else do you need to make a decision?"

- "Isn't this the kind of club in which you could see yourself working out?"

- "Do you feel that we can help you achieve your fitness goals?"

Although it resembles a definite attempt to close, the trial close is used to probe and to reveal how far along the prospect has gone in the decision-making process. You do not need to ask a closing question if you know the prospect is not ready to join. The time to ask for the order is when the prospect is fully ready to join. You can, however, ask for an *opinion* at any time.

A Closing Question

A *closing question*, in contrast to the trial close, is designed to produce an answer that confirms the fact that the prospect has joined. Look at these three examples:

1. I will go ahead and give you the appropriate aerobics class schedule depending on when you will be coming in. You want to work out in the morning, right?

2. We can go ahead and set up your free personal training appointment for this week. Is Thursday a good day for the appointment?

3. Which of these two memberships is best for you?

Chapter 13 — Closing the Sale

When you ask a closing question, say *nothing* else until the prospect gives an answer. The pressure of silence is enormous. Silence is golden because of what it brings you in terms of the information you need. *Never miss the opportunity not to say something.* If you can remain silent after asking the closing question, only two outcomes are possible: 1) the prospect says yes or 2) the prospect gives a reason for not wanting to join. In either instance, you are better off than you were before you asked the question. If the answer is yes, you have a sale. If the prospect gives you a reason for not joining, a concern has surfaced that you can convert into another opportunity to close.

TYPES OF CLOSES

Become familiar with as many types of closing techniques as possible. One or two standard closes are not enough in the competitive selling arena that is filled with many different kinds of buyers, all with varying needs and personalities. You need a specific close for every occasion and for every type of prospect. If you attempt to use the same close for every prospect, you will walk away from much of the business that should be yours. The sales plan for each prospect calls for a specific type of presentation strategy; your plan should also extend to the type of close you use. However, just as circumstances often dictate some changes in your presentation, they also point up the need for shifts in your closing plans. Your *sales call plan* should provide the preferred closing routine to fit with the presentation you expect to deliver. Be sure to plan some alternative closing routines you can use in the event you find it is necessary to modify your presentation to fit into some special situation you encounter when the guest arrives for the appointment.

A master fitness colsultant with a full repertoire of closing techniques merely chooses one that fits the revised situation and moves on as though nothing unusual is occurring. The various closing methods shown in Exhibit 13.3 and described here are not the only methods available. Most of them are subject to combination with other methods to fit with your unique personality and your club's environment. Learn the principles upon which these techniques rest and adapt them to your needs.

Assumptive Closes

In a sense, every close is assumptive. You do not attempt to close until you have received one or more buying signals from the prospect and have reason to believe you have a better than even chance of success. When you enter every

Exhibit 13.3

Successful Closing Techniques

Assumptive close

Throughout the presentation, assuming that the prospect will join allows the prospect to make the decision more easily by presenting opportunities to make smaller or easier choices. Common assumptive closes include the continuous-yes close, the order-blank close, and the alternate of choice close.

Impending-event close

Stress the urgency to make a decision because something is about to happen that means the opportunity to join with the present advantages may be lost.

Balance-sheet close

You take an active part in the decision-making process to help the prospect understand that the reasons for joining heavily outweigh reasons not to join.

Direct close

Make a straightforward request for the order. Many buyers appreciate a no-nonsense approach, but be mindful of each prospect's behavioral style and use this approach only with those who welcome such tactics.

Summary close

Review the features and benefits of the offering with particular emphasis on selling points that generated the most prospect interest earlier in the presentation.

Call-back close

A few of your sales may not close on the first attempt. Offer to call back on a prospect or have them return with a specific purpose in mind and with new information.

Secondary Question Close

Pose the decision to join with a question, then ask a secondary minor point question. When the prospect answers the minor point question, the major question is actually carried with it.

Reassurance Close

You appeal to the prospect's emotional reasons for joining. If your prospect is indecisive, and you feel that you are losing them, give them a reason that may help overcome their hesitancy.

Similar Situation Close

Give an example of another member who was in a similar situation as your customer is. Remind the prospect that they, too, were hesitant but decided to join and now are so happy that they did.

Instruction Close

Prospects sometimes just need to be told what they should do. You are not forcing them; rather, you are providing instruction to the apprehensive prospect to help them get over that little hill of uncertainty.

Chapter 13 — Closing the Sale

sales situation with a positive expectation of success, you are assuming that the prospect will join at the close. Your attitude throughout the interview is assumptive. Say, "*When* you use the free weights" and "*As* your training program progresses." Avoid words like *if* and *should* because they are conditional and block closing action.

The assumptive approach to closing establishes a positive environment in which the prospect can more easily say yes. These closes work well with indecisive buyers who tend to be nervous about making a final decision. They ask the prospect for low-pressure commitments without putting them on the defensive. Asking questions such as the ones below prepares them for an eventual, "YES" response, and helps them see themselves as members:

- "Will you be using the club during the day or the evening?"

- "Will your wife be working out with you?"

- "How many aerobic classes do you plan on taking each week?"

Present them with minor decisions that give them the opportunity to appear decisive in a small matter while they are actually painlessly making the bigger decision at the same time.

The closes described below are common assumptive closes.

Continuous-Yes Close. By asking a series of questions throughout the sales presentation, all of which are designed to be answered in the affirmative, it becomes more difficult for buyers to say no when they've already said yes a number of times. That is why you must get agreement on minor points before you ask for the membership.

These questions begin in need discovery. For example: "I'd like to ask you a few questions that help me understand your particular needs. Would that be okay with you?" *Yes*. Continue them during the presentation: "Do you like the idea of having so many different aerobics classes to choose from?" *Yes*. During the closing phase you may ask: "Are you satisfied with the personal service we provide on the gym floor?" *Yes*. "Does the membership agreement seem fair and understandable to you?" *Yes*. "Then it seems we can go ahead and get you started today." *Yes*. These are all closed-end type questions, so you must be confident that you will receive an affirmative response before you ask them. When the final closing question is asked, the prospect is inclined to keep on agreeing with you. You have a sale.

Order-Blank Close. Begin to ask the prospect a series of questions and write the answers on the membership contract or agreement form. This is a very basic close, but works so well in this industry. Immediately following the prospect's selection of a membership, you simply reach for an agreement or a membership card and begin to fill it out. If they do not stop you then the membership has been sold. There are two parts to this technique. First, you must say something when reaching for the agreement or membership card such as:

- *"Let me show you how this looks on paper."*
- *"Let me take out a membership card for you."*

Then, ask a final closing question and begin filling out the membership agreement or the card.

- *"What is the correct spelling of your last name?"*
- *"What is your current address?"*

Continue to fill out the information and then ask for a signature. *"Now that we have reached agreement, I know you will want to get started using the club right away. Just indicate your approval by signing right here."*

Alternate of Choice Close. In general, people like to exercise their freedom of choice and salespeople like to lead their buyers toward an easy agreement. This well-known close consists of giving the prospect a choice between two positive alternatives. Here are some suggestions:

- *Which membership is best for you, the GOLD or the GOLD PLUS?*

- *Do you prefer to make a one time paid-in-full investment or is our monthly plan more convenient for you?*

- *When would you like your free personal training session — tomorrow or Friday?*

Chapter 13 — Closing the Sale 242

The idea behind the alternate of choice close is to offer the prospect a choice between A and B instead of a choice between joining or not joining. The question is not "Will you join?" but "Which plan?" or "When will you start?"

Impending Event Close

This close uses the sense of urgency that is suggested by some impending event such as a promotional membership package that will affect the terms of the decision. Use this close with discretion. It must be based on truth and must not seem manipulative. The most common inducements are concerns that membership prices are going up.

> *The club has announced that membership packages are as low as they have ever been, but won't stay this low for long. If we can sign you up today, you can benefit from this great promotion.*

Never use this close deceptively! Whatever the impending event is, it must be real and in the prospect's best interests to take advantage of a membership placed now. Because this close is often abused by unscrupulous salespeople, prospects are likely to be skeptical of it. Properly applied, this close can work wonders for your long-term credibility.

The Balance-Sheet Close

This practical, decision-making format is familiar to most prospects, and they will feel comfortable as you use it. The procedure involves using a blank sheet of paper with a line drawn down the center to form two columns. In the first column, list all the reasons for making an affirmative decision in favor of joining. These are the assets. In the second column, list all the questions or concerns about joining—the *liabilities* involved in saying yes. The closing process is an analysis of the two columns to show the prospect that the reasons for joining the club heavily outweigh the reasons for not joining. Give the prospect the opportunity to express agreement with your conclusions. The prospect must take an active part in the decision-making process.

As you build the balance sheet, resist the temptation to hurry. As you list each advantage for buying, pause and allow time for the prospect to absorb the idea. Be sure that you have many more ideas in favor of buying than opposed to it so that the number of reasons will be so impressive that you won't have to deal with the relative weights of individual reasons. To use the balance-sheet method, you can begin like this:

 Mrs. Bakker, the decision you are about to make is important. I know you want to be sure you are making a sensible choice. So that we will be sure to make the decision that is best for you, let's look at all the reasons in favor of signing up with us today and any questions or concerns about it. We can then determine which side weighs more and make your decision accordingly. Let's begin with the ideas that favor a positive decision today. Is that fair enough?

Take out a sheet of paper and begin to list the reasons for membership. Be sure to avoid the word *objection*. Instead of talking about the prospect's objections, state them as concerns or questions to be answered: "You expressed concern about the gym being too crowded ." When you use the word *objection* out loud, you are setting up the prospect and yourself as adversaries; if you are adversaries, one of you must win and the other must lose. You are looking for a win-win solution to the buying decision.

The Direct Close

The direct close is a straightforward request for membership. Once you have covered all the necessary features and benefits of your club and matched them with the buyer's dominant buying motives, you can ask with confidence, "Are you ready to get started today?" Many buyers appreciate a no-nonsense approach. Of course, be mindful of the buyer's behavioral style. *Amiables*, for example, could find this approach threatening. Be sure to keep the direct close positive. Avoid the word *don't*. "Why don't we begin today?" and "Why don't you try out an aerobics class this evening?" are open invitations to additional objections. Insertion of a negative into the close may implant doubt where none existed, and the prospect may try to tell you why not. Use positive statements like these:

1. *May I pencil you in with a personal training consultation for Tuesday of next week?*

2. *Would you prefer to rent a locker, or just use a day locker?*

3. *Let's go over the group aerobics schedule to decide when you will take your first class.*

When you use this type of closing statement, then you and your customer can make positive plans together.

The Summary Close

One of the best closing tactics is to summarize the major selling points made during the presentation. This method is especially good when the prospect must defend the membership to someone else such as a spouse. The repetition of benefits at this point overcomes the prospect's tendency to forget or overlook points previously identified as important to satisfying existing needs. Avoid mentioning any new benefits during this close. Bring up additional points only if the summary fails and you need more ammunition to answer new objections.

Concentrate in the summary close on those items that were of most interest to the prospect and that related directly to the dominant buying motives. For example:

 Mr. Cameron, let's review the major points on which we have agreed:

1. *Our circuit training will provide you with a quick and simple way to get a total body workout on your tight schedule.*

2. *Your wife will love our group aerobics classes.*

3. *We saw that several members who shared fitness concerns similar to yours have had much success with us here (review testimonials or case histories).*

4. *Our staff will help you any time you need assistance on the gym floor.*

5. *You'll receive a free personal training consultation for both you and your wife. These services are included in our basic price.*

This summary puts into capsule form the highlights of your sales story. It gives both you and the prospect an opportunity to reconsider what was covered throughout the sales interview.

Give the prospect an opportunity to agree that the summary is correct. Once agreement has been expressed, the prospect is in a positive frame of mind, and the time is ripe to get some sort of formal commitment. The summary close must be combined with some other closing technique to complete the sale. For example, you might use *the alternate of choice close* like this:

 Mr. Cameron, with all of these major benefits available, you can see that joining with us is a sound investment. If we've covered everything, can I go ahead and get you started today with a monthly payment plan or would you prefer to pay in full?

245 THE OFFICIAL HANDBOOK FOR HEALTH CLUB SALES

Call-Back Close

Many sales opportunities are lost every day because salespeople take the prospect's decision not to join as permanent. Studies show that many memberships are won by fitness consultants who call numerous times on the same prospect. Each time you call them, stop by their office, or they return to see you, you must present new information or ideas that will stimulate them to join. If you have the same old story told in the same old way, you probably will not make a new impression. If they walk in and you say, "Well, have you thought it over?" the prospect's natural tendency is to restate the original objection: "Yes, and I still feel it is not a good time to spend the money." In other words, "No deal." Here is an effective plan for a call-back situation:

1. *Approach.* Begin by giving a reason for calling back: "Mrs. Murphy, after I left the other day, I realized that there is some information I did not give you that has real bearing on your situation." Be sure you do have something different to present—new benefits, additional testimonials, or whatever. Be sure it is pertinent and logical.

2. *Review.* Next, review the whole presentation. Begin with, "Let me review briefly the items about the club we talked about last time." The last meeting may be fresh in your mind, but the prospect will not remember ten percent of what you presented. Throughout the review, use phrases like *as you remember, you will recall*, and *we said that* to suggest points of agreement from the previous meeting.

This approach may not always work, but you know that you cannot sell to someone without face-to-face contact. Being there gives you the only opportunity you will ever have to sell this prospect.

Secondary Question Close

This close is a simplistic one that involves posing the major decision to join with a question, then without pausing, ask a secondary minor point question. When the prospect answers the minor point question, the major question is actually carried with it. Here is an example:

> *Mr. LaBoy, as I see it we have only one decision to make today and that is how soon do you want to start to reach your fitness goals. By the way, would you prefer a permanent locker or a temporary one?*

Reassurance Close

This is another simple close that appeals to the prospects' emotional reasons for joining. If your prospects are on the fence, cannot make up their minds, and you feel that you are losing them, try a response like this:

> "You know this is the best thing you can do for yourself and for your wife. She will be so proud of you. Go ahead, give it a try.

Similar Situation Close

Another useful close is the similar situation close. Relate examples of current members who were in a situation similar to the one your guest is facing. Remind your guest that they, too, were hesitant but decided to join and now are so happy that they did. Remember, any testimonials you give must be true and be able to be backed up by someone else in the club.

Instruction Close

This close is excellent, especially for potential members who have little to no workout or gym experience. These prospects sometimes just need to be told what they should do. You are not forcing them; rather, you are providing instruction to apprehensive prospects to help them get over that little hill of uncertainty with a close such as:

> "You want to trim those hips and thighs, right? (prospect nods head in agreement). I know you do! So here is what you've got to do…"

After the Close

Once you have closed the sale and have completed any necessary paperwork, you have no further business with the prospect at this time. Learn to end the appointment gracefully. You may be tempted to have them stay and enjoy the company of a new member you especially like. You feel like celebrating a successful membership sale. However, the member has other work to do, and so do you! If you allow them to linger around, you invite second thoughts and perhaps even regret. They need to leave with good thoughts about you and your efficient, professional manner. Thank the new member for joining and sincerely say that you are looking forward to seeing them in the club.

Closing the Sale
REFOCUS

- Closing the sale is a natural conclusion to a carefully prepared and well-conducted presentation to a qualified prospect. Successful closing is often a matter of attitude.

- Learn to recognize buying signals. These enable you to close at the earliest possible point in the presentation. Learn the CHEF technique.

- The most threatening element in the sale for many salespeople is the fear of rejection. Develop a plan for dealing with rejection.

- Both verbal and nonverbal clues point to the prospect's readiness to join. The buying signals often suggest the type of close that would be appropriate.

- Close when the prospect is ready to join.

- One effective tactic is a trial close that asks for an opinion rather than a commitment; this allows the salesperson to determine just how ready the prospect is to say yes!

- Use words like "when" or "as" during the close. Avoid words such as "if" and "should" because they are conditional and block closing action.

- The summary close consists of restating the major selling points made during the presentation. This repetition of benefits overcomes the prospect's tendency to forget or neglect main points.

- The balance sheet close works well because it also allows you to present a summary of the main selling points, but in a pro-and-con format. Many of us tend to think this way, but this close is especially well received by the analytical and amiable social styles.

Chapter 13 — Closing the Sale

Part V

Management Aspects: Personal and Organizational

Keeping customers happy and coming back takes more than smiles and thank-yous; it takes outrageous service.

Chapter 14

Service After the Sale

FOCAL POINTS

- The purpose of total customer service.
- What constitutes service quality.
- When and how to service.
- Your role in servicing.
- Upgrading and cross-selling current members.
- A systematic plan for follow-up activities.

BUILDING PARTNERSHIPS WITH TOTAL CUSTOMER SERVICE

Increased Expectations

How do you sell memberships and keep your members sold when there are so many others fighting to do the same thing? Total customer service is the answer. More and more clubs are turning to *service quality* as a strategy to acquire and maintain members. Your job as a fitness consultant requires you to look at your job differently. That is, your task is not to just get people in the door and sell them a membership, *but to do what is best for the member no matter what.*

Customer satisfaction has to be the ultimate objective of every athletic club. You may think that your club makes membership sales every month, but you really make satisfied customers every month. The customer absolutely defines quality in every transaction. Don't talk customer service – *live* perfect service.

Chapter 14 — Service After the Sale   252

Because meeting and exceeding member expectations is so vital to success, clubs must develop customer service strategies. This involves customizing your offering to members because individuals have different fitness needs. You can go out of business if you provide too much assistance to the wrong people, or if you fail to help the members who need it most. So you must inform your new members what kind of service they can expect, and the key to success is exceeding what you promise. Keeping them happy, and coming back, takes more than smiles and nods. It takes *outrageous service*. Health club members have an increasing rate of expectation for services and a decreasing tolerance for poor service, and as a result are more likely to migrate to the gyms who provide the best and most expert assistance.

> "A lot of people have fancy things to say about customer service, including me, but it's just a day-in, day-out, ongoing, never-ending, unremitting, persevering, compassionate type of activity."
>
> — Leon Gorman, L.L. Bean

Second-mile Service

Be willing to give your members more than they demand, more than they expect, even more than they deserve. Act from the desire to serve – not the desire to gain. When this is your policy, you will do whatever you must to be of service to your clients and members.

Scott Clark, author of *Beating the Odds: 10 Smart Steps To Small Business Success*, suggests that it doesn't matter how much, or how big the competition is. The key factor for any business is an emphasis on service! Service will always equate to satisfied members, and satisfied members are always willing to help out. They are consistent users, they bring in guests, refer friends, and talk positively about the club.

What exactly is good service? We know what service isn't. Exeptional customer service is more than simply offering towels, valet parking, car washing, or opening the front door. Small club managers and consultants should think of service as an intangible, such as a smiling receptionist to greet every member and guest, fitness instructors who provide service beyond normal expectations, and staff recognizing members by their first name. Personal touches like these add up to a

THE OFFICIAL HANDBOOK FOR HEALTH CLUB SALES

feeling of friendliness and comfort. As a fitness consultant, your goal should be this:

> "Every member should be feeling better when they leave your club than when they came in."

Second-Mile Service

Moments of Truth

Awareness of *quality service* by your members and prospects can be a great advantage. Salespeople are far more likely to make a sale when they can truthfully say, *"If you join our club, we will never let you down. Servicing your fitness needs is our top priority."* Jan Carlzon, president of Scandinavian Airlines (SAS), writes in his book *Moments of Truth*, "Each of our 10 million customers come in contact with an average of five SAS employees. Each contact lasts about 15 seconds. Thus, SAS is *created* in the minds of our customers 50 million times per year, 15 seconds at a time."

Those "moments of truth," when customers are made aware of service quality, are the moments that ultimately determine the success of your club. All employees must realize and care that their work affects customers' perception. Customer satisfaction is measured as moments in time. Plenty of members do not come back unless the service and assistance you provide is consistently better than the service provided by competitors.

> Customer service is like a daily election and customers vote with their feet.

CUSTOMER SERVICE TECHNIQUES THAT SUPPORT THE RELATIONSHIP

Value Added

Jim Jewett, author of *Discovering Fast Track Success*, attributes salespeople's success to their ability to engage in value-added thinking. He defines this concept as "seeking out every possible opportunity to add customer value." Recognizing value added is much easier than defining it. When you are in the position of the customer, you recognize value added when you receive it – and you remember it!

Another way to appreciate the importance of customers' loyalty is to take a long-term view of their value. Instead of considering a person's worth in terms of a single membership transaction, you should factor in all of the possible renewals and referrals over their lifetime. The professional fitness consultant has numerous opportunities for follow-up activities that determine whether particular customers will renew their memberships as well as whether they will tell others of their satisfaction or provide you with referrals. The relationship sales rep is sincerely and unselfishly helpful to members and prospects alike. Value-added service costs nothing except thoughtfulness and a few minutes of your time.

Get More From Current Customers

Always strive aggressively to obtain referrals from your members because they generate 75 percent of a club's new business. If you follow the recommendations in this section you will obtain more referral sales with less effort. In this area of

255 *THE OFFICIAL HANDBOOK FOR HEALTH CLUB SALES*

the business, you must change your status from a "go getter" to a "go giver". Your rewards in life will always be equal to the level of service you provide. If you wish to increase your rewards, you must increase the value of your service. Referral programs are designed to work best when members like you and appreciate the level of service they receive.

Here are 9 ways to provide a level of service that should be offered to all new members that will build lasting rapport, establish a sense of obligation to your referral programs, and provide testimonials:

1. Welcome and greet all members by their first name as they arrive.

2. Make sure new members feel comfortable about coming to the facility. Introduce them to the entire staff and some of the regular members.

3. Take new members through one or two complete workouts. These workouts must be entered into the daily workout log book so the receptionist can confirm appointments.

4. Give every new member an initial fitness test consisting of body composition and measurements, and blood pressure.

5. Have the person at the front desk ask members how their program is going and if they need any help. If help is required, a trainer must be notified immediately, or the original consultant who enrolled the member should take this person through a workout.

6. Any member who asks for help must immediately receive help, whatever the problem may be. We must all become expert problem solvers.

7. Any members having a problem should speak to the manager as soon as possible. You may not be able to help all the time but you can listen and demonstrate genuine concern.

8. Don't play favorites. Float while your on the floor. Service and acknowledge all the members equally.

9. All employees should wear a name tag. Something as simple as wearing a name tag makes you more approachable and puts you on a more intimate level with members.

Chapter 14 — Service After the Sale

The key to getting the most out of your members is *service, service and more service*. Although small clubs can't afford valet parking, they can provide more service than larger competitors. Give it a try and your club's referral program will take off!

Upgrading or Up-selling. Upgrading, also known as up-selling, is the process of persuading an individual to purchase a longer membership or bigger club package. Upgrading is largely a matter of selling your club and emphasizing the quality aspects of your facility. You ask for the upgrade because the new membership package will serve the needs of the client better than the less expensive membership. Most clubs have memberships that vary in price and duration. And most buyers like to have choices when making a purchase. The only way you can succeed in upgrading is to believe one hundred percent in what you're doing, think ahead, and create win-win relationships.

Cross-selling. Cross-selling is the process of selling products or services that are not directly connected to the primary membership. For example, your club may be connected to a nutrition or diet company or have an affiliation with a nearby tanning salon. By mentioning these services, you foster relationships with other local businesses and provide additional services to your members.

Cross-selling and upgrading have become increasingly important to many clubs in this information age. Customers have to be convinced that what you have available is going to solve a problem for them. To be truly customer-focused you have to make as many channels available as your customers are demanding. To do the best job of fostering lifetime loyalty, you need to know exactly what your customers are thinking.

RETAIN OR WIN BACK UNHAPPY CUSTOMERS

A customer comes into the club and launches into a tirade, complaining and whining about everything. Who needs a member like this? But then you stop, catch your breath, and think – "When members are rude it's usually because they are having a problem with some aspect of our club or its services." No matter how badly they behave, avoid responding angrily. You must learn not to take their rudeness personally. Maintain a positive attitude and an even tone of voice. This serves to disarm them and they will generally follow your lead.

THE OFFICIAL HANDBOOK FOR HEALTH CLUB SALES

Restate concerns to demonstrate that you were listening. Employ empathy by putting yourself in their shoes and seeing it from *their perspective*. Remember that members are reacting to a real or perceived problem with the club that they feel has let them down. Thank them for bringing the issue to your attention and then recommend a plan to solve it. Make sure your proposed solution meets with the customer's approval. Lastly, follow up to ensure the issue has been resolved and the person is completely satisfied. This tends to build a stronger relationship and greater loyalty with members.

Service in Response to Needs

When you are practicing ongoing service, you can anticipate complaints and handle them promptly before they become serious sources of dissatisfaction. A customer who is dissatisfied with a health club tells an estimated nine or ten other people. Always respond immediately to the possibility of a complaint or to one that is actually expressed. Complaints can be customer-saving opportunities. The salesperson who assumes that members must be satisfied because they have voiced no gripes over an extended period, is living in an unreal world.

Technical Assistance Research Programs, Inc. (TARP), based in Washington, D.C., conducted research that produced overwhelming evidence of the value not only of "handling" complaints but also of going out of the way to encourage and then remedy complaints. TARP's key findings include these:

1. Of unhappy customers, only four percent complain to company management. For every complaint received, the average company has 26 customers with problems, six of which are "serious," who do *not* complain.

2. Among customers with problems, complainers are more likely than non-complainers to do business with the club again, even if the problem isn't satisfactorily resolved.

3. Between 54 and 70 percent of complainers will give repeat business if their complaint is resolved, but a staggering 95 percent are repeat customers if they feel the complaint was resolved quickly.

4. Dissatisfied customers tell 9 or 10 people about their experience. 13 percent recount the incident to more than 20 people.

5. Customers who have their complaints satisfactorily resolved tell an average of five people about the treatment they received.

Retaining Existing Customers

All the efforts to retain customers is certainly not without benefits. Membership retention results from customer satisfaction. It has been estimated that reducing customer defections by as little as five percent can double a company's profits. A bad experience can be a bitter and enduring memory. There is no substitute for fitness consultants asking their customer base how they feel about the service the club is providing.

> "Those who enter to buy support me. Those who come to flatter please me. Those who complain teach me how I may please others so that more will come. Those only hurt me who are displeased but do not complain. They refuse me permission to correct my errors and thus improve my service."
>
> — Marshall Field

Win Back Those Angry Customers

No club enjoys losing a member. Winning back a customer who has turned to a competitor helps your self-confidence as well as your pocket book. The first step in regaining a customer is to discover why you lost the membership. Almost 80 percent of members leave because they feel they've been badly treated. It is your responsibility to mend this relationship. Exhibit 14.1 gives some of the most common "excuses" given by salespeople for losing members.

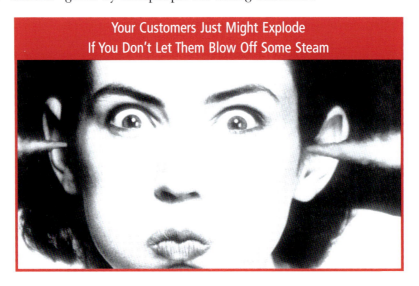

Exhibit 14.1

"Excuses" Salespeople Give for Losing Memberships

It's not my fault I lost that member . . .

- If it isn't price, then it's because the competition uses unfair or unethical tactics.

- That member is just too difficult for anyone to get along with.

- The member never cared about anything but price, so I was helpless.

- I just don't have time to give the member the service I would have liked to give.

- There can't be anything wrong with my sales techniques. I'm doing exactly what I've been doing for years.

Listen carefully to what the customer says to you. Do not contradict what the customer has told you, argue, or become angry yourself, no matter how unreasonable the customer may seem.

When faced with angry customers, you have two choices. One – you can walk away and consider them lost; or two – you can resolve the conflict and further reinforce the relationship. If you listen politely, ask additional questions, and probe for hidden feelings, the mere act of telling you what is wrong often defuses their negative feelings. The former satisfaction experienced in dealing with you surfaces and the individual may be quite happy to consider reestablishing the relationship with you and the club.

Do your best to glean every bit of current information you can regarding this angry person, along with what you know of your relationship with the individual in the past, in order to decide what went wrong. Here are some possible reasons that you might lose a membership.

1. **Something you have done**
   No one is at top effectiveness all the time. Without intending to do so, you may have said or done something that offended the customer or damaged your credibility in some way. Exhibit 14.2 illustrates a sure-fire way to offend a mem-

Chapter 14 — Service After the Sale   260

ber and destroy a relationship. The old slogan for Arpege perfume began, "Promise her anything, but...." For you, the "but" must be followed by "don't promise what you can't deliver."

Exhibit 14.2

Destroying Credibility with the Customer

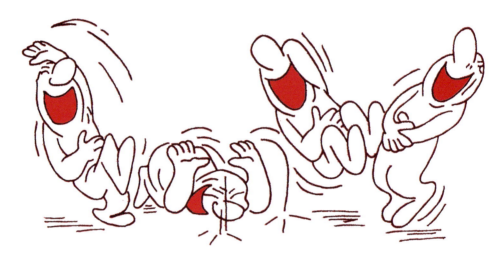

2. **Something you fail to do**
   Failing to tell the full story about what the club can provide, failure to keep the customer informed about membership changes or privileges, failure to meet promises, failing to follow up or waiting too long to follow up—all these omissions destroy the individual's faith in you and your club.

3. **Something the club does**
   If the club drafts the member's account twice in one month or makes errors in billing, the person may become dissatisfied enough to change clubs.

4. **Something the club fails to do**
   The club may fail to keep the locker rooms clean, change the hours of operation without warning, or fail to provide an adequate number of trainers so that making an appointment is very difficult. To avoid such problems, stay abreast of any internal changes.

Take some time for problem solving. Until you discover and acknowledge the real problem, you cannot solve it. Sometimes the answer is unpleasant. If the problem lies in your actions or attitudes, you must accept responsibility so that you are free to solve the problem and regain the member's loyalty. If you deny your obvious responsibility, you escape into excuse making and are blinded to the options available for regaining the customer's goodwill. When you know what the problem is, you can plan strategies for rebuilding the relationship.

FOLLOW-UP ACTIVITIES FOR MEMBERSHIP RETENTION

Before starting any new retention program, you must understand that nearly 20 percent of your customer base will turnover each year due to relocation. This is called uncontrollable attrition.

Making new club members feel at ease is a crucial aspect of member retention. Clubs spend so much time and invest so much money in marketing and recruiting new members only to forget about them once they are enrolled. The services, quality product, and pleasant atmosphere you provide will enhance membership retention.

The tracking system you develop for servicing should be as well-organized as your prospecting system. Set up a rotating file by dates of expected contact for each customer. Use a card file or computer program. The file method chosen should list member names, the dates they joined, the fitness consultant who signed them up, and some personal information about their goals. Whatever organizing system you choose, be sure to have a *specific, written* plan for servicing. Your plan should include these four elements:

1. Stay Informed

The process of buying and selling does not end with the membership purchase—unless you intend for that to be the only transaction you will ever have with this customer or with anyone this individual influences. Service is the activities you do to keep customers sold permanently. Your job is not complete until the customer is satisfied.

Regular calls to existing members help you keep up with their overall satisfaction. If you consistently keep up with their progress, a relationship can be developed and your credibility established before you ask for a membership renewal. Keep-

Chapter 14 — Service After the Sale 262

ing up with members' improvements and progress not only helps you solidify your presence with them, but also gives you credibility with any references they supply to you.

> ## Gaining a New Customer
> ## Costs Five Times More
> ## than Keeping a Current One

2. Make Phone Calls

The most viable method of retaining members is to simply stay in contact with them. The telephone is one of your best service tools for this purpose. Members will be impressed if you call them periodically just to see how things are going. It is absolutely pertinent that you set up a system of follow-up calls. Exhibit 14.3 is a sample Business Building Card that provides space for information about a new member and a contact schedule that will keep you in touch with that person during the most difficult times of their membership up to the critical renewal time.

The first call you make should simply be to confirm an initial workout appointment. The fitness consultant who enrolled that member must then follow up after the first workout, first week, first month, sixty, ninety days, and so on of the membership.

Activity reports should be printed from the club's computerized check-in system so that follow up calls can be made if a person is missing in action for 14 days or more. As soon as attendance becomes slack, contact that member to see what the problem might be. Ask, *"Did we do something to keep you from returning?"* Get the problem right out into the open.

This process allows you to give members personalized attention with less investment of time for both you and them. Individuals respond positively to the fact that you are interested in them and how the club is meeting their needs, and they are also pleased that they did not need to spend half an hour in a personal visit with you.

263   *THE OFFICIAL HANDBOOK FOR HEALTH CLUB SALES*

Exhibit 14.3

Business Building Card

Fitness Consultant:_____ New Member:_____

Enrollment Date: _____ / _____ / _____ Renewal Date:_____ / _____ / _____

Phone Number: H#(_____)_____-_____ W# (_____)_____-_____

Address: _____

Birth date:_____ / _____ / _____ Reason for enrolling (Goals):_____

Membership Type: Gold( ) Gold Plus ( ) Monthly ( ) Advance Pay ( ) $ Other

Hobbies/Interests: _____

Spouse's Name:_____ Birth date: _____ / _____ / _____

Reason for enrolling (Goals): _____

Membership Type: Gold( ) Gold Plus( ) Monthly( ) Advance Pay( ) $ Other

Children/Pets:_____

Follow-Up Procedure
(Track progress, are goals being achieved, personal training, overall satisfaction, etc)

7 days _____	15 days _____
30 days _____	60 days _____
90 days _____	120 days _____
160 days _____	190 days _____
220 days _____	260 days _____

Chapter 14 — Service After the Sale

3. Send Mail (Letter or Card)

Follow up your phone calls with periodic mailings to members. Here are some ideas for mailings that will help you keep in touch:

- Thank you notes for new members
- Birthday cards to all members
- Thorough program orientation pamphlets
- Equipment orientation information
- Notices of upcoming social events
- Overall satisfaction feedback forms

4. Be a Problem Solver

The relationship salesperson is a problem solver. The first application of problem-solving skill comes in the sales process at the point of need discovery and application of the club's services to their specific needs. Your problem-solving abilities operates in at least two areas.

Coordination Within Your Club. You are responsible for coordination of all services necessary to ensure that the member is satisfied. Any question regarding weight training, machines, payment terms, or other questions regarding the facility is your concern.

Assistance With Training. If members are new to working out or this is the first time they have joined a gym, this may require some extra assistance on your part. Your role, then, becomes that of coordinator—notifying the appropriate individuals, such as personal trainers, that additional help may be required and following up regularly and often to track their progress. Your efforts after the initial sale of the membership makes all the difference in producing a positive club environment.

Give close attention to the effectiveness of each type of service contact you offer to your customers. Discard methods that do not work, and repeat methods that do. Keep your service records as meticulously as you do your data on prospecting. Know what you have done for each customer, what you plan to do next, and when.

265   *THE OFFICIAL HANDBOOK FOR HEALTH CLUB SALES*

Service After the Sale
REFOCUS

- The right kind of customer service brings you repeat members over time. A membership buying decision is a one-time action unless you turn it into a habit with effective follow-up.

- Service after the sale adds value by showing the member that you are willing to take care of any problems. Service after the sale is more important to your members than the actual sale itself.

- After-sale service gives you an opportunity to keep up with the new member's progress so you will know what additional opportunities you have for upgrading or cross-selling.

- Service is an ongoing activity. It is never too soon or too long after the sale to provide service.

- Plan, execute, and track any personal visits, telephone calls, and mailings to your customers and measure how effective they were.

- Service is the key to winning back lost memberships. Contact the former customer with genuine concern and interest.

Chapter 14 — Service After the Sale

Time Saving Tips

Be sure to handle each piece of paper only once.

— Alan Lakein, author of *How to Get Control of Your Time and Your Life*

To keep staff meetings short, I always try to sandwich them between two scheduled appointments.

— Dan McNamee, president, McNamee Consulting Company

I look for the kind of guy who says, "Forget that, it'll take ten years. Here's what we gotta do now."

— Lee Iacocca, from *Iacocca: An Autobiography*

Put a dollar value on what you have to do; if it doesn't add up in dollars and cents, don't do it.

— Edward J. Feeney, consultant, Edward J. Feeney Associates

Simplify expense reports by keeping an envelope in your pocket. Write the date, city, and names of customers to be visited on the flap; note expenditures on the envelope; then put each day's receipts inside.

— Merrill Douglas, chairman, Time Management Center, Inc.

Yesterday is a canceled check: forget it. Tomorrow is a promissory note: don't count on it. Today is ready cash: use it!

— Edwin C. Bliss from *Doing It Now*

THE OFFICIAL HANDBOOK FOR HEALTH CLUB SALES

Chapter 15
Time Management

FOCUS

- A time management attitude.
- Organizing your activities and environment.
- An effective organizing system.
- Identifying priorities.
- Maintaining a positive attitude towards time.

DEVELOPING A TIME MANAGEMENT ATTITUDE

Time is perhaps your most precious commodity. Although a continuous supply of time is available, it cannot be stored for future use, and it cannot be reclaimed if it is wasted. When you realize that life itself consists of time, the value of time becomes clear. We loudly denounce attitudes or practices that show a lack of respect for human life, but we seem not to notice when we throw away priceless hours—the fabric of life—in useless activity or idleness. Begin your program of managing time by asking yourself a question posed by Alan Lakein in his book *How to Get Control of Your Time and Your Life*: "What is the best use of my time right now?"

The term time *management* is a misnomer. Because *every* minute has sixty seconds and *every* hour has sixty minutes, time itself cannot be managed. It can only be used. What can be managed, however, are you and

Chapter 15 — Time Management   268

your activities in the club. Time management, then, is actually personal organization as well as self-management. It involves three areas:

- Self-management (self-discipline)
- Planning and organizing
- Systems and techniques to automate routine

Use your time instead of simply spending it. Time is made up of a series of events. The key to managing time is controlling these events to your advantage. Time control and self-management can be learned. You have the ability to control your present thoughts and actions and to decide how to use your time.

> **Dost thou love life? Then do not squander time, for that's the stuff life is made of.**
> **— Benjamin Franklin**

Get a firm grip on the reality of the worth of time. Pretend that the president of your bank informs you that you have been chosen to receive a special prize: Every day for the rest of your life $86,400 will be deposited into your account. The only stipulation is that it must all be spent every day. Anything left at the end of the business day goes back to the bank. You can't hold anything over from one day to the next. Those first weeks are exhilarating. By the end of the first month, you have received over $2 million. After a while, however, you begin to have trouble spending that much every day. Think how you would feel the first time $20,000 slipped away from you and went back to the bank because you failed to spend it all. You would quickly realize that using this much money every day calls for some serious planning.

This imaginary scenario is not entirely fantasy. The old adage is true: Time is money. Every day 86,400 seconds are deposited in your account and in that of everyone else. You cannot save any unused time for another day. How many— or how few—of your 86,400 seconds go back to the "bank" unused depends on your skill in planning and managing your time. The important questions are these:

1. How will you spend your time?
2. How will you invest your time?
3. How much time will go to business, to service for others, to family, to leisure?
4. How much time will be reserved just for yourself — for the things you want to do?

THE OFFICIAL HANDBOOK FOR HEALTH CLUB SALES

Your most important asset is time, and how you use it is crucial to your success. Noted speaker Ira Hayes says,

> *"The inability or lack of desire to become organized is responsible for the vast majority of failures. It is why otherwise bright people turn out to be only mediocre performers and achieve only a small degree of the success that they rightfully could achieve. A disorganized desk, car, or way of life leads to rushing around and confusion and generally results in a poor attitude which makes people around you question the advisability of doing business with you."*

Everybody has the *ability* to manage time. The *desire* is the variable that makes the difference, and taking charge of your life depends on your personal choice.

Nearly everything that we think, say or do is governed by patterns of behavior that we have developed over the years. We develop most of them early in life and rarely change them. The only way to lose a habit is to stop practicing it. Stop practicing negative habits and start practicing positive ones, and your life will improve automatically. If you want to achieve good results in professional health and fitness sales, establish good habit patterns.

In sales, more than in many other profession, the management of time is a matter of personal choice and responsibility. Here's an idea for you to try: get to work by 5 a.m. three times a week, and you'll gain an extra day. You will realize a great feeling of satisfaction at 8 a.m. when you've already finished the paperwork that would have taken you hours to do after 8 a.m. because of interruptions. Now you are free to perform income producing activities such as putting out lead boxes and calling prospects.

Attitudes Toward Time

Mental preparation is necessary to win the race against time. Developing a time management attitude helps to overcome life's obstacles. Just as Olympic champions practice diligently and relentlessly to perfect their athletic techniques, you can practice time management techniques and maximize the benefits to be enjoyed from both professional and personal pursuits.

You can let the whole subject of time management assume such proportions that the mere thought of attempting to master it becomes frustrating. It is estimated that the typical fitness consultant spends an average of only two hours a day in productive membership sales. However, just increasing the time spent with a member doesn't do very much for you, it's what you do with the time that's important. Focus your time so that it matches opportunity.

Keep a positive perspective toward time and your use of it. Here are some suggestions for establishing the kind of time attitudes that will bring you success:

1. Make a list of the activities you want to complete during the next week to achieve the results you desire.

2. For an entire week, keep an hour-by-hour record of exactly what you do with your time. Summarize your record and compare what you actually do to the list you made of what you want to do to achieve your goals. (Exhibit 15.1 illustrates a form you can use for this purpose.)

3. At the end of each day and at the end of each week, take a personal accounting of what you have accomplished compared to what you set out to do.

4. List the five habits or attitudes that were the biggest obstacles to the achievement of the results you wanted. Write out a plan for changing these habits or attitudes. Conduct an additional time analysis study three months from now and compare the two. Determine whether you are making progress in replacing these habits or attitudes with new ones.

Conducting a detailed personal time-analysis study at least twice a year is a good habit to establish. Just as you schedule a regular medical checkup, plan for a time management checkup to keep you aware of how well you are using your time resources.

PROCEDURE FOR GETTING ORGANIZED

Before you can gain any measure of control over your time, you must address your need for laying the groundwork to handle the onslaught of information you encounter every day. Several techniques can help you.

THE OFFICIAL HANDBOOK FOR HEALTH CLUB SALES

Exhibit 15.1

Daily Time Summary

Record time every hour or more frequently to ensure an accurate record. Keep the record for an entire week. Activities listed are typical for fitness consultants.

	Internal Prospecting	External Prospecting	Telephone Time	Club Presentations	Servicing members	Meetings	Sales Training	Paperwork	Preparing for Club Tours			
6 am												
7 am												
8 am												
9 am												
10 am												
11 am												
12 noon												
1 pm												
2 pm												
3 pm												
4 pm												
5 pm												
6 pm												
7 pm												
8 pm												
9 pm												
10 pm												

Chapter 15 — Time Management

Remove the Clutter

You can think more clearly and more creatively if you remove as much clutter as possible from your life and your living space. Remove unnecessary papers from your work area—your desk, your car. Even if the stacks of paper are neat and appear to be well organized, they promote a subconscious psychological tendency to review and think through the items in sight. In a very few seconds you can think through all of the tasks or incompletions that are represented by a sizable stack of paper. For all practical purposes, however, your mind does not differentiate between doing a task physically and doing it mentally. If you mentally review a big stack of paper a dozen times a day in the process of deciding which one to tackle next, or which one to avoid, you are exhausted long before the day is over.

Once you decide to dispense with clutter, tackle the job at once. Follow this plan:

1. **Collect the Clutter.** Gather up all the clutter that affects you and take it to one convenient work area. Empty your car, bedside table, pockets, and any other cubbyhole where you stick things that are waiting to be done. Dump all the clutter into one container.

2. **Sort the Clutter.** Divide the clutter into two categories: time-critical material (that is, items with a specific due date) and "someday" material.

3. **Deal With Priorities.** Deal first with the time-critical items, such as appointments you have with potential members that day or that week. Provide a series of thirty-one folders to represent the days of the month. (This is commonly called a *1-31 file*.) Examine each of the items you have identified as time critical. If it involves a specific hour of the day, write it on your calendar. Then put each item in the folder for the day that the first action must be taken to meet the due date. Each day check the appropriate folder as you make your daily to do list.

4. **Set Up Working Categories for the Rest.** Now begin to organize the someday material. Set up two convenient files—the stacked "in-out file boxes" are handy. Label these files *reading* and *projects*. Go through your someday items and sort them in the two files according to their nature.

Handle Interruptions

To handle them properly, you must first determine whether an occurrence is truly an interruption or part of your job. Only when you understand this difference are you able to control your attitude toward the people and the circumstances that threaten to get in your way as you are doing your job. Once you determine that an interruption is part of your job, decide whether it is more important than what you are currently doing or whether it should be postponed. This determination helps you keep your priorities straight and reduces procrastination.

Interruptions typically fall into three categories, each of which you can handle with the right attitude. The following is a list of the three types of interruptions – people, paper, and environment – and examples of the most common ways that fitness consultants experience them.

People	Paper	Environmental
• Superior	• Notes	• Telephone calls
• Associate	• Memos	• Visual distractions
• Subordinate	• Correspondence	• Comfort factors
• Members	• Periodicals	– temperature
	• Messages	– light
	• Projects	– clothing

People Interruptions. People interruptions are the most frustrating because they are the most difficult to solve, and who the person is makes a difference in the way you respond. If you are interrupted by your club manager, remember that that person probably has the right to interrupt you. If you are working on something of extreme importance or have a prospect walking into the club for an appointment, however, you can properly ask respectfully whether your superior might wait until your project or call is completed. As your work is presumably important to the success of the club, and therefore to your sales manager as well, most bosses consider such a request to be a mark of both effectiveness and self-confidence on your part.

When a member interrupts you either by phone or in person, adopt the attitude that this contact is not an interruption. You do not automatically put your full day at the disposal of a member's whim, but you do give full attention while the individual is talking and then do whatever is necessary to take care of the situation.

Paper Interruptions. People who work in a disorganized environment experience both confusion and frustration when confronted with necessary club paperwork. They feel confused because they have no automatic method for handling the item; they spend too long thinking about how to handle it. Then, because they dislike feeling confused, they become frustrated with the repeated inroads made on their time by additional paperwork. Before very long, disorganized people decide they just hate all paperwork. Fitness consultants are often among those who say they hate paperwork because they feel that it is less important in producing their income than their direct selling activities in the club.

Environmental Interruptions. Distractions in your work space can wreak havoc on your productivity if not properly addressed and controlled. Instead of feeling overwhelmed by environmental distractions such as frequent phone calls or customer walk-ins, schedule a specific telephone time each day to set up appointments for sales presentations and take care of other sales-related business. Then the remainder of the day is free for those vital selling contacts.

AN ORGANIZING SYSTEM

Once you remove the clutter and the incompletions from your work area and get a firm grip on controlling interruptions, three simple tools will help you organize your activities.

The Master Calendar

Many fitness consultants prefer a pocket-sized book that is always available to note an appointment. Whatever its size, the calendar should list only specific time commitments such as appointments with members and club tours. All the information needed for those specific commitments is collected in the 1-31 file folders or recorded on the computer master calendar until it is needed for the appointment or other commitment.

Daily To-Do List

The second time-organizational tool you will need is a daily to-do list. Be sure to prioritize each item on your list. Highlight those activities completed, and carry forward the uncompleted items. A familiar story about Charles Schwab, former president of Bethlehem Steel, confirms the real impact of this simple tool. Schwab called in consultant Ivy Lee and proposed, "Show me a way to get more done with my time, and I'll pay you any fee within reason."

"Fine," said Lee, "I'll give you something in twenty minutes that will increase your output at least fifty percent." Lee then handed Schwab a blank sheet of paper and said, "Write down the six most important tasks that you have to do tomorrow and number them in order of their importance. Now put this paper in your pocket, and the first thing tomorrow morning look at item one. Work on it until you finish it. Then do item two, and so on. Do this until quitting time. Don't be concerned if you have finished only one or two. You'll be working on the most important items. If you can't finish them all by this method, you couldn't have finished them by any other method either; and without some system, you'd probably not even decide which was the most important."

Lee continued, "Use this system every working day. After you've convinced yourself of the value of the system, have your men try it. Try it as long as you wish and then send me a check for what you think it's worth." Several weeks later, Lee received Schwab's check for $10,000—a much more impressive sum around the turn of the 20th century than it sounds now.

Remember you can't alter time. The trick to managing your time is to manage not your time, but your activities. The value of a to-do list is apparent, but it becomes even more valuable when you use it not only to identify needed tasks but to establish priorities for them. Putting top priorities first is the only way to be sure that your activities are making a direct impact on your goals. Sales success depends on establishing and steadfastly pursuing a series of goals. When you develop specific and measurable *growth goals*, you gain the determination and drive it takes to succeed. Figure 15.1 is an example of a format you can use for your to-do list. If you are using a computerized master calendar, you can print out your daily to-do list. The form is not nearly as important as the practice!

The Integrated System

The 1-31 reminder file, the master calendar, and the to-do list together constitute a place your mind can trust and a place where you can store all the reminders that must surface at a given time in the future. You can safely forget about incompletions until they surface in your system. Together these organizing tools form a system that makes organization of your daily activities an automatic process. At the close of each day's work, transfer any left-over items from today's to-do list to the new list for tomorrow. Then consult your 1-31 file and your master calendar to find all the items you have scheduled for tomorrow. Note any specific times associated with those items, such as the time for an appointment or meeting. Now you are ready to begin work tomorrow without even thinking about what to do first. You are ready to begin your day with the task of highest importance.

Figure 15.1

A To-do List with a Daily Plan to List Appointments

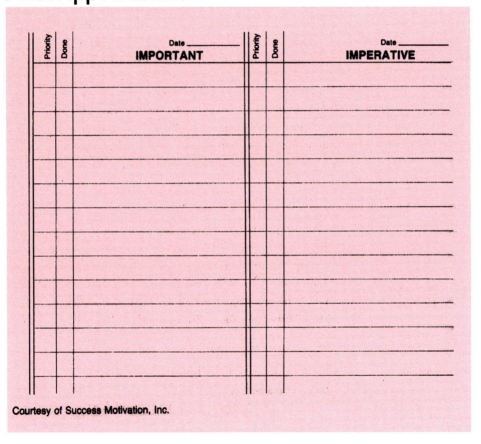

Identifying Priorities

An important concept for good time managers to understand is the Pareto principle. It states that 80 percent of the value (or the frustration) of any group of related items is generally concentrated in only 20 percent of them. In other words, "a minority of the input produces a majority of the results." The principle, named for the Italian economist who proposed it, holds true for many areas of today's experience. For example:

In Measuring Value, You Receive . . .

80% of:

- Sales
- Productivity
- Profit
- Referrals
- Commisson Income

from 20% of:

- Customers
- Activity
- Products
- Clients
- Orders

In Measuring Frustration, You Experience . . .

80% of:

- Absenteeism
- Errors
- Servicing Problems

from 20% of:

- Employees
- Workers
- Customers

Likewise, 80 percent of your success comes through the achievement of the top 20 percent of your goals. In managing your time effectively, you must recognize that *which* items you complete, not *how* many items you complete, determine your success.

To identify the special 20 percent of your activities that have the potential for producing the greatest success, establish different categories of priorities.

"A" priorities are the most pressing. They include the items that must be done by a specific date if you are to reach one of your major goals and items that would damage the reputation of your club or your personal credibility if you failed to accomplish them.

"B" priority items are any items that can be done at any time within the next week or month without causing any repercussions.

"C" priority items would be nice to do at some time when you have nothing else pressing to do, but you would suffer no real loss if you never got around to them.

Obviously, you want to give first attention to your **"A" priorities** and carefully number them in the order of their importance. Your goal is to complete as many **"A" priorities** as you possibly can each day and then supplement them with any **"B"** items you can.

Time Goals

Once you have established the habit of using a to-do list, begin to record next to each item your estimate of the amount of time you will need to complete it. Estimating the required time lets you judge whether you can complete everything. Time studies have shown that even people who know which items are most important and set priorities still waste an average of fifteen minutes between items of work in simple procrastination or in trying to decide what to do next.

A second benefit of estimating completion times is to help in avoiding procrastination. A deadline – even an informal estimate of the time required – pushes you to complete the work in the allotted time. Northcote Parkinson is noted for his observation that *work expands to fill the time allowed for its completion*. Something about a stated time allotment seems to establish a mental set that causes you to use just that amount of time. If the time is short, you work efficiently and push for completion. If the time allowance is too generous, you procrastinate, spend extra time getting ready to work, and find a dozen small interruptions to make sure you don't finish too early. By estimating times for completion, you eliminate the tendency to procrastinate.

MAINTAINING A POSITIVE ATTITUDE TOWARD TIME

Anyone who expects sales success in the health and fitness industry should anticipate hard work and long hours. If you always seem to have more work than working hours, though, you may be due for a refresher course in time management. These techniques can't give you more time, but they can help you make the most of what you've got. Follow them to help you get—and keep—time on your side.

Set Deadlines — and Beat Them. When you've got a lot to do and not a lot of time to do it in, deadlines can help you to stay on schedule. Prioritize your tasks, then draw up a schedule for completing them.

Place a Time Limit on Meetings. If you or the other fitness consultants in your club tend to dread meetings, maybe it's because they drag on too long and accomplish too little. Knowing your meeting will last a specific amount of time should help keep things moving. Before each meeting, decide on a limited number of topics to discuss and a limited time period for discussing them.

Take Advantage of Your Peak Time. To be most efficient at the jobs you like least, tackle them at the time of day when you feel most productive. Pay attention to your moods and work output throughout the day to find out when you're most productive, and save your worst jobs for when you're at your best.

Decide to Delegate. Don't feel guilty about delegating responsibility—if you take on a responsibility that someone else could handle more effectively, you're not making the best use of your club's resources.

Put It in Writing. To remember phone numbers, important dates or anything else, write them down. Freeing your mind of clutter helps you think more clearly, and concentration is key to productivity.

Don't Overload on Overtime. If your work week consistently exceeds a reasonable number of hours, ask yourself why. Identify the tasks that take up the most time and look for ways to complete them more efficiently. Also, compare the number of hours you're working to what you're actually getting done. A too-small return on your time investment indicates a problem.

Learn to Say "No". When it comes to time management, many of us are our own worst enemy. You'll never have enough time to finish your work if you're always biting off more than you can chew. When people ask you do favors for them that they should be doing themselves, they are *putting uneccesary burden and stress on your shoulders*. If you agree to take on too many jobs for others, you are soon carrying an impossible load of monkeys and accomplish nothing.

Time is like talent—you can't create more of it, you just have to make the most of what you've got. You need self-discipline from the time you wake up in the morning until you go to bed that night. Spending your time more wisely starts with paying attention to how you spend it. Once you decide to take control of your time, you'll have the power to stop squandering it.

Time Management
REFOCUS

- The ability to manage time efficiently and effectively is largely a matter of attitude. Time is money. If you seek advancement and a comfortable income, managing time properly is one of the best skills you can develop.

- Interruptions are time wasters, so handle them with planning and control. Interruptions in the club arise from people, paper, and environmental factors.

- A workable system for time management includes at least three elements:

1. A master calendar for scheduling commitments.

2. A daily to-do list to record activities to be done each day to reach your goals.

3. A reminder file to hold items that will become important at a specific later date.

- Following simple time management techniques won't make more time, but it will help you make the most of every moment you have.

Chapter 15 — Time Management   282

Notes

Notes

Notes

Notes

Notes

Notes

Notes